studies in jazz

Institute of Jazz Studies
Rutgers—The State University of New Jersey
General Editors: Dan Morgenstern and Edward Berger

1. BENNY CARTER: A Life in American Music, *by Morroe* *Edward Berger, and James Patrick, 2 vols., 1982*
2. ART TATUM: A Guide to His Recorded Music, *by Arnol* *Ray Spencer, 1982*
3. ERROLL GARNER: The Most Happy Piano, *by James M*
4. JAMES P. JOHNSON: A Case of Mistaken Identity, *by S* Discography 1917–1950, *by Robert Hilbert, 1986*
5. PEE WEE ERWIN: This Horn for Hire, *as told to Warren W. Vaché Sr., 1987*
6. BENNY GOODMAN: Listen to His Legacy, *by D. Russell Connor, 1988*
7. ELLINGTONIA: The Recorded Music of Duke Ellington and His Sidemen, *by W. E. Timner, 1988; 4th ed., 1996*
8. THE GLENN MILLER ARMY AIR FORCE BAND: Sustineo Alas / I Sustain the Wings, *by Edward F. Polic; Foreword by George T. Simon, 1989*
9. SWING LEGACY, *by Chip Deffaa, 1989*
10. REMINISCING IN TEMPO: The Life and Times of a Jazz Hustler, *by Teddy Reig, with Edward Berger, 1990*
11. IN THE MAINSTREAM: 18 Portraits in Jazz, *by Chip Deffaa, 1992*
12. BUDDY DeFRANCO: A Biographical Portrait and Discography, *by John Kuehn and Arne Astrup, 1993*
13. PEE WEE SPEAKS: A Discography of Pee Wee Russell, *by Robert Hilbert, with David Niven, 1992*
14. SYLVESTER AHOLA: The Gloucester Gabriel, *by Dick Hill, 1993*
15. THE POLICE CARD DISCORD, *by Maxwell T. Cohen, 1993*
16. TRADITIONALISTS AND REVIVALISTS IN JAZZ, *by Chip Deffaa, 1993*
17. BASSICALLY SPEAKING: An Oral History of George Duvivier, *by Edward Berger; musical analysis by David Chevan, 1993*
18. TRAM: The Frank Trumbauer Story, *by Philip R. Evans and Larry F. Kiner, with William Trumbauer, 1994*
19. TOMMY DORSEY: On the Side, *by Robert L. Stockdale, 1995*
20. JOHN COLTRANE: A Discography and Musical Biography, *by Yasuhiro Fujioka, with Lewis Porter and Yoh-ichi Hamada, 1995*
21. RED HEAD: A Chronological Survey of "Red" Nichols and His Five Pennies, *by Stephen M. Stroff, 1996*

The Contradictions of Jazz

Paul Rinzler

Studies in Jazz, No. 57

The Scarecrow Press, Inc.
Lanham, Maryland • Toronto • Plymouth, UK
2008

SCARECROW PRESS, INC.

Published in the United States of America
by Scarecrow Press, Inc.
A wholly owned subsidiary of
The Rowman & Littlefield Publishing Group, Inc.
4501 Forbes Boulevard, Suite 200, Lanham, Maryland 20706
www.scarecrowpress.com

Estover Road
Plymouth PL6 7PY
United Kingdom

British Library Cataloguing in Publication Information Available

Library of Congress Cataloging-in-Publication Data

Rinzler, Paul E., 1953–
   The contradictions of jazz / Paul Rinzler.
     p. cm. — (Studies in jazz ; no. 57)
   Includes bibliographical references and index.
   ISBN-13: 978-0-8108-6143-5 (pbk. : alk. paper)
   ISBN-10: 0-8108-6143-7 (pbk. : alk. paper)
   eISBN-13: 978-0-8108-6215-9
   eISBN-10: 0-8108-6215-8
   1. Jazz—Philosophy and aesthetics. I. Title.
   ML3800.R54 2008
   781.65—dc22   2008018975

It is the stretched soul that makes music, and souls are stretched by the pull of opposites—opposite bents, tastes, yearnings, loyalties. Where there is no polarity—where energies flow smoothly in one direction—there will be much doing but no music.

—Eric Hoffer, *Between the Devil and the Dragon*

Contents

Editor's Foreword

Paul Rinzler's name and work were familiar to me, from his contributions to the *Annual Review of Jazz Studies* and his excellent book *Jazz Arranging and Performance Practice* (from Scarecrow Press), but *The Contradictions of Jazz* reveals bright new facets of this distinguished teacher, player, and scholar.

This is not a fat tome, but it is loaded with intellectual nourishment. Much writing about jazz, be it scholarly or journalistic, is hermetic or provincial, but Rinzler digs deeply in his quest for answers to the music's seeming contradiction—to simplify—between the individual and the collective.

This plays out on many levels, illuminating what the author calls "the incredible interconnectedness in jazz." And making connections is something he excels at, as in clinching choruses in a solo.

Refreshingly free of academic jargon, Rinzler's prose engages the reader throughout, and his frame of reference is startlingly wide, yet never pretentious. We encounter, among others, Joyce, Emerson, Churchill, Einstein, Husserl, Hesse, Dylan, Norman Podhoretz, and the Firesign Theater—the latter an indication that a sense of humor is blessedly in evidence, as in one of my favorites among the chapter epigraphs, Yogi Berra's immortal "When you come to a fork in the road, take it."

But don't get me wrong—this is serious reading. I doubt that anyone interested in the wonderful and mysterious music we call jazz, no matter how seasoned, will come away from this book without having gleaned new insights. I confess that I approached it with some trepidation, but soon found myself deeply interested and involved. Rinzler's ability to draw on his experience as an accomplished pianist is a great advantage, akin to a jazz imprimatur.

This is a book that will make you think about the music and make you a better listener, and, I would strongly surmise, a better player as well.

—Dan Morgenstern

Preface

The most important thing about jazz—to me, at least—is how it sounds. Jazz is music, and music, in general, is meant to be heard and enjoyed. But after the sounds die away, as they must, curiosity can lead us to start thinking about those sounds and how they were produced. Jazz is performed in a particular way in a particular set of musical conditions and circumstances (such as the ubiquity of improvisation, the chorus form, the rhythm section, and more) that help to distinguish it from other styles of music. These aspects of jazz express certain values, such as the value of individualism through solo improvisation. Admittedly, these values are sometimes not immediately apparent when listening to or performing jazz. In the moment, jazz, like all music, is sound, and listeners can be swept away (and might prefer to be swept away) by the ongoing rush of one sound following another, or by the sonorous qualities of beautiful or fascinating music. But when we stop and think about it, when we consider how jazz is created and what is happening in jazz improvisation, we are led to the significance and meaning of those sounds and the values that get expressed. The aim of this book is to explore some of these values, the contradictions that occur between the values, and the meaning and significance of the contradictions.

SYNOPSIS

This book examines eight values that are expressed in jazz:

- individualism
- interconnectedness

- assertion
- openness
- freedom
- responsibility
- creativity
- tradition

In part one, I will explain how each of these eight values is expressed in jazz, first by identifying more detailed aspects of those eight values, then by showing how the musical conditions and circumstances of jazz express these values. Plainly and by themselves, these eight values tell us a lot about the meaning of jazz and its significance. But they are also related and can be grouped into four pairs that are often oppositional:

Individualism and interconnectedness are opposites because interconnectedness requires at least one other person to whom one is connected, whereas individualism concerns only a single person.

Assertion and openness are opposites regarding the direction of their influence: assertion means that something within a person is projected out into the world, while openness means that something from the world is received by a person.

Freedom and responsibility are opposites because responsibility calls for some requirement or limit on a person's behavior, and freedom is the absence of limits.

Creativity and tradition are opposites because innovation seeks to change that which tradition would maintain.

That such contradictions are a part of jazz is remarkable, but even more remarkable are the different ways in which such contradictions are expressed. Opposites such as assertion and openness and freedom and responsibility are not opposed to each other merely by one opposite completely negating the other. Rather, opposites can be opposed in various ways:

- mutual exclusion (one negates the other)
- perspective (different sides of an object or a situation)
- inverse proportion (a zero-sum game)
- gradation (a gradual blend)
- propagation (an offspring from parents)
- juxtaposition (two opposites side by side)
- dynamic tension (opposites fully present but clashing)

In part two, I will show how opposition other than mutual exclusion is present between various detailed aspects of the four pairs of opposite values. Jazz is even more remarkable because, in some cases, the form of opposition is dynamic tension, in which not only are both contradictory aspects fully present, but their opposition is not resolved.

There are other contradictions beyond these four pairs of opposite values in jazz, and in part three I will discuss their broader meanings. This discussion depends on the distinction between composition and improvisation. I will offer an aesthetic for jazz based on the opposition between two groups of ideas: in one is improvisation, process, experience, imperfection, phenomenology, and existentialism and in the other is composition, product, perfection, and science.

Throughout this book, I focus on jazz improvisation. But while improvisation is of central importance in jazz, jazz and improvisation are not equal. There are many types of music other than jazz that are improvised, and not everything in jazz is improvised. To some extent, what I claim for jazz in this book applies to other improvised music. It is not my purpose here to compare such claims, nor even to imply that what I claim for jazz is unique to jazz. Instead of making such a comparison between jazz and other improvised music, I only want to say something about jazz, and I will leave it to others to decide whether these ideas might apply to other styles.

I will also contrast improvisation and composition, as well as other ideas. It is important to understand, however, that these contrasts are generalizations and are therefore imprecise to some extent. Nevertheless, it is my hope that this book will convince readers of the usefulness of these generalizations.

I will use the word "instrument" to refer to the medium by which all jazz musicians produce sound, even though jazz vocalists do not play an instrument. There is no term in English that covers all musical instruments and the voice (considered as the "instrument," or medium, that a vocalist uses).

ACKNOWLEDGMENTS

I thank Alyson McLamore, Peter Reinholdsson, Marc Sabatella, and, most importantly, my wife, Robin, for their invaluable help in preparing the manuscript of this book.

Acknowledging these starting points, I hope to illuminate some aspects of jazz that are contradictory. In order to do this, it is necessary first to view opposition from a broad perspective. Toward that beginning, chapter 1 will outline various types of opposition besides the commonplace idea of mutual exclusion and will discuss opposition as an element of dialectic reasoning.

Part One

INTRODUCTION

1

♫

Opposition

Our mind is capable of passing beyond the dividing line we have drawn for it. Beyond the pairs of opposites of which the world consists, other, new insights begin.

—Hermann Hesse

This book explores how certain aspects of jazz are opposed to each other, as well as the nature of this opposition. Ultimately, the contradictions in these opposites in jazz will serve as a crucial part of an aesthetic theory of jazz. This aesthetic theory contrasts improvisation, process, experience, imperfection, phenomenology, and existentialism with composition, product, perfection, and science.

In order to appreciate the role that opposition and contradiction play in jazz, it is necessary to view opposition in a broad context. We begin with a brief survey of different types of opposition, followed by a short discussion of dialectics.

BEYOND MUTUAL EXCLUSION

Two contradictory items may stand in opposition to each other in several different ways, but it seems that opposition is too often understood only in terms of mutual exclusion, what is sometimes called "either/or thinking." While mutual exclusion is perhaps the strongest form of opposition, assuming that all opposition is in the form of mutual exclusion can prevent considering the possibility that opposites can coexist in some fashion. For instance, even though we can call two corners in a room opposite corners, they are not mutually exclusive of each other in the sense that both exist as part of the same room. In fact, they both *must* exist in order for there to be a room at all.

One example of either/or thinking is the following criticism of studying individuality in jazz by Daniel Fischlin and Ajay Heble:

> What troubles us . . . is that in [two authors'] haste to promulgate arguments about improvisation as a life-strategy for expressions of individuality, originality and creativity, they fail to account for the ways in which jazz improvisation and creative improvised music have always (certainly in their most resilient and most provocative historical instances: bebop, free jazz, AACM, Pan Afrikan Peoples Arkestra, Feminist Improvising Group, and so on, all addressed in this book) been about community building (rather than individual self-expression), about fostering new ways of thinking about, and participating in, human relationships.[1]

However, there is nothing troubling about failing to account for community building. Even though individuality can be seen as opposed to community and relationship, it does not deny them. Only if one is limited to viewing opposition as mutual exclusion, and not any of the other forms of opposition outlined below, might individuality deny community and relationship. There are many diverse people in the world with many diverse interests, and all of them may address various topics that contribute to knowledge and understanding.

The underlying assumption of Fischlin and Heble's criticism is that the opposite of a valuable topic is not valuable, but this assumption relies on mutual exclusion, and opposites may be related through other means. One may argue that one *should* focus on a particular topic instead of another, such as community instead of individuality, but that is a particular claim that may or may not be true, and it must be demonstrated in any event by specifying what goal is served by such a preference. In the quotation above, individuality is criticized merely for not accounting for community. This, however, is like condemning red for not being blue. Of course, one way around this problem is to address both sides of an opposition and to understand how they relate to each other through their opposition; these are important goals of this book.

TYPES OF OPPOSITES

Opposites may be related in several distinct ways, summarized in the following (this is not intended to be an exhaustive list). I will offer examples

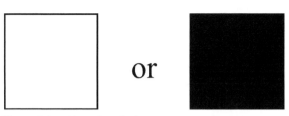

Figure 1.1.   Mutual exclusion.

from jazz to illustrate some of these types of opposition (every possible type need not be present in jazz or in any particular discipline).

Mutual Exclusion (A or B)

In mutual exclusion (see fig. 1.1), two opposites cannot coexist: for instance, a thing is either a guitar or not; it is impossible to be a guitar and not be a guitar at the same time.[2] Other examples of opposites that are mutually exclusive are odd and even natural numbers, and true and false. An example of an either/or, mutually exclusive relationship in human affairs is sports, where one team wins (completely) and the other team loses (completely). The term I will use to identify either of two elements in mutual exclusion is "negation."

While it is not the purpose of this book to focus on mutual exclusion, it does appear sometimes in jazz. For instance, the value of community in jazz is found in the big band, but the usual conformity in a big-band performance (rigorous adherence to musical norms such as precise coordination of articulations, dynamics, and intonation) is mutually exclusive of the value of individuality. When one conforms in a big band, one is not expressing one's individuality (see "Sections in a Big Band" in chapter 10).

Inverse Proportion (A Plus B Equals 100 percent)

As one side in a zero-sum game is increased, the other is necessarily decreased. The opposites are inversely proportional to each other, as shown in figure 1.2. In a zero-sum game there is a fixed amount of benefit, resource,

Figure 1.2.   Inverse proportion.

prize, or goal that only can be divided among the interests involved. To the extent that one side wins, the other side must lose proportionately. For instance, dividing a household budget between different bills (rent, mortgage, food, utilities, and the like) is a zero-sum game. Given an initial budget, any money that is used to pay one bill cannot be used to pay another.

In jazz, this type of opposition can be seen when tradition is opposed to creativity as a new style of jazz is being created. For instance, bebop accepted certain characteristics of the swing era (the basic chord progression for "I Got Rhythm," for instance, served as the chord progression for many bebop compositions). To the extent that bebop adopted characteristics of swing, it expressed tradition and was not creative; to the extent that bebop departed from the characteristics of swing, it was creative and not traditional.

Gradation (A and B Blend into Each Other)

When opposites blend (see fig. 1.3), they are placed on the far ends of a continuum, and between the two extremes there is a gradation that mixes the two opposites. For instance, black and white blend into each other through shades of gray. As the amount of white decreases through shades of gray, the amount of black increases. The two opposites are always in a proportional relationship, but at any point along the continuum there is some amount of each (except at the very extremes). In contrast, a zero-sum game also establishes a proportional relationship, but at any point along the continuum there is only one or the other, black or white, and each retains its full identity. In a blend, pure black and pure white are diluted when combined into gray. They both lose their identity; gray is not black and it is not white.

Propagation (A and B Create C)

Opposites can combine such that the combination does not resemble either of the contributors, even while some aspects or characteristics from

Figure 1.3.   Gradation.

Figure 1.4. Propagation.

the contributors may be discernible (see fig. 1.4). The combination is creative in the sense that it has characteristics that are not apparent in either of its progenitors. The combination is more than the sum of its parts, and transcends the progenitors. In this graphic, the pattern of black and white in the speckled square is not predictable from the white and black squares (although, of course, one aspect of the white and black progenitor squares—their colors—is predictable and apparent in the combination).

This type of fusing of opposites is commonly seen in parents and children. A child may inherit a mother's nose or a father's eyes, but the mother and father are not recognizable as complete identities in the child. One can identify elements of the parents in the child, but the combination of characteristics of the offspring is not present in either of the parents. The randomness of the combination of genetic material from the parents is partially responsible for producing a new set of characteristics in the offspring.

A more extreme example is a chemical compound made of two or more elements. Water is a combination of hydrogen and oxygen but at room temperature has none of the characteristics of pure hydrogen or pure oxygen, which are gases at room temperature (while water is a liquid at room temperature).

Perspective (A or B, Depending on One's Position)

One may see either black or white, depending on one's perspective, as shown in figure 1.5. Black and white coexist, but not when viewed from a single position. The fable about the blind men who each perceive an elephant in a different way (touching different parts of the elephant) and draw very different conclusions about the nature of it illustrates how opposing perspectives can be valid simultaneously. In this form of opposition, one can only view either the black or the white side, but cannot see both sides at the same time (see "Juxtaposition," following).

Juxtaposition (A and B Side by Side)

It is sometimes said that part of maturity is being able to hold two opposite ideas, as illustrated in figure 1.6. For instance, one can both love and

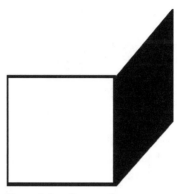

Figure 1.5.   Perspective.

hate another person. One may love how a spouse is emotionally supportive but hate how he or she cleans the house. Such love does not necessarily have any effect on such hate, and vice versa. Because the love and the
hate are directed toward two areas not necessarily related, they can remain independent of each other and thus fully coexist without any dilu-
tion or conflict.

An example of juxtaposition in jazz is the opposite improvisational tendencies of Miles Davis and John Coltrane within the same jazz combo.
Davis was renowned for his minimalistic style of improvisation, while
Coltrane was typically a busy improviser, playing many notes. Their opposing styles were juxtaposed when one's solo followed the other's (to
very successful musical results).

Dynamic Tension (A and B Opposed but Fully Expressed)

In dynamic tension (see fig. 1.7), two opposites are present and are fully
expressed, yet are in conflict. This can be compared with juxtaposition, in
which two opposites are present but are not in conflict; the contradiction
between the two opposites is not engaged.

A physical form of dynamic tension can be understood by trying to
bring together two magnets at their opposite magnetic poles. The mag-

Figure 1.6.   Juxtaposition.

Figure 1.7. Dynamic tension.

nets will resist being brought together, and one can feel in one's hands this resistance. The tension created by the opposition between the two magnets is a physical manifestation of dynamic tension.

Another example of dynamic tension is liking pain. Most people have at one time or another scratched an itch or picked at a scab on their bodies so much that it began to be slightly painful, but continued scratching and picking anyway. While there may be several reasons why a person might do that, one reason is that one may like or prefer the sensation of mild pain. This also can be a form of dynamic tension. At a slight level of pain, there can be a deliciousness in feeling pain. This is an example of dynamic tension because there is a contradiction (the pleasure of pain) in which both sides of an opposition are present but the conflict is not hidden or absent. The sensation when someone likes pain is somehow painful and pleasurable at the same time. It is as if one is able to turn a negative (pain) into a positive (pleasure), but somehow it remains a negative at the same time.

A musical example of dynamic tension is interaction in jazz, in which a jazz musician initiates or responds to unplanned, improvised musical ideas. Interaction can be viewed as simultaneous in/out information processing: the musician improvises, sending out musical ideas to which other musicians in the ensemble might respond, and the musician must listen as well, taking in the musical ideas that others in the ensemble offer and responding appropriately. These two opposite processes can occur simultaneously, and others have noted the tension involved in doing so (see "Dynamic Tension" in chapter 11).

Dynamic tension is a way in which the conflict between opposites is fully active, and even savored. I hope that this book helps the reader to appreciate the dynamic tension in the contradictions of jazz. Contradiction is commonly imagined as something to be avoided, resolved, or eliminated, but dynamic tension shows that there can be a positive side to contradiction. Something that is not contradictory may be stable, solid, and reliable, but dynamic tension and contradiction can be exciting, active, and vibrant.

A fuller discussion of the specific forms of opposition (dynamic tension, mutual exclusion, and others) between contradictory elements in jazz is presented in part two.

OPPOSITES AS NEGATIONS

The forms of opposition that are not mutual exclusion are the focus of this book. Four pairs of opposite values in jazz—individualism and interconnectedness, assertion and openness, freedom and responsibility, and creativity and tradition—are primarily opposed to each other through means other than mutual exclusion. This fact can be highlighted by contrasting these eight values with their true negations, with which they are related by mutual exclusion. However, in order to do so, it is first necessary to define the four pairs of values briefly.

Individualism. Focus on a person as a single person, without regard to social relations.

Interconnectedness. The relationships between two or more people, especially the music created when a musician improvises in the context of what other musicians in the ensemble have improvised.

Assertion. Taking the initiative and putting oneself forward confidently, as a form of self-expression, attempting to make a positive statement or contribution.

Openness. Being receptive, accepting the unknown, being nonjudgmental.

Freedom. Individual sovereignty, having choices and the ability to choose, negative freedom (from external restriction) and positive freedom (an expression of one's internal character).

Responsibility. The requirement to fulfill one's duties and obligations, usually to others.

Creativity. The production of (artistic) novelty.

Tradition. That which is preserved and which forms the foundation for a discipline.

Figure 1.8 outlines the four pairs of opposite values and their true negations.[3]

THE VALUE OF NEGATIONS

As I will show, jazz expresses four pairs of opposite values and not, generally, their negations. This is not to say, however, that negations are worthless. For instance, in contrast to individualism, it can be an exhilarating experience to be swept up in a crowd at, say, a rock concert, or at a sports event, and to feel the surge of energy as part of a large mass of people. Also, it is unrealistic to expect a young child to be as responsible as an adult, so children are appropriately freed of some responsibilities. In contrast to assertion, sometimes doing nothing is the best course.

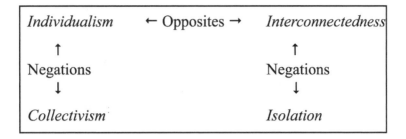

Individualism	← Opposites →	Interconnectedness
↑		↑
Negations		Negations
↓		↓
Collectivism		Isolation

Assertion	← Opposites →	Openness
↑		↑
Negations		Negations
↓		↓
Passivity		Narrowness

Freedom	← Opposites →	Responsibility
↑		↑
Negations		Negations
↓		↓
Restriction		Irresponsibility

Creativity	← Opposites →	Tradition
↑		↑
Negations		Negations
↓		↓
Prosaicism		Iconoclasm

Figure 1.8. Four pairs of opposite values and their negations.

Furthermore, the negations of the four pairs of opposite values are not completely absent from jazz. Any value may, at times, be present or appropriate in most if not all realms of human activity. For instance, solo jazz musicians have a long and great tradition within jazz, even though jazz is not fundamentally a solo idiom: the typical jazz group, a combo, contains more than one individual. Perhaps jazz's greatest virtuoso is pianist Art Tatum, whose reputation is built largely on his solo performances. Solo musicians reflect the value of isolation, and not interconnectedness, insofar as they do not perform with other musicians. However, even though the negation of one of the four pairs of opposite values may be fully expressed at one time or in a certain circumstance, the position that the original eight values hold in jazz may still remain.

DIALECTICS

That people often don't imagine different types of opposition is a testament to the strength in Western culture of what has been called *demonstrative reasoning*, as opposed to *dialectic reasoning*. Joseph Rychlak defines the core features of demonstrative reasoning as "singularity, linearity, unidirectionality, and non-contradiction."[4] Demonstrative reasoning can be traced back to Aristotle's famous syllogism "All men are mortal; Socrates is a man; therefore, Socrates is mortal." Given the premises of human mortality and Socrates' humanity, it would be an unallowable contradiction to claim that Socrates was not mortal. This illustrates the logic that says A cannot be not-A. Demonstrative reasoning is the foundation of science and mathematics. As Rychlak says, "The greatest strides in human reason these past four centuries (the Age of Science) have been made with the clear recognition that demonstrative strategies have been employed."[5]

On the other hand, Rychlak notes that "the core feature of dialectic is oppositionality . . . conflict and dynamic alternatives [cf. dynamic tension] are generated within the totality of such descriptions."[6] In contrast to Rychlak's core features of demonstrative logic, dialectics include multiplicity, multidimensionality, bi- or multidirectionality, and contradiction. Dialectic reasoning joins opposites together. Rychlak asks, "Can we truly learn what *up* is without necessarily understanding what *down* is?"[7] The dialectic was first recognized in ancient India and China, and later in the West by the early Greek philosophers.

Erika Lindemann and Daniel Anderson contrast dialectic thinking with earlier forms of reasoning in a person's intellectual development.[8] Adolescents tend to rely on universals, absolutes, and dualisms first. Eventually they adopt a naïve relativism in which all options are equally good. Finally, their mature thinking becomes dialectic: provisional, relative, contextual, and accepting of inconsistencies or contradictions. William Cobb contrasts dialectic reasoning with demonstrative reasoning through games:

> Here's an example of discursive [demonstrative] reasoning about this: Winning . . . is good, therefore its opposite, losing, is bad. It's better to have what's good than what's bad, so I want to win as often as possible. Thus, the handicapping system is a nuisance, and I should understate my rating so that I can win more often. . . . Here's dialectical reasoning applied to the same example: Winning . . . is good. Yet, winning is also bad. You learn more when you lose, and winning can lead to gloating and arrogance. Perhaps, then, winning is both good and bad, but if winning is not an unqualified good maybe it is not the real point of playing. Thus, one aim of the handicapping system may be to make us realize that winning is not the point of playing. Well, then. What is the reason for playing? And is winning both good and bad or neither good nor bad?[9]

Another good example of a dialectic approach is conflict resolution, or mediation. The opposing parties in a conflict often initially view the conflict with demonstrative logic and in mutually exclusive terms: each side believes that its side is right and the other side is wrong—period. With the help of a mediator, however, it is common for both parties to gain the perspective that both sides are right in at least some ways. When both sides can see validity in the other's position, a win-win solution is often the resolution of the conflict.

In true dialectic fashion, I don't intend to exclude demonstrative reasoning and use only dialectics in this book. I hope that I will demonstrate various conclusions about jazz that will be persuasive in a logical manner. But it is the opposites of jazz, its dialectic, that are the particular focus of this book. As William Talbot says, "Not all arguments are, or purport to be, proofs. In most contexts, reasoning is not meant to prove things, but to make sense of things. . . . Dialectical reasoning is non-demonstrative reasoning by which we attempt to improve the coherence of our beliefs (so they make more sense)."[10] I hope less to prove something about jazz than to create a coherent way of looking at some important and defining aspects of jazz.

NOTES

1. Daniel Fischlin and Ajay Heble, "The Other Side of Nowhere," in *The Other Side of Nowhere: Jazz, Improvisation, and Communities in Dialogue* (Middletown, Conn.: Wesleyan University Press, 2004), 23.

2. Mutual exclusion implies that the same considerations or context be applied to both X and not-X. For instance, a telephone is clearly not a guitar, but I was able to stretch the cord between the handset and the console of my telephone tightly enough to be able to produce a pitch when I plucked it. One might claim that any taut string or wire that one plucks to produce a discernable pitch is a kind of guitar. However, to claim that a telephone is not a guitar (in the context of the everyday conception of a telephone) and that a telephone is also a guitar (in the context of a creative use of the elements that make up a telephone) is to apply different contexts. Within the context of everyday conception, a telephone is not a guitar.

3. I will use the word "collective" in this book in a way that should be distinguished from "collectivism." In collectivism (and things collectivistic), the group is primary and individuality is lost, but the word "collective" is often used in jazz when individuals retain their individuality while being part of a larger group.

4. Joseph Rychlak, *The Psychology of Rigorous Humanism* (New York: John Wiley and Sons, 1977), 501.

5. Rychlak, *The Psychology of Rigorous Humanism*, 74.

6. Rychlak, *The Psychology of Rigorous Humanism*, 501.

7. Rychlak, *The Psychology of Rigorous Humanism*, 59.

8. Erika Lindemann and Daniel Anderson, *A Rhetoric for Writing Teachers*, 4th ed. (New York: Oxford University Press, 2001), 101.

9. William Cobb, "The Empty Board #13: The Dialectic of Go," *American Go Journal* 33, no. 1 (Winter 1999): 8.

10. William Talbott, "PHIL 102A, Test of Transparencies for Week #1 (Sept. 30–Oct. 4)," http://faculty.washington.edu/wtalbott/phil102/trweek1.htm (accessed September 3, 2005). I have altered some of the capitalization of the original.

Part Two

THE VALUES OF JAZZ

2

♫

Individualism

It is easy in the world to live after the world's opinion; it is easy in solitude to live after our own; but the great man is he who in the midst of the crowd keeps with perfect sweetness the independence of solitude.

—Ralph Waldo Emerson, *Self-Reliance*

In order to discuss how the four pairs of values in jazz are opposed, I will first explain what those values are. This chapter and the seven succeeding chapters will outline some details of these values so that they may be better understood in and of themselves, in preparation for understanding how they may be in opposition.

Individualism defined: Oyserman, Coon, and Kemmelmeier reviewed several researchers' definitions of individualism, and found a common thread: "These definitions all conceptualize individualism as a worldview that centralizes the personal—personal goals, personal uniqueness, and personal control—and peripheralizes the social."[1] Individualism places focus on a single person and his or her own desires, choices, interests, and goals, based on the specific idiosyncrasies of his or her own personality. The individual is a single person considered separate from any social relations. In individualism, it is the individual that has the power to make decisions and has full authority to carry out those decisions. It is perhaps no accident that individualism is an important part of jazz because jazz was created in the United States, which is widely regarded as being one of the most individualistic countries in the world.

Individualism's opposite: Individualism and interconnectedness are opposites because individualism concerns the single person, but interconnectedness requires more than one person.

A SINGLE PERSON: THE SOLOIST

The fundamental aspect of individualism is the number of people concerned: namely, one. This is an important consideration. A group of many people may contain a complex web of relationships that are present to a much lesser degree in a smaller group, and the difference in the complexity of the relationships between smaller and larger groups of people may well be fascinating or significant. But any collection of two or more people, no matter how large, is sharply distinguished from a collection that contains only a single person because there are no other people in that collection with whom to have any relationship.

One of the hallmarks of jazz is solo improvisation, but that hasn't always been the case. Before the dominance of Louis Armstrong, jazz was focused on the group rather than the individual. This was reflected in the common practice of frontline collective improvisation in New Orleans and Chicago jazz in the 1910s and 1920s. Ted Gioia says that "unlike later jazz, with its democratic reliance on individual solos, New Orleans pioneers created music in which the *group* was primary, in which each instrument was expected to play a specific role, not assert its independence."[2] The front line, typically consisting of a trumpet (or cornet), trombone, and clarinet, would improvise together at the same time. The trumpet would play the primary melody or improvise a variation on it; the trombone would play an accompanying melody that was pitched lower, moved more slowly, and was harmonically more basic; and the clarinet would play a high, fast, agile obbligato part. Because each instrument played a melody with different characteristics and thus fulfilled a different musical function, the collective improvisation remained coherent. (In contrast, imagine trying to listen to three people talking at the same time.) Even though each individual was improvising to a greater or lesser extent, it was the collective aspect of the front line—simultaneous improvisation—that was emphasized.

Louis Armstrong, however, changed jazz fundamentally in this regard. His unparalleled virtuosity, his melodic genius, his infectious spirit, and the sheer force of his musical personality so outstripped his contemporaries that he nearly single-handedly put the focus of jazz on the individual, not on the collective. His improvisations were that astonishing. Gioia agrees, saying that "[Armstrong], more than anyone else, showed the way to a more complex and sophisticated conception of the jazz solo, a conception that would change the music forever."[3] So does Martin Williams, who notes that "Armstrong's achievement was also more responsible than anything else for the fact that jazz irrevocably became not so much a collective ensemble style as a soloist's art."[4] With significant exceptions, such as free jazz and such ensembles as Weather Report, the individual soloist has remained a central focal point in jazz.

THE PERSONAL

An Improvisation and Its Person

Individualism in jazz connects the improviser, as a person, to the music that is improvised. An improvisation is inextricably linked with the improviser. This has been recognized even by those who reject improvisation. Composer Gavin Bryars says,

> One of the main reasons I am against improvisation now is that in any improvising position the person creating the music is identified with the music. The two things are seen to be synonymous. The creator is there making the music and is identified with the music and the music with the person. It's like standing a painter next to his picture so that every time you see the painting you see the painter as well and you can not see it without him.[5]

It makes sense that a composer, and less so a performer of composed music, might have an opinion about improvisation in this regard. Both the composer and the improviser are responsible for the conception of fundamental aspects of the music to be performed, but the composer is typically not a part of the performance of a composition. Performers are linked to their performances, like improvisers are, but not to the conception of the work, as improvisers and composers are. So composers are correct to view improvisers as conceivers, as well as to notice that the person of the conceiver is apparent in improvisation but not in composition. For a fuller discussion of the relationship between the performer, the composer, and the improviser, see "Perfection and Structural Complexity" in chapter 17.

A Personal Sound

Individualism implies the personal in the sense of being distinct or unique. A personal, custom-made product fits the specific requirements or conditions of an individual. Each jazz musician is expected to develop a highly personal, individual sound. Eric Nisenson holds that "the most important thing in jazz is to establish your own distinctive sound, one that is uniquely yours. . . . In order to be a great jazz artist, you must find out who you really are."[6] Developing a unique sound or approach is widely regarded as the central ambition for a jazz musician, defining that musician as an artist. Nisenson has defined the distinction between this aesthetic and that of European classical music thus: "European music is composed for an instrument or an ensemble; the performer's job is to play the music hopefully as close to the conception of the composer as possible. . . . [E]verything the jazz soloist plays is an expression of his personality, experience, deepest feelings and desire."[7]

Contradictorily, finding a personal sound might well include a learning period in which the style of past masters is imitated and absorbed. However, to stay at that level and not ever develop a personal sound would relegate a musician to second-class artistic status. Sam Rivers took the imitation of other jazz musicians seriously, but in a way that served the ultimate goal of finding a personal sound for himself: "I listened to everyone I could hear to make sure I didn't sound like them. I wasn't taking any chances; I wanted to be sure I didn't sound like anyone else."[8]

Immediate Identification through a Personal Sound

A jazz musician's individualistic personality can be apparent in his or her music so effectively that it is often possible for listeners to determine who is playing after hearing only a few seconds or a few notes, in the way one can recognize a friend's voice on the telephone after only a few words. A good example is the sound that Miles Davis produced in the 1950s with a Harmon mute. Many listeners can accurately recognize this sound as Davis's very quickly.

Personal Technique

Musical technique can also be personal. If a musician's sound should be personal and individual, then perhaps the means to achieve that sound can be personal and individual as well. Unusual or unorthodox technique is rare in classical music, and when it does appear, it is usually viewed as a deviation from orthodoxy. Andy Hamilton has written that "both Stan Tracey (jazz) and Vladimir Horowitz (classical) play with straight, flat fingers. This aberration on Horowitz's part is regarded as an eccentricity of genius; people wonder how it works, but it does, and it's the method Horowitz has chosen."[9] In jazz, however, there is little or no technical orthodoxy because technique is nearly always seen as being in service to the individual creating a unique and personal sound. The requirement that one stay true to one's unique personal characteristics holds true for technique, then, as well. Hamilton continues: "If Tracey did use a more classical technique [curved, and not straight, flat fingers] he might be a more obviously fluent player, in the style of Bill Evans, perhaps; but he would not then be Stan Tracey (with the angular lines, stabbing chords, etc.)."[10]

DIVERSITY

Individualism Leads to Diversity

Diversity is a direct result of individualism. To the extent that individuals are different from each other, their characteristics and the choices they make will be different. When individualism is encouraged, diversity will be present as well.

Diverse Substyles

Jazz has created a wide assortment of music in its many substyles (New Orleans, Chicago, swing, bebop, hard bop, cool, third stream, free, jazz/rock, neoclassical, smooth jazz, and more). It has sometimes been noticed that the history of jazz has been so varied that in one century it has paralleled (or even surpassed) the diversity of the entire history of common practice classical music from approximately 1600 to 1900. Jazz has produced an amazing amount of diverse music in a relatively short amount of time. The music that is gathered under the label "jazz" can be very different: in some significant ways, Jelly Roll Morton sounds very little like Kenny G.[11]

Combining aspects of different styles of music in order to create a new style or substyle is called fusion, and is one particular method of achieving diversity. Eric Nisenson quotes jazz composer George Russell: "Jazz was born as a fusion of music—fusion is the real 'jazz tradition,' fusing together various types of music and creating a new whole."[12] Russell's comment referred to the controversy over the style of jazz/rock, a style also called "fusion" because it combined jazz and rock, but even the birth of jazz in New Orleans at the beginning of the 1900s was a fusion of diverse styles and cultures, mainly African, English, French, and Spanish. Jazz has always been interested in taking what it can from nearly any other conceivable musical resource or style and seeing if such borrowing can be fruitful.

Lack of Diversity

Most of the time, diversity in jazz is highly valued. But sometimes, even jazz recoils at supporting diversity. There have been several styles of jazz—bebop, free jazz, and jazz/rock—which, when they were initially developed, created great disagreement. The antagonism against these controversial styles of jazz is contrary to the tendency in jazz to embrace diversity. Even though all jazz musicians have not always supported all types of fusion, there is great diversity within the music that is called "jazz."

ANTIAUTHORITARIANISM

Authority can be considered an aspect of collectivism, the negation of individualism. In collectivism, authority is given to someone who decides, speaks, or acts for the entire group, such as political leaders, religious leaders, or law enforcement officials (the authorities). Some principle, such as birthright, age, gender, might or power, social role, or even a democratic process, endows that person with the power to express the group's will or to impose his or her will on the group.

In general, jazz rejects the authority of an outside person in fundamental ways and gives to the individual the freedom and the responsibility that an authority would otherwise hold. This rejection of authority is based on the improvisational and spontaneous nature of jazz. Daniel Belgrad says, "This deconstruction of authority is an implicit political feature of spontaneous art. Like the recovery of human values neglected in the progress of Western civilization, and the struggle against corporate liberalism's growing social power, it is one of the social meanings of the aesthetic of spontaneity."[13]

Authorities Denied

Jazz has an antiauthoritarian element to some extent because figures such as the composer and past jazz masters, who may be mistaken for authorities, actually are not. In these cases, jazz places authority in the hands of the individual instead. Examining these supposed authorities will help illuminate the antiauthoritarian tendency of jazz.

The Composer

Perhaps the greatest potential authority in jazz, in musical terms, is the composer. A composer conceives the music, and the performer interprets the music of the composer. In a mainstream jazz combo, however, a composer does not tell the jazz musician what to play and how to play it, but only offers a starting point. The composer provides the broad outline—the chorus, the composed melody, and the chord progression—that the improviser uses in whatever manner he or she desires. The jazz composer loses the authoritative position enjoyed in nonimprovisatory styles because nearly all aspects of jazz are under the direct and complete control of the improviser. As David Lichtenstein says, "When the soloist improvises, he confronts the authority of the melody. To the extent that the improvisations ring true, they contain figures that achieve an equivalence with that authority."[14]

Past Jazz Masters

One might consider the past masters of jazz to be musical authorities. Giants of jazz such as Louis Armstrong, Charlie Parker, Miles Davis, and John Coltrane are commonly revered by aspiring or professional jazz musicians as well as by fans and listeners. The fanatical devotion that is common when one begins to learn the subtleties of jazz carries with it a near-religious worship of the musicians whose music provides the inspiration for the student of jazz. Neil Leonard has described this devotion in explicitly religious terms, likening early jazz, bebop, and free jazz to religious sects in tension with a dominant (non-jazz) theology, and likening "innovative jazzmen who inspired jazz sects [to] prophetic performers whose role harked back to the shaman."[15] In my own case, I was enthralled with the music of McCoy Tyner and studied his music in great detail and to a level that I have rarely matched since. That study was powered by an almost fanatical desire to understand why Tyner sounded the way he did so that I could duplicate his sound. Fans of jazz, as distinct from practicing musicians, can be similarly devoted to their favorites.

However, such musical figures are not really authorities of power, but are examples of what sociologist Max Weber called "charismatic authorities," people who gain authority through personal characteristics or qualities, and who can be distinguished from legal/rational authorities, such as a judge, and traditional authorities, such as a patriarch.[16] While jazz musicians may still devote themselves to studying the past masters (especially since trumpeter Wynton Marsalis has led the neoconservative movement that explicitly reveres those earlier jazz greats), very few jazz musicians would consider such study sufficient. Absorbing what the past masters have done cannot be the end of the study of jazz for a jazz musician, as if the past masters laid down what must be absorbed and what style must be played as a musical authority of power might. Jazz musicians are too concerned with creatively making their own sound, or developing their own unique approach, to accept such authority and end their studies at mere imitation of the older stars in the pantheon. Some masters themselves agree; McCoy Tyner has said, "[W]hen young pianists tell me, 'Wow, I really love what you're doing,' I tell them, 'That's wonderful, but allow yourself to come out, too.' Something I do may lead you to something, but it shouldn't distract you from finding your own sound."[17]

Jazz as an Outsider

Closely related to antiauthoritarianism is the idea of the outsider. An outsider is an individualist who is not part of the mainstream. In some ways, jazz itself is an outsider. On one hand, jazz has been on the outside throughout a large part of its history if only because a large number of its best musicians have been African American, and racism placed African Americans outside the mainstream of American society. One small indication that jazz was outside the norm is that jazz musicians were included with marijuana users in an early sociological study of deviance.[18]

On the other hand, jazz was once solidly in the center of U.S. culture during the swing era, in which it was America's popular music. Recently, after experiencing a decline in popularity, jazz has begun moving back into the mainstream. The abundance of jazz programs and ensembles in public schools, colleges, and universities positions jazz firmly within American education. The neoconservative movement of the past twenty years or so has exposed many people to a more popular but still authentic form of jazz. When the music of John Coltrane is used to sell a luxury car, as I once saw on a television commercial, then jazz is moving further into the mainstream. However, jazz recordings currently make up only about 3 percent of all albums sold in the United States.[19] Despite its current status, jazz is not quite "America's music" like the Dallas Cowboys football team was said to be "America's team." Jazz is said to be "America's classical music," but it has just about the same low percentage of album sales as classical music, which prevents either from truly being "America's music." Jazz may be respected enough to be represented in education and to sell automobiles, but it remains on the fringe of mainstream American culture to some extent.

Self-reliance

A jazz improviser is a self-reliant musician, fulfilling the roles of the performer and the composer all at once. In 1841, long before jazz was created, Ralph Waldo Emerson identified spontaneity—a primary aspect of improvisation—as fundamental to self-reliance:

> The magnetism which all original action exerts is explained when we inquire the reason of self-trust. Who is the Trustee? What is the aboriginal Self, on which a universal reliance may be grounded? What is the nature and power

of that science-baffling star, without parallax, without calculable elements, which shoots a ray of beauty even into trivial and impure actions, if the least mark of independence appear? The inquiry leads us to that source, at once the essence of genius, of virtue, and of life, which we call *Spontaneity or Instinct* [emphasis added]. We denote this primary wisdom as Intuition, whilst all later teachings are tuitions. In that deep force, the last fact behind which analysis can not go, all things find their common origin.[20]

It is not surprising that one of the great American thinkers should speak to one of the great American art forms even before that art form was created. Furthermore, when Emerson recognizes the importance of individualism and self-reliance by saying, "No kernel of nourishing corn can come to him but through his toil bestowed on that plot of ground which is given to him to till,"[21] the jazz improviser would agree, saying, "No phrase of nourishing music can come to the improviser but through his toil bestowed on that section of the tune which is given to him to improvise."

In summary, then, individualism is expressed in jazz through the ubiquity of the individual improvised solo, through the aesthetic of a personalized sound and technique, through the great diversity of substyles of jazz, and through antiauthoritarianism and self-reliance. While people are obviously social animals, it is also true that people are separate individuals, and it is this truth that forms the basis of individualism. Jazz acknowledges this by giving the individual the opportunity to prove that he or she actually is an individual through the improvised solo and through the development of a personal, individualized sound. This is achieved through self-reliance as well as by minimizing the authority of the composer, and even past jazz masters, so that the individual retains sovereignty. Even though individualism is strong in jazz, it is complemented by the presence of the value of interconnectedness, which will be examined in the next chapter.

NOTES

1. Daphna Oyserman, Heather M. Cooñ, and Markus Kemmelmeier, "Rethinking Individualism and Collectivism: Evaluation of Theoretical Assumptions and Meta-Analyses," *Psychological Bulletin* 128, no. 1 (2002): 5.

2. Ted Gioia, *The History of Jazz* (New York: Oxford University Press, 1997), 50.

3. Gioia, *The History of Jazz*, 51.

4. Martin Williams, *The Jazz Tradition* (Oxford: Oxford University Press, 1983), 55.

5. Quoted in Derek Bailey, *Musical Improvisation: Its Nature and Practice in Music* (New York: Da Capo Press, 1993), 115.

6. Eric Nisenson, *The Making of Kind of Blue: Miles Davis and His Masterpiece* (New York: St. Martin's Press, 2000), 25.

7. Nisenson, *The Making of Kind of Blue*, 22.

8. Sam Rivers, *Dimensions and Extensions* (Blue Note BST 84261, 1986), liner notes, quoted in Andy Hamilton, "The Art of Improvisation and the Aesthetics of Imperfection," *British Journal of Aesthetics* 40, no. 1 (January 2000): 174.

9. Andy Hamilton, "The Aesthetics of Imperfection," *Philosophy* 65, no. 253 (July 1990): 332.

10. Hamilton, "The Aesthetics of Imperfection," 332.

11. However, because there is some rational basis to group together all the music that is collected under the label "jazz," there are basic similarities between musicians widely separated in time and sound such as Morton and Kenny G.

12. Eric Nisenson, *Blue: The Murder of Jazz* (New York: St. Martin's Press, 1997), 191.

13. Daniel Belgrad, *The Culture of Spontaneity: Improvisation and the Arts in Postwar America* (Chicago: University of Chicago Press, 1998), 43.

14. David Lichtenstein, "The Rhetoric of Improvisation," *American Imago* 50, no. 2 (Summer 1993): 240.

15. Neil Leonard, *Jazz: Myth and Religion* (New York: Oxford University Press, 1987), 35.

16. Max Weber, *Economy and Society*, vol. 1 (New York: Bedminster Press, 1968), 215.

17. Bob Doerschuk, "McCoy Tyner," *Keyboard* 7, no. 8 (August 1981): 36.

18. Howard Becker, *Outsiders: Studies in the Sociology of Deviance* (New York: Free Press, 1963).

19. Recording Industry Association of America, "2003 Consumer Profile," www.riaa.com/news/marketingdata/pdf/2003ConsumerProfile.pdf.

20. Ralph Waldo Emerson, "Self-Reliance," in *The Complete Essays and Other Writings of Ralph Waldo Emerson*, edited by Brooks Atkinson (New York: Random House, 1940), 155.

21. Emerson, "Self-Reliance," 146.

3

♫

Interconnectedness

Without relationships, no matter how much wealth, fame, power, prestige and seeming success by the standards and opinions of the world one has, happiness will constantly elude him.

—Sidney Madwed, http://www.madwed.com/
Quotations/, "relationships"

In contrast to the focus in chapter 2 on individualism, it is the purpose of this chapter to emphasize the value of interconnectedness. People are social animals (even though we are individuals as well), and the connections and relationships we make throughout our lives are, excepting mere physical survival, perhaps the most important thing we do. Jazz reflects this importance by establishing conditions in which a group of musicians may interconnect musically. Interconnectedness in jazz can be profound and intimate. This emotional depth is one indication that jazz strongly expresses the value of connecting with others.

Definition of interconnectedness: Interconnectedness refers to mutual relations among people. It includes the interactions among two or more people as well as the influences people may have on each other. Richard Schmitt has called interconnectedness "being-in-relation."[1] For the opposite of interconnectedness, see chapter 2, Individualism.

As forms of interconnectedness, interpersonal relationships among jazz musicians who perform together may be distinguished from the relationships within the music created by those musicians. That is, jazz musicians who perform together, like anyone, may have any type of social relationship with each other, from strangers who have never met before they perform together (at a jam session, perhaps), to acquaintances, to friends, to good friends, to best friends, to lifelong friends, and the like. These interpersonal relationships, however, are distinct from the music that a jazz musician generates and that is created and conceived in relationship to what others in the ensemble have performed. Of course, the musical interconnectedness of jazz musicians may be influenced by the type and depth of the interpersonal relationships among those jazz musicians. But it is musical interconnectedness, and not interpersonal connectedness, that is the primary focus under study here.

Musical interconnectedness makes an ensemble more than just a collection of individuals. For instance, all the members of a musical ensemble could individually align the placement of their rhythms only with regard to an external beat, provided, say, by a metronome or a conductor. But the members of a jazz ensemble are interconnected when they align their rhythms in relation to how the others in the ensemble align their rhythms in relation to an underlying pulse. The resulting rhythmic consensus is interconnected, having been mutually and reciprocally negotiated.

THE GROOVE

One of the most important musical relationships in jazz is the groove. The groove can be defined as a regular and consistent articulation of rhythms in relation not only to an underlying background pulse (audible or not) but in relation to how other musicians in the ensemble articulate their rhythms. When a groove is established, listeners report its effect as similar to a type of forward momentum through which the music seems to flow effortlessly. The groove can be defined by whether the rhythms are slightly ahead of, right on, or behind a real or imagined background pulse. These variations are usually described as "pushing ahead," being on top," and "laying back." Differences in these types of grooves, and whether a groove occurs or not, is determined within very small time frames (typically hundredths of seconds or less). The groove establishes the most basic type of rhythmic relationship. Most jazz musicians consider the groove to be fundamental to jazz.[2]

Forming a Consensus

Normally, all musicians must be in accord as to how they relate to the beat and to each other rhythmically. This basic question—how well the ensemble will create a groove, and whether the ensemble will interpret the groove before, on, or after the beat—is a fundamental one that is no less important for usually being spontaneously and nonverbally negotiated. If the musicians have played together before, they may have already established a relationship and thus can anticipate how the groove will be played based on their past experience with each other. Drummer A and bassist B may both tend to lay back against the beat, so they may strike a laid-back groove immediately and successfully. If drummer A lays back but bassist B plays on top of the beat, they will need to negotiate the groove. One might fully adjust to the other, or they may compromise somewhere in the middle, or change their approach for certain types of pieces (laying back less, for instance, in more rhythmically aggressive styles such as hard bop).

Consistency

Another important aspect of the groove is the consistency of the rhythmic relationships among the background pulse and the musicians. Once those relationships are established, the groove is heightened when those rhythms are repeated over and over again, creating a dependable groove. In order to produce a strong groove, musicians must perform their rhythms consistently in whatever way (ahead of, on top of, or behind the beat) has been previously established.

It is a testament to the incredible interconnectedness in jazz that a groove must be consistent, within hundredths of a second, over many, many beats. To take a rough estimate, if we assume that, at one type of typical jazz gig, an ensemble might play three sets over three hours (with two short breaks), with about forty-five minutes of actual music performed per set (discounting breaks between tunes), with an average tempo of 160 beats per minute, then the number of beats performed would be $160 \times 40 \times 3 = 19,200$. The vast majority of these beats, for competent professionals, would be in the groove and performed within mere hundredths of a second of those of another musician.

Depth

Not only is the groove fundamental, but the connection between musicians who establish a groove is emotional and intense. No better statement of the intensity of the interconnectedness of musicians creating a groove can be offered than the following: " 'You play every beat in complete rhythmic unison with the drummer,' [bassist] Chuck Israels explains, 'thousands upon thousands of notes together, night after night after night. If it's working, it brings you very close. It's a kind of emotional empathy that you develop very quickly. The relationship is very intimate.'"[3] Israels's use of the word "intimate" indicates how being musically interconnected through the groove is analogous to being interconnected through deep, personal relationships. As Charli Persip says, "The drummer and the bass player must be married."[4]

INTERACTION

Interaction in jazz involves the spontaneous and improvised musical reactions of one musician to what another musician in the ensemble has performed. Interaction can either be an isolated incident in which one musical statement elicits a single response, or it can be an ongoing, ever-evolving process in which one musical idea triggers a response that prompts yet another response, and the process continues on and on. It can also be multidimensional because it need not be limited to two people; interaction can involve all members of the ensemble. This also means that any one musical phrase may bring out a different reaction from multiple musicians.

Interconnectedness is a rich and complex aspect of jazz, as evidenced by the number of different combinations of musicians that may interact, the possibility for ongoing change in interaction, and individual differences in interaction. For a quartet (an average-sized jazz combo), there are dozens of possible configurations of musicians participating in interaction. In table 3.1, each member of a quartet is indicated by the letters A, B, C, or D, and each of the different configurations of interaction, numbered from one to forty-six, is represented under the "Responders" column as a group of one or more letters. An "initiator" is a musician who introduces a musical idea, and a "responder" is a musician who answers a musical idea another musician has performed. The first four rows of table 3.1

Table 3.1. Configurations of Interaction, Single Set

Initiators			Responders		
A	1. B	2. C	3. D	4. B,C	5. C,D	6. B,C,D
B	7. A	8. C	9. D	10. A,C	11. A,D	12. A,C,D
C	13. A	14. B	15. D	16. A,B	17. A,D	18. A,B,D
D	19. A	20. B	21. C	22. A,B	23. A,C	24. A,B,C
A,B	25. C	26. D	27. C,D			
A,C	28. B	29. D	30. B,D			
A,D	31. B	32. C	33. B,C			
B,C	34. A	35. D	36. A,D			
B,D	37. A	38. C	39. B,C			
C,D	40. A	41. B	42. A,B			
A,B,C	43. D					
B,C,D	44. A					
A,B,D	45. C					
A,C,D	46. B					

show all the combinations of musicians who may respond if a single other musician initiates a musical idea. One letter indicates a response by a single musician, and a group of letters indicates a response by two or more musicians. The next six rows show all the combinations of responders if two musicians are jointly performing the initial musical idea (for instance, a crescendo) that the responders may answer. The next four lines show the single possibility for response if three musicians are performing a musical idea to which the remaining musician might respond.

All the possibilities in table 3.1 apply to a single musical idea offered by an initiator. However, a quartet is not limited to one musical idea to which others might respond. Musician A may respond to what musician B has just played at the same time that musician C is responding to what musician D has just played. Such multiple sets of interaction are shown in table 3.2. Each distinct configuration of interaction is numbered one through twelve. Each line in a single configuration in table 3.2 is a separate set of initiator and responder. For instance, the first two lines of table 3.2

Table 3.2.   Configurations of Interaction, Multiple Sets

Initiators	*Responders*
1. A	C
B	D
2. A	D
B	C
3. A	B
C	D
4. A	D
C	B
5. A	B
D	C
6. A	C
D	B
7. B	A
C	D
8. B	D
C	A
9. B	A
D	C
10. B	C
D	A
11. C	A
D	B
12. C	B
D	A

comprise a single configuration of interaction; musician C is responding to musician A while musician D is responding to musician B.

In total, then, there are fifty-eight different configurations of interaction possible in a jazz quartet. This creates the potential for a great amount of complexity, but there are two other factors that add even more complexity. First, the possibilities for interaction are always subject to change as time unfolds. There is a continuous, moment-by-moment possibility of changing the configuration of who is responding to whom, vastly increasing the potential for interaction in a quartet. Second, multiple responses need not be musically similar. If the drummer plays a particularly interesting polyrhythm, the bassist may decide to duplicate one line of that polyrhythm, while the pianist might add a new polyrhythmic line to cross the others. The great degree of complexity possible in interaction creates a rich environment and many opportunities to express and illustrate interconnectedness in jazz.

COMMUNITY

Relationship sometimes implies a connection between only two people, but community refers specifically to the relationships within a group of people. In jazz, one obvious community is the jazz ensemble, a group of musicians who are united in order to accomplish the musical goal of playing, at a bare minimum, the next tune. This community may last only until the end of that next tune, or it may last years and years in the case of musicians who regularly play together over a long period of time.

The Ensemble: Combo versus Big Band

There are two primary types of jazz ensembles: the combo and the big band. (We can dispense with the case of a solo musician for our discussion of jazz ensembles as musical communities because a community requires more than one person.) The combo and the big band express community in quite different musical ways as a result of the different sizes of these two ensembles and the role of the composer in each.

A combo is typically three to six people, while a big band can have eighteen members or more. The smaller number of musicians in a combo and their distinct roles mean that the composer predetermines relatively little of the entire performance, usually just the composed melody and its accompanying chord progression. Even though the chords will be used throughout the entire piece, the majority of what the ensemble plays is improvised and therefore not predetermined by the composer, whether it is the specific voicing that a guitarist uses to play a chord in the chord progression, or the specific notes that the bass player uses to walk a bass line from one chord to the next. Even when a jazz musician in a combo plays the composed melody, it is usually improvisatorially embellished to some degree. On the other hand, in a standard big-band arrangement, all the musicians are expected to play nearly everything exactly as written, as indicated by the composer. Even for improvised solos in a big-band arrangement, the composer can specify the order, length, and placement of the improvisations.

The crucial role of the composer in a conventional big band and the lesser role of the composer in a combo create two types of communities. In a combo, an interconnected community can be generated from the bottom up in a spontaneous and individualistic manner. Interaction is one way in which this can happen. The community of the big band, on the other hand, is imposed from the top down, starting with the composer and going through the conductor or director, in an authoritarian, collectivistic manner. The composer is the musical authority to whom the musicians submit by virtue of performing the composition as written.

However, even though the big band incorporates collectivism, which is mutually exclusive with individualism, the big band still expresses interconnectedness as a musical community. The members of a big band are tightly interconnected because they are strictly coordinated with each other. Especially for the winds—the trumpets, trombones, and saxophones—their intonation, timing, and articulations are aligned within exacting limits, on a scale of microseconds and similar to that of the groove. To coordinate with so many other musicians with such precision means that one must be solidly locked in—very tightly interconnected—with everyone else.

Despite the fact that playing the groove and playing a standard big-band arrangement allows for little if any significant or creative spontaneous change from the performers (except for improvised solos), interconnectedness is still expressed by both. One rarely if ever would play a groove that spontaneously and frequently changes; the whole point of a groove is to consistently approach the beat in a unified manner. Similarly, one does not spontaneously change what note one plays, for instance, in a harmonically complex shout chorus of a big-band chart. In a standard big-band chart, the composer has already made those decisions. But musicians in both types of ensembles are no less interconnected because of the very different foundations (individualistic versus collectivistic) on which the interconnectedness rests. Because the big band submits to the single authority of the composer, the interconnectedness in a big band is rigid, predetermined, and collectivistic, whereas interconnectedness in a combo is flexible, spontaneous, and individualistic.

Interconnected Strangers

Jazz musicians are well known for being able to perform at a very high level without any rehearsal, even with musicians who have never played together before. This is possible because jazz has a common practice and an assumed base of knowledge, approach, and procedure. One might consider the ease with which strangers can play jazz, however, to be contrary to community. Who could be less interconnected than people who have never met before? Actually, the ability of jazz musicians who are strangers to play together effectively reflects interconnection very strongly. Standard jazz practice enables jazz musicians who have never met before to come together and connect in musically intimate ways immediately, quickly, and deeply.

DEMOCRACY

Jazz can be considered a democratic form of music because, typically, there is no conductor: all members are responsible for creating the music collectively. As Max Roach says,

> When a piece is performed, everybody in the group has the opportunity to speak on it, to comment on it through their performance. It is a democratic process, as opposed to most European classical music in which the two most important people are the composer and the conductor. They are like the king and the queen. In a sense, the conductor is also the military official who is there to see that the wishes of the masters—the composers—are adhered to (as interpreted by the conductor). However, in a jazz performance, everyone has an opportunity to create a thing of beauty collectively, based on their own musical personalities.[5]

In practice, however, each member of the group may not be equal in every way. Paul Berliner notes that some jazz ensembles take the approach of "stressing the mutual interdependence of players and somewhat limiting individual freedom," and that leaders sometimes exercise an undemocratic authority in some ensembles. However, he also notes that "characteristically, the jazz community emphasizes freedom of expression in music making," as a statement of the ideals of democracy.[6] While some groups may not function completely as democracies, the principle of democracy is strong in jazz.

In solo jazz improvisation, the spotlight is turned on the individual, who not only usually commands the listener's attention, but also requires the support of the rest of the ensemble. It is the ensemble's responsibility to provide a background for the soloist. Although doing so creates an unequal, undemocratic situation, democracy is still expressed in jazz because the soloist's power is like the power of voters in a democracy: it is equally distributed. In a democracy, everyone can vote; in jazz, everyone can solo (in principle). While it is not uncommon in practice for a headliner to be featured and for backup musicians to take fewer solos, it is still uncharacteristic for a jazz musician, even a backup musician, to take no solos on a jazz gig.

An exception to the democratic ideal in jazz is the distinction between the rhythm section (typically piano and/or guitar, drums, and bass) and the horn section (any wind or melodic instrument, such as saxophone, trumpet, trombone, and voice). The rhythm section has the secondary role of supporting the horns when the horns play the composed melody as well as when one of the horns (or any member of the rhythm section) takes an improvised solo. The distinction between the soloist and the rhythm section creates an undemocratic hierarchy (even though this inequality can be transcended through interaction).

CONSENSUS

"Consensus" is a broad synonym for "agreement," but I intend a more specific meaning to consensus that comes from the decision-making process used by Quakers. Consensus is a process of eliciting views and perspectives from group members on a particular topic, exploring the ways in which the members may be in agreement or not, and finding a way to create a single view to which all can agree, despite any initial differences. Consensus thus seeks to interconnect the members of a group, and such a process can be seen in jazz, too. (In Quaker practice, if complete agreement is not possible, then at least the remaining differences are acknowledged, at which point the dissenters either relent as a loyal opposition whose disagreement is not enough to prevent action, or no action is taken. Note that voting is not part of this process.)

Applying this form of consensus to jazz, we must realize that the content of a musical consensus is a different thing than a consensus in a meeting about an idea or issue. The content of jazz is not material or semantic, but is more abstract. However, the essential process of consensus building may still be seen in jazz. Everyone in the ensemble presents his or her ideas or approach, and adjustments may be required when approaches differ so that the entire group may move forward.

Consensus is different in jazz as well because it can occur spontaneously and nonverbally. In a meeting, issues can be discussed and time is available, usually, for working through any differences. However, a musical performance happens in real time, and in jazz it is expected that players who have never played together before should sound as if they have. Furthermore, many issues arise during a performance that must be resolved during that performance, leaving little opportunity for a verbal discussion or preagreement. This time restraint means that a consensus must sometimes be negotiated nonverbally as the performance happens.

Now, it is true that some aspects of a jazz performance may be negotiated beforehand. Certainly, established jazz groups, either through discussion or through tradition and experience, will predetermine to some extent various aspects of their ensemble performance, such as, for instance, what type of ending will be played for a particular piece. However, in improvised music, things can always change, so jazz musicians are usually watchful for the unexpected, even if it might be contrary to a long tradition and much experience. There are also cases in which jazz musicians have not predetermined some aspects of a performance because they have not played together before. In these cases, some things must be collectively improvised, and this group process is similar to consensus building.

We can examine how a jazz group might use consensus to improvise an ending for a piece. One common ending is inserting a chord a half-step above the last chord, and then resolving that inserted chord by playing the last chord. This insertion is easily done if the band also sustains the next-to-last chord indefinitely, setting up the inserted chord and the last chord. Let's assume that the last two chords in a jazz piece are B♭7 and E♭Maj7. One ending for this piece might be

next-to-last chord	B♭7
inserted chord	EMaj7
last chord	E♭Maj7

If the piano player, for instance, spontaneously inserts the EMaj7 chord, he or she can be considered to have contributed his or her opinion, as part of a consensus-building process, on what the end of the piece will be.[7] The rest of the ensemble will have to react to this spontaneous (but not completely unheard of) development. If the saxophonist is contributing fills (improvised, ornate figurations) at the ending, then he or she probably will adjust the notes played to fit the inserted chord, the EMaj7, and not the one expected, the E♭Maj7. However, the saxophonist may contribute an idea on top of the pianist's inserted chord; if the pianist has lengthened the ending by inserting the EMaj7 as an extra chord, perhaps the saxophonist will play fills for an extended length of time, which in turn might force the piano player to support the saxophonist's fills with more voicings or iterations of the EMaj7 chord than the pianist may have originally anticipated. It is this type of give-and-take that makes interconnectedness in jazz similar to consensus: everyone must react to and take into account what everyone else is doing, and somehow, out of this mix, a coherent direction is determined and the group moves forward.

In summary, we have seen that jazz expresses musical interconnection through (1) the groove, a very intimate type of rhythmic connectedness; (2) interaction, in which an improvisation is created in relation to what others are improvising; (3) the community of the jazz ensemble; and (4) democracy and consensus that represent how jazz musicians make musical decisions together. Interconnectedness is thus a significant issue in jazz improvisation and is a value that jazz strongly expresses.

NOTES

1. Richard Schmitt, *Beyond Separateness: The Social Nature of Human Beings—Their Autonomy, Knowledge, and Power* (Boulder, Colo.: Westview Press, 1995), 3.

2. Paul Berliner, *Thinking in Jazz: The Infinite Art of Improvisation* (Chicago: University of Chicago Press, 1994), 349.

3. Berliner, *Thinking in Jazz*, 349–50.

4. Quoted in Berliner, *Thinking in Jazz*, 349.

5. Quoted in Berliner, *Thinking in Jazz*, 417.

6. Berliner, *Thinking in Jazz*, 417–18.

7. One difference between a musical consensus in jazz and an issue-oriented consensus at a meeting is that once something has been contributed musically, it is impossible to take back (to change one's opinion). Once played, it stays played. However, in terms of others' responses, the situation is much the same: the rest of the group has to deal with any individual's contribution. It is the responses, more than the initial statement, that establish interconnection because an initial statement only requires a single person, whereas a response implies two or more people who are interconnected through the response.

4

♫

Assertion

It was from Handel that I learned that style consists in force of assertion.

—George Bernard Shaw

There are four aspects of assertion—affirmation, initiative, self-expression, and fulfillment—that are present in jazz improvisation and will be explored in this chapter. Assertion is a primary value in jazz improvisation because improvisation (1) is an affirmation of whatever meaning or emotion the improviser is able to create or communicate to the listener; (2) is an act that requires initiative; (3) allows the improviser to express himself or herself musically; and (4) allows the improviser to fulfill his or her musical desires.

Definition of assertion: Assertion has been differentiated from aggression and submission as follows:

Aggression   Behavior that violates another person's rights or dignity
Submission   Behavior that allows another person to violate one's rights or dignity
Assertion   Behavior that insists on one's rights and dignity without violating the rights and dignity of others[1]

While the specific issues of rights and dignity do not apply when considering assertion in music, much of the flavor of assertion in this definition does. One cannot assert when one submits, but one must not violate another when asserting, either. Assertion is thus neutral with regard to others, and what is left as a result of this neutrality is just the positive expression of one's individuality, neither suppressed nor suppressing.

Opposite of assertion: Assertion and openness are opposites by virtue of the direction of their influence. Assertion moves from a person out to the world, whereas openness concerns influence or information from the world moving into and being received by a person.

AFFIRMATION IS POSITIVE

An affirmation is nearly the same as an assertion: "affirm: to state or assert positively: maintain as true."[2] If a decision, a belief, or a position is asserted, one has also affirmed that decision, belief, or position.

The word "positively" quoted above can mean "with confidence," but its other meaning—positive as the opposite of negative—is relevant. An affirmation states what is true, not what is false, as indicated in the definition quoted above. In this sense, an affirmation is positive, not in the sense of stating a conclusion confidently, but in the sense of not expressing an idea in negative terms. The word "affirmative" also carries this connotation; when we answer in the affirmative, we say "Yes," and not "No." The positive nature of affirmation is also reflected in its recent use in New Age practice as a means to make positive change within oneself, a mantra that attempts to create inner transformation for the better. An affirmation thus springs from within oneself—it might be something as profound as affirming a belief in honesty, or something as mundane as indicating a preference for chocolate over vanilla. A positive assertion or affirmation can be contrasted with a limitation or a restriction. Telling someone to stop, or hindering another's actions, are not affirmations. They may be entirely appropriate and necessary (for instance, stopping a child from running into the street), but they are not affirmations.

A Great Affirmation

In my opinion, one of the greatest acts of affirmation and assertion in art (literary, musical, or otherwise) that will help illustrate the positive character of affirmation is the very end of James Joyce's *Ulysses* in which the character Molly Bloom, as part of a long stream-of-consciousness passage, reiterates the word "yes" (the purest affirmation, the essential positive) several times:

> . . . and the sea the sea crimson sometimes like fire and the glorious sunsets and the fig trees in the Alameda gardens yes and all the queer little streets and pink and blue and yellow houses and the rose gardens and the jessamine

and geraniums and cactuses and Gibraltar as a girl where I was a Flower of
the mountain yes when I put the rose in my hair like the Andalusian girls
used or shall I wear a red yes and how he kissed me under the Moorish wall
and I thought well as well him as another and then I asked him with my eyes
to ask again yes and then he asked me would I yes to say yes my mountain
flower and first I put my arms around him yes and drew him down to me so
he could feel my breasts all perfume yes and his heart was going like mad
and yes I said yes I will Yes.[3]

Nonverbal Affirmation

An affirmation is usually expressed in words, as a credo or a statement of
one's belief, opinion, or position. However, more broadly, an affirmation
can also be an act. If one tells the truth in difficult circumstances, one has
affirmed a belief in honesty by one's actions and without making an explicit statement to that effect. This broader view of affirmation is necessary to understand how affirmation can apply to music. A jazz musician
who plays swing dance music and who swings well and thus motivates
the dancers is affirming the joy of rhythm through the music. Putting specific words to exactly what part of the music is doing the affirming and
exactly what is getting affirmed can be difficult because music, as sound,
can lack semantic content. So even though determining the specifics of affirmation in music can be subjective and open to interpretation, it means
no less that jazz, and music and art in general, can be affirmations. To the
extent that a performance is a positive experience, the musicians who perform, as well as their audience, affirm the value of music. No matter what
is getting affirmed, jazz improvisers affirm and assert their musical ideas
when they improvise and perform.

INITIATIVE

Assertion implies initiative. One dictionary defines the verb "assert" as
"to put (oneself) forward boldly and insistently."[4] Putting oneself forward
boldly requires initiative and an internal reservoir of strength and confidence. One could decide not to assert oneself, to withdraw and not contribute. Asserting oneself, however, requires an affirmative decision to
seize the opportunity and to put oneself into the fray. Taking the initiative
is not a reaction, that is, a response to a specific stimulus. Telling someone
to stop, or hindering another's actions, are reactions to specific stimuli.
Taking the initiative characteristically begins with an internal motivation,
as something done for intrinsic reasons and not as an immediate response
to something external.

By definition, initiative does not have to happen: it is optional and voluntary. It can be easier sometimes to sit back and just go along with the crowd. Doing something entails the risk of making a mistake and suffering criticism, and it takes energy and resources. Because assertion is optional and not required or automatic, one must make an affirmative decision and exercise some initiative in order to be assertive, and that is what jazz musicians do. They do so despite significant barriers sometimes, but these barriers only reinforce the necessity for initiative. In order to overcome a barrier such as stage fright, a performer must take the initiative and actively resist or somehow accommodate the stage fright; otherwise, it would be too easy to give in to the fear and give up.

I was once standing backstage with the composer of a composition in which I was the featured soloist, waiting for our cue to go onstage (the composer was conducting). We fell silent in that common situation in which one works whatever magic one has to in order to overcome the tension of stage fright (although, at that point, I was fairly comfortable in my management of whatever fear of going onstage I had). Somehow sensing this, I broke the silence and the tension by saying, "Tell me again, why do we do this?" We both laughed because my question acknowledged the tension we were both feeling, but an actual answer to my question would identify our motivations and the source of our initiative. There must be some very powerful internal, intrinsic motivators to get people out on stage and perform the high-wire act that is music, an act that may not require highly refined judgments of space and balance like tightrope walkers, but requires equally amazing judgments about time, harmony, and other aspects of music. Those motivators allow us to take the initiative and to enact the complex and subtle behaviors that are a musical performance.

Taking the initiative in jazz is easily seen through a counterexample. In the college jazz ensembles that I direct, I will sometimes open up a solo section, making it available for any member of the ensemble to take an improvised solo. On some occasions, not one student volunteers. Now, a lack of student volunteers can be a problem in any university class, particularly with nonmajors whose motivation may not be as high as it is in classes in their major. But I am always more disheartened at a lack of volunteers to take a solo in my jazz ensembles than for any other class I teach. The ideal for jazz is that musicians, especially students, should be champing at the bit to have a chance to assert themselves by taking a solo. Of course, there are many reasons why a student in one of my ensembles might not volunteer; the point is that, in jazz, the standard and the ideal is that one should take the initiative to assert oneself through improvisation.

Improvisers Must Have Something to Say

If an improviser does not have the internal motivation to want to express something, then that improviser probably will be a poor one. Even if, as a professional, the improviser fakes it now and again, at least the fake should be convincing enough to fool us. A jazz improviser needs to have something *to say*, that is, to assert, by taking the initiative, and making the choice to do so.

PUBLIC ASSERTION

A complicating factor of assertion in jazz improvisation is that jazz, as a performing art, is public, not private. The jazz musician is normally expected to have his or her music disseminated to an audience publicly, usually through live concerts or recordings. It would be a much different thing to take the initiative and improvise creatively but keep that creation private and never reveal it to anyone than to create something in public and make it known to others. A weaker form of assertion might include private initiative and creation, but the stronger form requires initiative and creation to be public and social, and that is the form that jazz generally adopts.

That jazz embraces public assertion and initiative is reflected in the long tradition of the jam session. The jam session was, for many years, an important method by which jazz musicians learned their craft. The approach of the jam session for learning how to improvise (and some might say the only way to learn) is to just get out there (publicly) and do it. It takes a good amount of confidence, courage, initiative, and assertiveness to learn one's craft in the public arena of a jam session, where anyone can hear the mistakes that are inevitable in the learning process.

SELF-EXPRESSION

From Within

When one takes the initiative and asserts or affirms some individual aspect of one's personality, one engages in self-expression. Assertion can be considered an expression of the uniqueness of the individual, moving from the internal idiosyncrasies of an individual's personality outward to the external world. When one asserts oneself, one makes a statement (literally or figuratively) because there is some internal aspect of one's personality that leads one to what is asserted. Assertion is not imposing oneself on the outside world, like a bull in a china shop; assertion is merely not being afraid to be oneself and to show that to others. J. R. Monterose states this idea in the following manner: "Why not play your own music if you're a jazz player? Jazz is supposed to be self-expression. You've got to have a need to say something on your instrument—to get it out. If I can't be myself, there's no point in being in jazz."[5]

Personal and Deep

Because assertion begins from internal sources, it can express very meaningful and personal things from very deep places within a person. Jazz musicians can tap into a deep unconscious well in order to improvise. They may talk about "laying it all out there" like sports teams do. It is not as though all jazz musicians always plumb the very depths of their souls in every solo they take; as with any craft or profession, they may be subject to daydreaming and other mundane distractions while working. But reaching deep inside oneself when improvising is one ideal in jazz as an art form—resulting in the intense, soul-wrenching solo—for both the musician as well as the audience (as opposed to the commercial goal of just getting through the gig in order to get paid). "Chuck Israels describes the emotion in Miles Davis' performance (with Cannonball Adderly) of 'Autumn Leaves' as 'extraordinary; what concentration—what commitment to the feeling of that piece! That's my idea of how to be a performer. When you give it all to the piece.' "[6] Jazz musician Pee Wee Russell is committed to playing every solo as if it were "the last one you were going to play in your life."[7] Pianist McCoy Tyner's belief that "music is as serious as your life" was used for the title of a book.[8]

SINCERITY

Ideally, a jazz musician has to mean it; playing an improvised solo has to matter to the musician. Jazz, in its highest form, requires the musician to feel something inside himself or herself sincerely. It would be possible (and I've had students do this) to go through the motions in a technically correct form but without feeling any emotion internally. Perhaps many, if not all, jazz improvisers have done this at some point or another. But a significant goal in jazz improvisation is to be able to reach that place inside oneself in which one feels something deeply and use that as the emotional pressure, so to speak, behind an improvisation or performance. Paul Berliner tells the story of a struggling jazz student who, upon breaking up with his girlfriend, played so emotionally during a lesson that his teacher, who had previously been very critical of the student's efforts, praised him highly, leaving him in shock.[9] Of course, a professional jazz musician may not need a personal or emotional crisis to be musically inspired, but Berliner's anecdote illustrates the role that a personal and sincere emotional experience can play in jazz improvisation.

FULFILLMENT

The verb "fulfill" means "to satisfy (requirements, obligations, etc.)." In the case of jazz improvisation and other arts, the word can be applied to the personal requirements of one's character or nature. One is fulfilled when one is satisfied by expressing one's character and personality. Assertion and fulfillment are linked, as the following anecdote illustrates. I was in the market to buy a house several years ago. In my search, I had found a very interesting house, but it had some flaws. Although initially I was excited about the house, it ultimately fell out of favor with me. My real estate agent, however, was pressuring me very strongly to buy it. I believe we had two different perspectives: he saw the house's many great features and thought that they made up for its negatives; I, on the other hand, would have rather had a house with few or no negatives, even if that meant it had fewer positives. My bottom line was that I didn't want to have to worry about very much with my new house, even if it meant sacrificing some nice features or a good financial deal. In the end, I nearly had to fight with my real estate agent in order not to buy the house. Had I not asserted myself in line with my true preferences, I would have taken the advice of my real estate agent, who was pressuring me heavily, and bought the house. However, that house wasn't right for me, and since I was the one buying it, it was appropriate for me to assert myself and my preferences. When I finally bought another house, I felt very fulfilled; I bought what was right for me.

That assertion can bring fulfillment is an important point because sometimes there are obstacles to fulfillment. An extreme example might be buying a used car. Used car salespeople are sometimes trained in techniques that do not encourage customers to buy exactly the right car for them (and so fulfill the customers' needs as much as possible), but merely make sure that some car is sold, even if it is inappropriate in some way for the customer. It is not uncommon for customers to fail to assert themselves when making a major purchase, if only out of ignorance of sales techniques.

Asserting one's needs and desires is the first step to fulfilling them. In the real world, it is common for desires and needs to go unmet. But jazz improvisation is a discipline that nearly demands that one assert oneself in order to be completely fulfilled.

Play What You Want

Jazz musicians, as improvisers, are more fulfilled musicians compared to others in one particular sense. It is common to feel emotionally fulfilled when enjoying music in general. Music is widely recognized as having great power over one's emotions; it "hath charms to soothe the savage breast." There is yet another level of fulfillment that a composer enjoys. The composer is able not only to hear the music that he or she has composed, but is also able to create it, expressing something of his or her own character and personality through the music. The improviser enjoys much of this fulfillment of the composer because the improviser takes over much of the role of the composer. But an improviser is in an even greater position than the composer in terms of fulfillment. The fulfillment of a jazz improviser is as complete as any musician because the improviser listens, creates, and performs, all of which are bound together in a single, unified act: improvisation. Stated simply, improvisers get to play exactly what they want, which is a high level of musical fulfillment.

Don't Play What You Don't Want to Play

In my teens and twenties, I was reluctant to play jazz standards because they weren't musically fulfilling for me. I favored the modal jazz played by John Coltrane, McCoy Tyner, and others because it seemed to me to be more substantial and deep, as opposed to the lightweight sentiments (reflected sometimes in the lyrics) that I heard in jazz standards at the time. Now, however, I can appreciate the great music that is inside jazz standards and I know that an improviser can assert his or her own great music from within those standards.

But jazz encourages the attitude of fulfilling oneself musically because it emphasizes improvisation, the activity in which you play exactly what you want. So we should not be too surprised when the ideal of fulfillment is turned back on jazz by those, like me in my teens and twenties, who reject jazz standards, or by anyone who has a particular idea of what fulfillment in jazz should look like. I still see this sentiment now and again in some students that I teach, and I can recognize myself in them. It is part of the contradiction of jazz that jazz educators can appropriately insist that their students learn to play jazz standards as a fundamental part of the idiom while still encouraging them to also play exactly what they want, but that discussion will be more fully presented in part II.

To summarize, assertion is expressed in jazz through affirmation, initiative, self-expression, and fulfillment. Jazz thus offers musicians an opportunity to become themselves more fully, and to thereby achieve musical satisfaction. *Ars longa, vita brevis,* but jazz improvisers take the fullest advantage of what their lives, as brief as all of ours, do offer when they seize the initiative to make a positive affirmation of the emotions that music can express so well, becoming fulfilled through the process of self-expression.

NOTES

1. Conflict Resolution Program of Santa Cruz County, *Conflict Management Tools & Skills: A One-Day Workshop.* Santa Cruz, Calif.: Conflict Resolution Program of Santa Cruz County, 1995.
2. *The Random House Webster's College Dictionary,* s.v. "affirm."
3. James Joyce, *Ulysses* (New York: Vintage Books, 1961), 768. For a surreal, gender-bending reading of this passage, hear The Firesign Theater's compact disc *How Can You Be in Two Places at Once When You're Not Anywhere at All* (Mobile Fidelity Sound Lab MFCD 834), from 27:09 to the end of track 1.
4. *The Random House Webster's College Dictionary,* s.v. "assert."
5. J. R. Monterose, *Straight Ahead* (Xanadu, 1975), liner notes, quoted in Andy Hamilton, "The Aesthetics of Imperfection," *Philosophy* 65, no. 253 (July 1990): 331.
6. Paul Berliner, *Thinking in Jazz: The Infinite Art of Improvisation* (Chicago: University of Chicago Press, 1994), 255.
7. Quoted in Whitney Balliett, *Improvising: Sixteen Jazz Musicians and Their Art* (New York: Oxford University Press, 1977), 89.
8. Valerie Wilmer, ed., *As Serious as Your Life: The Story of the New Jazz* (Westport, Conn.: Lawrence Hill & Company, 1980).
9. Berliner, *Thinking in Jazz,* 259.

5

♫

Openness

Rabinovich and Abramovich went to the Rabbi to settle a dispute over a particular tract of land. Rabinovich said, "O Wise One, you must tell Abramovich to return this parcel of land. It has belonged to my family for generations and you cannot allow this thief to steal it." The Rabbi nodded solemnly and said, "Yes, yes, you are right." But then Abramovich turns to the Rabbi and says, "O Wise One, my family has used this land as a wheat field for generations. If not for us the land would have gone to ruin." Hearing this, the Rabbi nods gravely and says, "Yes, yes, you are right." Afterward, a third party, Yankelevich, who has been listening to the conversation, turns to the Rabbi and says, "This all seems very complicated. Everyone says you are very wise, but I saw you agree to two totally contradictory claims." The Rabbi nods solemnly and says, "Yes, yes, you are right."[1]

Openness is aligned with other important jazz values, notably freedom (chapter 6) and creativity (chapter 8). Freedom means that options are open for choosing, and creativity requires an openness to possibilities not imagined. Openness, therefore, is a fundamental value in jazz not only for its own sake, but also for the way in which it supports other jazz values such as freedom and creativity.

Definition of openness: There are many definitions of the word "open," but at least four in particular have relevance for jazz:

Receptivity	Acceptance of input, as in open-minded
The unknown	An open destination, or open questions

| Continuation | An open-ended ticket |
| Being nonjudgmental | Open to any way |

For the opposite of openness, see chapter 4, Assertion.

RECEPTIVITY

Receptivity is perhaps the fundamental aspect of openness. To be receptive means that one is ready, willing, and able to gather and accept input or information that some part of the environment happens to be sending one's way.

If the first requirement for a jazz musician is to play notes and rhythms, that is, to perform, then the second requirement, not too far behind the first, is to listen. When so much of the musical character of a performance is left undefined, it is essential for the jazz musician to listen carefully to everyone in the ensemble in order to determine in what direction the music might go. To establish a groove, to decide whether a solo should continue, to reach a climax or to calm the music, and the like, are all matters that require jazz musicians to listen actively and to be open and receptive to the emerging group consensus about how the music should proceed. Active listening can even apply to such basics as the key of a piece. I recall playing publicly with some other musicians in a pick-up group—I had never played with them before—and they called a piece that I had not only never played before, but had never even *heard* before. I was fairly confident of my ability to grasp most of the chord progression after hearing it once while the others performed it (and while mumbling my way through it the first time), but I thought that it would be a good idea to have at least a starting point, which would be knowing in what key the piece would be played. I asked the leader what the key was, but the only answer I got was "One—two—one, two, three, four," which was the count-off, and the piece immediately began. So there I was, without any starting point whatsoever (except for the tempo). In such a circumstance, listening is essential.

In addition to being essential, listening in a jazz ensemble is highly refined. Jazz musicians sometimes must make subtle musical judgments very quickly. For instance, if a pianist plays a substitute chord, it is common to expect that the soloist will recognize it and perhaps alter his or her improvisation to fit the substitute chord (or the soloist may choose to clash with it). The time span required for such reactions can be fractions of a second. It is a measure of the ability to be open in jazz that such quick responses are often made.

THE UNKNOWN

Being open can mean that one does not know exactly to what one is open. In order to be comfortable with being open, one must be comfortable with the unknown. Jazz improvisation is an unknown because, ultimately, there are no rules that require how a jazz solo must unfold. Of course, there are rules of thumb as well as standard operating procedures. For instance, a jazz solo often starts out calmly and increases in intensity as it progresses. There may be psychological or aesthetic reasons for this, but it is not required that such a rule of thumb must be applied, nor any other rule of thumb. It is always up to the jazz improviser to decide whether to adhere to a rule of thumb or not. A jazz improvisation is fundamentally unknown, despite the given chord progression and the general tendencies that might allow making accurate predictions about a solo (for instance, that a solo will be more intense at its end than at its beginning). It is a meta-rule that any rule need not be followed in any particular circumstance.

Unpredictability

Jazz as an Experiment

Jazz improvisation is like an experiment in the sense that an improviser may try something and not know if it will be worthwhile. John Corbett says, "Jazz experiments . . . Is the second word a noun or a verb . . . ? [E]xperimenting is what jazz does."[2] This experimental aspect introduces an ever-present chance of unpredictability and the unknown. Furthermore, musicians are in control of how unpredictable a jazz performance may be. If everyone in a jazz band is more or less on autopilot and merely plays standard and well-worn licks with no attention to interaction or other creative possibilities, not much will be unpredictable. If instead, the musicians decide to push the envelope and try out new ideas, the performance may be highly unpredictable.

Chaos Theory and the Emergent

Chaos theory seeks to explain how very small changes in initial conditions can unpredictably create large changes in later conditions, as if a butterfly flapping its wings could trigger a hurricane a continent away. David Borgo provides a jazz analogue to chaos theory. While his example comes from free jazz, it still applies to all of jazz. "In the case of the free improvisation quintet, if one player adopts an expressive vibrato, it may trigger the other musicians to explore a similar vibrato effect until the expressive device becomes the organizing musical force for the next few minutes of improvisation. Without a preconceived musical score . . . , small changes in the performance of a free improvisation ensemble may amplify via positive feedback in iteration to create radically divergent effects."[3] Because jazz musicians may actively listen to one another, even a small or seemingly insignificant creative effort can blossom into a radically new sound that was difficult to predict.

Emergence also entails unpredictability. R. Keith Sawyer refers to George Mead's definition of emergence and applies the idea of emergence to improvisation: "In a series of lectures at Berkeley in 1930, G. H. Mead elaborated a pragmatist theory of emergence: 'The emergent when it appears is always found to follow from the past, but before it appears, it does not, by definition, follow from the past.' Mead was commenting on the contingency of improvisational interaction: although a retrospective examination reveals a coherent interaction, each social act provides a range of creative options, any one of which could have resulted in a radically different performance."[4] Sawyer's point is that an agent could have taken any of a number of different paths, so the one that is taken is not predictable beforehand. The path taken is also contingent in that it responds to a set of conditions that, because the performance is improvised, were not foreseen at the beginning of the performance. For instance, what a jazz ensemble might improvise at the beginning of a chorus late in a piece may well depend on what the group improvised at the beginnings of previous choruses.

Embracing the Unknown

The advantage of openness is that new results are always possible, but the disadvantage is the risk of failure. As John Corbett has said, "the performer does not *know* for certain what will be played going into the performance, since the music is by definition undefined; the risk of failure, or complete collapse, is everywhere present."[5] While few would actively seek failure or collapse, jazz offers an opportunity to face the possibility of failure courageously. John Litweiler says that Ornette Coleman "makes clear that uncertainty is the content of life, and even things that we take for certainties . . . are ever altering shape and character. By turns he fears or embraces this ambiguity; but he constantly faces it, and by his example, he condemns those who seek resolution or finality as timid."[6] David Borgo interprets a large and growing body of recent scientific work in chaos theory and dynamical systems theory (complex dynamical systems, fluid dynamics, quantum electrodynamics, and fractal geometry) as a trend "in which uncertainty may be revered rather than feared."[7]

The Unknown Requires Strength

Sometimes, when people are open and receptive, it is seen as a kind of weakness, perhaps because openness is easily contrasted with aggression, in which strength and ability are demonstrated in an obvious manner. Openness is sometimes seen as a prime characteristic of a milquetoast, someone who is excessively submissive and will do or accept what anyone else requests. But openness requires strength, competence, and confidence. In order to be open in general and comfortable with the unknown in particular, one must have a strong foundation of internal strength and security. The unknown can legitimately induce fear because there is always the possibility of some danger being present. So, in order to face danger securely, one must have sufficient internal resources and confidence. However, those resources and confidence can be invisible because they are held in reserve; there is only the potential for their need because the unknown is only potentially dangerous. Openness does not necessarily mean weakness; it can simply mean that strength may not be outwardly visible.

Improvisation as a Journey

A common metaphor for the unknown and openness is the journey. On some journeys, there is little that is unknown; but the largest journey, life itself, is deeply unknown. While our everyday lives are mostly routine, anything can happen at any time, as the history of the world and the history of our lives easily show. Despite whatever success we enjoy at prediction, the future is perhaps the greatest unknown. Our journey through time is fundamentally unknowable, and we cannot help but be open to it. We have no choice but to accept our journey into the future as it is gradually revealed to us.

A common metaphor for jazz improvisation is also a journey, the end of which is not determined at its beginning. Christopher Small has looked at improvisation in this way by contrasting it with composition:

> Western composed music resembles an account of a journey of exploration that has been taken by the composer, who comes back, as it were, from "Out There," and tells us something, as best he can, of what it was like. The journey may have been a long, arduous and fascinating one, and we may be excited, moved, even amused by it, but we can not enter fully into the experience with him because the experience was over and he was safely home before we came to hear of it. . . . In improvising, on the other hand, the musician takes us with him on his journey; we negotiate with him every twist and turn, every precipice and danger. We may not know how long the trip is going to be, or even necessarily where we are going. It may be that we shall

not enter any new territory at all, or even if we do, that it will prove just a dismal swamp that no-one will wish to revisit, but every now and then we obtain glimpses of glittering new lands, are dazzled by the sight of beauty and meaning which is all the more astonishing for being unexpected. . . . In short, composed music is the account of the journey of exploration, which might well have been momentous, but is over before we learn of it, while improvisation is the journey itself.[8]

Coltrane as Sisyphus

One of the best examples of a jazz musician who embodied the idea of jazz improvisation as a journey is John Coltrane. Coltrane's music consistently exhibited a sense of journey and restless, constant progression. Joachim Berendt expresses this by contrasting Coltrane with Ornette Coleman, comparing them to characters from mythology:

If Ornette Coleman is the phoenix whose music from the start was revealed to us—if not in its mature form, then at least in its basic conception—as if it had sprung from the head of Zeus, then Coltrane was a Sisyphus, who again and again—from the very bottom up to the mountaintop—had to roll the hard, cumbersome rock of knowledge. And perhaps, whenever Coltrane got to the top, Coleman would already be standing there in his resplendent circus suit, playing his beautiful melodies. But the music John Coltrane would blow then, from the top of the mountain—standing next to Ornette—was imbued with the power of the pilgrim who had reached yet another station on the long, thorny road to knowledge (or might we better say—because it was Coltrane's conviction—to God).[9]

One can understand Coltrane's journey through one of his masterpieces, his composition "Giant Steps." The modulations in "Giant Steps" are especially awkward and present a challenge to the improviser. By composing "Giant Steps," Coltrane set upon a journey toward one of the most difficult chord progressions in jazz. "Giant Steps" was like a challenge out on the horizon and gave Coltrane a goal for his continuing musical journey. When Coltrane recorded "Giant Steps," he proved that he had mastered its chord progression. But then what? Once one arrives, the journey is over. Coltrane faced a dead end with regard to difficult chord progressions. What was next, devise an even more difficult progression? The better answer, one that Coltrane adopted, reinforces the idea of an ongoing journey even better than a more difficult chord progression could have. The way to continue a journey that has come to a dead end is to aim for a completely different point on the horizon, rather than just trying to go farther in the same direction. That different direction for Coltrane was modal jazz, something that he was already playing with Miles Davis even as he recorded "Giant Steps." Modal jazz gave Coltrane a new direction for his ongoing journey. It became his second main style, following hard bop, and one that would gradually transform into his last style, free jazz. Eric Nisenson has also identified the journey in Coltrane's career: "As he wandered farther and farther outside [into free jazz], I was forced to realize that Coltrane simply had to continue moving on, even if it meant making music that was considerably less perfect than his earlier work."[10] Coltrane's free-jazz album *Ascension* enshrines in its title what was perhaps the ultimate journey for Coltrane, a religious journey to know God.

CONTINUATION

Openness can be defined as not reaching the end of a process in time. The ongoing nature of openness is a part of viewing a journey as a metaphor for jazz.

In jazz, an improvisation is and is not a finished thing. In one sense, an improvisation during a performance of a jazz piece literally ends at some point, as does the piece itself. However, in another sense, an improvisation is only the current manifestation of all of an improviser's improvisations on that piece. A jazz musician performs another version of his or her approach to a piece every time he or she has occasion to improvise on it. In this sense, improvisation is an ongoing process, connecting all of the improviser's improvisations on a particular piece. They are linked because the piece determines, through its harmonic and formal structure, the broad outline of what the improvisation will be: it establishes the lay of the land that the improviser must traverse in the improvisation. An improvisation can be considered a work in progress, and we hear one version of this work in progress on stage. The improviser has the advantage of getting a second chance, a third chance, and more chances in an ongoing process every time he or she performs the same piece.

One might contest this view of improvisation by attempting to graft the ongoing nature of improvisation onto the process of composition. One might argue that, similar to an improviser, a composer also continually refines his or her craft with each subsequent composition. This idea, however, ultimately fails because in the case of the improviser, reference back to the original piece on which he or she is improvising is necessary: there is no doubt, by definition, that it is the same piece on which the improviser is improvising, and so each improvisation is linked as another version of the improviser's approach on that original piece. In contrast, each successive attempt at refinement of craft by the composer does not necessarily entail revision of the same composition; rather, each composition is normally considered to be a new work with no necessary connection to any previous composition. The composer starts from a blank slate in a way that the improviser, when improvising on a piece multiple times, does not.

BEING NONJUDGMENTAL

Being nonjudgmental refers to rejecting the idea that there is right and wrong. There are several different ways of being nonjudgmental, ways in which the distinction between right and wrong does not apply:

All options are equal. For instance, if one is going out to the movies, and all movies available are equally appealing, then it does not matter which movie is chosen, and therefore there is no right or wrong choice.

Neutrality. One may decide not to make a judgment as to what is right or wrong even when one thing may very well be right and the other wrong. There are times in which not making a judgment and behaving neutrally is important. A mediator, for instance, may refuse to make a judgment as to whether one side in a conflict is right or wrong (even if the mediator has a personal opinion as to which side is right) because such a judgment would destroy neutrality, a crucial part of mediation.

Perspectives. A final judgment as to what is right or wrong may not be possible because of the equivalence of different perspectives. The fable about the group of blind men who conclude very different things about an elephant after they examine different parts of it shows that different perspectives, while individually not a complete picture, may all be correct even if they conflict. None of the blind men who examined the elephant were wrong insofar as they accurately described what they perceived; their mistake was in imagining that their limited perspective was the entirety.

Another way to say that there is no right or wrong is one of the titles from my jazz piano trio CD *Active Listening*, "Everyone Is Right."[11] Of course, at first glance, it is obvious that everyone is *not* right: people make mistakes and people can disagree. However, this title exaggerates in order to make the point that what may seem like a matter of right and wrong may very well not be so. Rather than a plain statement of absolute fact, this title is an alert that, many times, what seems plainly to be right or wrong may not be once perspectives and assumptions are shared.

Right and Wrong Notes

To acknowledge those times in which there is no right or wrong is not to admit it at all times. Saying "1 + 1 = 3," in the absence of any other specific conditions, and in the context of mathematics, is clearly wrong. So sometimes there is a right and wrong, and sometimes there is not. Being judgmental—having unyielding and absolute ideas about what is right and wrong—may be appropriate sometimes, but it cannot be considered an aspect of openness.

Right and wrong in jazz is a complicated situation, and its contradictions are perhaps no better illustrated than in what Hugh Roberts has called Thelonious Monk's personal motto, "Wrong is right."[12] So the question of whether or not a note is right is an important one in jazz.

At first, there are right and wrong notes in jazz, at the stage when students of jazz learn which notes and scales fit with which chords. Students learn, in effect, a catalog of the correct notes and scales that accompany jazz chords. But ultimately, any note may be played over any chord. If an improviser creates some musical relationship by using a note that would be wrong according to a mere classification of the correct notes and scales that accompany jazz chords, then that note is correct. One way to do this is through embellishment:

> Miles Davis recalls his argument with Charlie Parker, who maintained that players could "do anything with chords. I disagreed, told him that you couldn't play d-natural in the fifth bar of a B♭ blues. He said you could. One night later at Birdland, I heard Lester Young do it, but he bent the note. Bird . . . just looked over at me with that 'I told you so' look."[13]

Another way to do this is through motivic development. The note B♭ is considered nominally wrong over a CMaj7 chord, but figure 5.1 shows how B♭ can be made to work over CMaj7 by repeating a motif with the B♭.

The note B♭ is dissonant against a CMaj7 chord, but by repeating the dissonance and the short phrase of which it is a part, a musical relationship is created, through motivic development, which is able to trump any consideration of the rightness or the wrongness of the note as defined through mere classification. Admittedly, the dissonance may be irritating, and this broadly drawn example is only for illustrative purposes. But the note is not wrong: ultimately, an improviser can use any note over any chord for some artistic purpose. Jazz is extremely tolerant in this regard: nearly any sound can be incorporated if it is done purposefully and with a strong musical sense.

There are no right and wrong notes even though jazz pedagogy, at least for beginners, establishes right and wrong notes. Beginning jazz theory could say, "These notes may be freely used over this chord, and these notes are more difficult to use over that same chord," but convenience may change this more subtle idea into a plain, straightforward, "These notes are correct, and these notes are not."

Figure 5.1. Motivic development: repeating a motif with the note B♭.

Openness teaches us to be receptive to whatever reality might offer us and to be ready to learn about it. Anything can happen, and the future is unknowable. Similarly, anything can potentially happen in a jazz improvisation, and where a jazz improvisation may go is ultimately unknowable, too (despite the characteristic tendencies of individual jazz musicians). The same humility that teaches us to be receptive and that is necessary when facing the unknown also tells us that we shouldn't make quick or easy judgments, that what is right or wrong can sometimes be a tricky issue. Openness not only reflects humility, but is also a strategic move, given an unknowable future.

NOTES

1. Tony Rothman and George Sudarshan, *Doubt and Certainty* (Reading, Mass.: Helix Books, 1989), 153–54.

2. John Corbett, "Jazz Experiments: Cutting Edge Research," *Downbeat* 61, no. 7 (July 1994): 50.

3. David Borgo, "Reverence for Uncertainty: Chaos, Order, and the Dynamics of Musical Free Improvisation" (Ph.D. diss., University of California, Los Angeles, 1999), 99.

4. R. Keith Sawyer, "Improvisation and the Creative Process: Dewey, Collingwood, and the Aesthetics of Spontaneity," *Journal of Aesthetics and Art Criticism* 58, no. 2 (Spring 2000): 152.

5. John Corbett, "Writing around Free Improvisation," in *Jazz among the Discourses*, edited by Krin Gabbard (Durham, N.C.: Duke University Press, 1995), 222.

6. John Litweiler, *The Freedom Principle: Jazz after 1958* (New York: William Morrow, 1984), 39.

7. Borgo, "Reverence for Uncertainty," 9.

8. Christopher Small, *Music, Education, Society* (London: John Calder, 1980), 176.

9. Joachim E. Berendt, *The Jazz Book: From Ragtime to Fusion and Beyond*, revised by Günther Huesmann, translated by H. and B. Bredigkeit with Dan Morgenstern and Tim Nevill (New York: Lawrence Hill Books, 1992), 127–28.

10. Eric Nisenson, *The Making of Kind of Blue: Miles Davis and His Masterpiece* (New York: St. Martin's Press, 2000), 7.

11. Paul Rinzler Trio, *Active Listening* (Sea Breeze Jazz SB-3039, 1999).

12. Hugh Roberts, "Improvisation, Individuation, Immanence: Thelonious Monk," *Black Sacred Music* 3, no. 2 (Fall 1989): 54.

13. Paul Berliner, *Thinking in Jazz: The Infinite Art of Improvisation* (Chicago: University of Chicago Press, 1994), 252.

6

♫

Freedom

Everything that is really great and inspiring is created by the individual who can labor in freedom.

—Albert Einstein

Freedom is widely considered to be precious. Jazz improvisation is a musical realization of this precious thing, a musical form in which freedom is given a high status and a strong role. Freedom might also be represented in music by dissonance, implying freedom from the rules of harmony, or through randomly chosen sounds. But certainly, one of the great attractions of jazz improvisation is the delight in hearing freedom made audible.

Definition of freedom: The following are some aspects of freedom that help define it in terms relevant for our discussion:

- sovereignty (the authority to make a choice);
- the presence of options;
- the capability to express or carry out a choice; and
- the distinction between positive and negative freedom (choices coming from internal motives versus external forces).[1]

Opposite of freedom: Freedom and responsibility are opposites because freedom explores options and multiplies possibilities, whereas responsibility limits action through obligation. Freedom fulfills one's own needs or desires and responsibility fulfills the needs or desires of others.

THE IMPROVISER AS SOVEREIGN

Improvisation is at the core of jazz, and the essence of improvisation is freedom and individual sovereignty. The improviser has the authority to play whatever he or she wants. This authority cannot be delegated without destroying the idea of improvisation (what would it mean for an improviser to delegate the authority to determine the music of an improvisation?). The freedom of an improviser stands in contrast to the relative lack of freedom for a performer who is playing a piece of music already composed and notated. The performer still has control over some areas of music—articulation, dynamics, and more—but the improviser has control over those areas as well. For a nonimprovising performer, the composer is sovereign over two of the most basic aspects of music—notes and rhythm—but the improviser is sovereign in the composer's place.

The improviser's sovereignty is not absolute, however. The improviser's musical decisions are heard in the context of what others in the ensemble, such as the rhythm section, are performing at the same time. The improviser may take some or all of the entire musical environment into account when making improvisational decisions. But the improviser still has sovereignty over those decisions, even if they occur within the context of others' contributions to the entire musical environment.

LIBERATION

Liberation implies being set free from something. For the improvising jazz musician, liberation means an escape from the "tyranny of the score." That is, the improviser does not have a score that dictates which notes and rhythms must be performed. A melody and a chord progression is predetermined by the composer, but the discussion of how those musical elements may limit or not limit the freedom of the improviser will occur later in this chapter (see "Limits of Freedom").

Some substyles of jazz also reflect liberation. One of the factors that helped create bebop was the desire to be liberated from the confines of popular big-band music of the late 1930s and early 1940s. Solo improvisation in swing-era big bands was sometimes limited by the composer/arranger, who exercised control through the written score. Bebop emphasized solo improvisation, small combos, and lack of musical scores, and thus achieved a liberation from the control of the composer/arranger. Also, free-jazz musicians elevated the concept of freedom and liberation in jazz above nearly all else; they sought liberation in particular from the chord progression, which determines the broad harmonic direction of a solo improvisation. Some free-jazz musicians, like Archie Shepp, made a connection between liberation in improvisation and political and social liberation during the civil rights struggles of the 1950s and 1960s.[2]

OPTIONS

Having more than one option is crucial for freedom. If only a single option is available, freedom to choose is meaningless because there is no real choice. If several options are available, however, then one may actually be free to choose.

Diversity, a value in jazz previously discussed (see "Diversity" in chapter 2), supports freedom because diversity leads to having a number of options from which to choose. In jazz, this can mean the freedom to play in any of the various substyles of jazz. In general, it is a valuable trait in the economic marketplace for a jazz musician to be versatile, that is, know as many forms of jazz as possible. While the most famous jazz musicians may not reveal the breadth of the options open to them because they are able to specialize and perform a smaller range of material according to their desires, it is common that, throughout a career in jazz, one has to pay a lot of dues and do many different things, including playing in many substyles, as well as composing, teaching, and more.

POSITIVE AND NEGATIVE FREEDOM

Freedom has been famously defined in negative and positive terms by Isaiah Berlin.[3] Negative freedom is the absence of outside restriction, interference, or coercion. Positive freedom is an expression of self-realization, of internal desires, or of the uniqueness of an individual. In positive freedom, the individual acts for his or her own internally defined purposes. Positive freedom is thus closely tied to assertion and affirmation, as well as individualism. Positive freedom can be understood by contrasting it with various ways in which people make choices for reasons other than the assertion of one's personality or character.

Trust. An expert or friend recommends a certain choice that one follows on the basis of trusting the other's judgment.

Tradition. That's how it's always been done.

Apathy. It doesn't really matter what one decides, so some random process, perhaps, is used.

These are not necessarily examples of coercion or a lack of freedom. They are examples of choices made freely, but are not examples of positive freedom.

The labels "positive" and "negative" are somewhat unfortunate, be-cause, as opposites, they seem to imply mutual exclusion, and the terms may imply value as well (negative = bad, positive = good). But neither implication is correct. Positive freedom is not better than negative free-dom. In fact, as a type of dialectic, positive freedom cannot occur without negative freedom. One cannot freely choose, as an assertive expression of one's personality, unless one is free from external restriction that might prevent that choice. Therefore, negative freedom is not a negative (bad) thing; no type of freedom can be exercised without it.

And yet, negative freedom is not the end of the matter, either. Some people, both listeners and musicians, may be attracted to jazz for its neg-ative freedom. One can imagine that a musician, frustrated with the con-trol that a conductor or composer exerts, might feel liberated upon dis-covering jazz improvisation. Liberation is an expression of negative freedom; it is always liberation *from* something, that is, from something external. However, once liberated, the question becomes "Now what?" (positive freedom). Positive freedom relies upon negative freedom, but to remain within negative freedom in jazz would mean merely improvising for the sake of being able to play anything. Once one has negative free-dom, the next step is to express positive freedom, which opens up a new, separate realm of self-expression, fulfillment, and individuality.

Adolescent Rebellion as Negative Freedom

A good example of negative freedom without positive freedom is ado-lescent rebellion. It is a general feature of adolescence that one rebels against parents and other adult figures in society as part of the process of gaining independence and becoming an autonomous adult. At least from the perspective of many parents, it often seems as if teenagers are rebelling for rebellion's sake. When the desire to be free of control be-comes a goal in and of itself, when it is a greater need than the specific content of the freedom being sought, negative freedom outweighs pos-itive freedom.

Rebellion expressed in rock music holds special appeal for adoles-cents because it expresses elements of such negative freedom. For ex-ample, consider the rock substyles of metal, speed metal, and thrash. These styles have a prominent feature of intense guitar improvisa-tions—dense, fast solos with a distorted tone color.[4] I suspect adoles-cents are drawn to these styles of rock in some measure not as an ex-pression of positive freedom, but because the style expresses the desire for negative freedom, for being free from the control of parents, school, and society in general, which can be important issues for adolescents as they find their individual identities.

Free Jazz

A particularly interesting case of freedom in jazz is free jazz, which was a controversial style of jazz and still is to some extent. The controversy over free jazz can be seen as a misinterpretation of positive freedom for nega-tive freedom.

Some free-jazz musicians acknowledged that freeing the individual to play nearly anything conceivable required a concomitant responsibility not only among the other performers (to create a unified whole out of many, sometimes conflicting, voices) but a responsibility to the audience as well. However, some in free jazz took freedom to be the end-all and be-all of the style. One absurdity to which this can lead is illustrated by the following an-ecdote related by Ekkehard Jost (perhaps apocryphal, perhaps not):

> A saxophonist was asked to take part in a "free" jazz session. When he turned up with his horn he was told to feel free to express himself, and to "do his own thing." Anyway, he must have been feeling a bit nautical, because he played "I Do Like to Be Beside the Seaside" throughout the entire session. Apparently, his associates were extremely angry about this and told him not to bother to come again.[5]

No doubt if the saxophonist had played shrieks and squawks instead, he would have been accepted. So even free jazz had stylistic norms and ex-pectations that did not allow such a ditty as "I Do Like to Be Beside the Seaside" to be played. These stylistic limitations reduced negative free-dom for improvisers wishing to use traditional materials. Not being able to play a traditional song in a free-jazz context is not an example of true freedom in exactly the same sense that, for instance, some early feminists did not accept women who chose more traditional goals in life, such as bearing children and child-rearing. While the range of choices available to people may be expanded, as in the case of feminism and the choices avail-able to women, such expansion does not require rejection of the earlier choices, even if there were fewer of them. If a woman can choose to be a homemaker under feminism, then a jazz musician can play "I Do Like to Be Beside the Seaside" at a free-jazz jam session.

Some critics of free jazz treated it as if it was merely expressing nega-tive freedom, as if it was only a rebellion against the established order, just as some view adolescent and rebellious children. While the history of mu-sical invective is centuries long, jazz had not seen such criticism as was as-sociated with free jazz:

> Roy Eldridge was quoted as saying about free jazz saxophonist Ornette Cole-man, "I listened to him high and I listened to him cold sober. I even played with him. I think he's jiving, baby. He's putting everybody on."[6]

Hell, just listen to what he writes and how he plays it. . . . If you're talking psychologically, the man [Ornette Coleman] is all screwed up inside.[7]

Such critics saw free jazz as merely a rejection of the established order, an expression of negative freedom. For them to hear free jazz as an expression of positive freedom, they would have had to comprehend what Ornette Coleman and others *were* doing, whereas the critics were only very clear on what they *were not* doing (they were not following standard harmonic structures and procedures in jazz). By not perceiving what Coleman was positively doing, they concluded he was doing nothing, and so saw Coleman as merely rejecting what had come before. No wonder the reaction was as vitriolic as it was. However, Coleman actually was incorporating significant parts of traditional jazz harmony into his improvisations. Free jazz is sometimes assumed to have no harmonic basis, or to be atonal. More accurately, however, free jazz has no *predetermined* harmonic basis, which means that traditional harmonies can very well occur, it's just that they are not planned, but happen spontaneously. One particularly clear moment of traditional harmony occurs in Ornette Coleman's improvised solo on his composition "Congeniality" at 2 minutes and 12 seconds.[8] Coleman repeats several times, with minor variations, a short phrase that has a clear harmonic basis: it's in the key of B♭. (In fig. 6.1, the repeated phrase is contained within the boxes.)

In his piece "Street Woman,"[9] as just one other example out of many, Coleman's tonal center is G, although he departs from that tonal center very freely sometimes.

So Coleman *is* doing something, he *does* use tonality (albeit in a different way than his predecessors and with few or no predetermined harmonies), he *is* expressing positive freedom. While Coleman could certainly express positive freedom with phrases that are atonal, his critics would have to admit that, if they consider it positive freedom when they play tonal phrases such as the one shown in figure 6.1, they must grant the same positive freedom to Coleman when he plays tonal phrases, even in the context of some other unplanned or even atonal phrases.

Figure 6.1. Coleman's repetition of a short phrase with a clear harmonic basis, in the key of B♭ (contained within the boxes).

LIMITS OF FREEDOM

Jazz is naïvely thought to be completely free. For an improviser to be able to express a musical idea spontaneously and freely, the technical skill to do so must appear transparent and effortless (or nearly so if the musician is challenging himself or herself to push the limits of his or her improvisational skill). But this transparency and effortlessness encourages the idea that jazz is completely free. However, no freedom is boundless, and the freedom of jazz musicians is limited through style and by the composition on which musicians improvise. Freedom remains one of the essential characteristics of jazz even if freedom in jazz is not absolute.

Style

Jazz musicians typically self-restrict the range of their improvisatory freedom in order to conform to various standards of style. For instance, when playing a bebop tune, streams of eighth notes at a fast tempo are stylistic; when playing a slow blues tune, expressive blue notes are stylistic. However, within a style, an improviser still has much freedom to play whatever notes, rhythms, phrasing, motives, or musical structure he or she desires. And ultimately, it is the improviser who makes the meta-decision as to which of the various standards of style the improviser will adhere and which may be stretched or broken.

Composition

The only way in which the composer remains sovereign is that the composition determines the melody and the chord progression on which the improviser bases the improvisation. In one sense, these musical elements limit the improviser's freedom somewhat and determine the broad harmonies of the improvisation. For instance, a chord progression may define the key of C major at a certain point in the piece. This is only a nominal restriction, however, because the improviser can play any melody within C major, which is not an insignificant amount of freedom. Within the constraints of the melody and the chord progression given by the composer, the improviser is still sovereign to exercise a great amount of freedom. An analogy for this situation might be driving: drivers have the freedom to determine what car to buy, how to drive the car, when to drive, when not to drive, and how fast to drive, but because a car is driven on roads, a car cannot go anywhere and so is constrained to stay on streets. (Perhaps free jazz would be analogous to an off-road vehicle?)

However, an improviser could choose to ignore or to subvert the given harmony. For instance, rather than improvising in the key of C major, the improviser could creatively modulate to other keys, even a harmonically distant one such as one a half-step away, a technique known as "side-slipping." (Most likely, the harmonic tension thus created would be resolved by modulating back to C major at some point.) In the end, the improviser has the freedom to ignore the initial set of conditions that the composer has defined, but doing so would still be heard in the context of the given key as performed by the rhythm section as an accompaniment to the improvisation. Countering expectations in a piece by subverting or ignoring the prevailing key or harmony is not the same as playing the same notes in a piece with no chord progression or predetermined key. In the former, there is a ground or foundation, played by the rhythm section, against which the subversion is heard, and in the latter, the background harmony or key is absent (or at least not predetermined).

COMPLETE FREEDOM

Beyond the limits of style and the composition, freedom itself is fundamentally limited. To believe that jazz or any art can be completely free is tempting, especially since freedom in jazz is such a central value, and freedom, in general, is attractive. But it is difficult to imagine a completely free or completely creative act. Any act, including musical ones, can be seen to rest or to be founded on some other act, and not, therefore, be completely free or original or creative. Even if a free-jazz saxophonist plays the most outrageous honks and squawks (without even discrete pitches or rhythms in meter)—something in which a listener might find absolutely no rhyme nor reason, and so may think is absolutely free— such music still rests, for instance, on the foundation of playing an instrument. It is, after all, still a saxophone making those sounds and therefore the improviser is limited at least by the physical nature of the instrument. There is always a way to delimit and define a boundary around any conception. If one wishes then to conceive of something still more free than shrieks and squawks on a saxophone, that is possible, but merely moving to the other side of the line does not mean that the ultimate boundary has been breached. There is always another line farther away that hasn't been crossed. Trying to eliminate all context is, apparently, impossible: one can always, it seems, find some prior context in which even the most radical act can be placed. And if there must always be some context or background against which even the most extreme act is conducted, it cannot be said to be completely free; the background or context is predetermined and thus is that part of the act that is not completely creative or free.

Statements by great artists on complete freedom must be taken with a grain of salt. When Charlie Parker says, "They teach you there's a boundary line to music. But, man, there's no boundary line to art,"[10] he is best understood to be speaking rhetorically, not precisely, because examination shows that any human conception does have a boundary. While great artists clearly have a special and valuable perspective on what they do, it must be remembered that the reason they are great artists is because of what they do, not because they necessarily have a special ability to articulate or interpret what it is they do in precise terms.

Boundaries Accepted or Challenged

If freedom always implies, ultimately, some boundary, a type of meta-freedom open to the jazz musician is to accept or push against a boundary to a greater or lesser extent. A boundary may be defined by the context of what has already been established in the piece being performed, or by what we normally call style, which creates a consistent approach to using the materials of music. This consistency defines a boundary, which then may or may not be challenged.

For instance, one of the most straight-ahead and mainstream jazz improvisations that stays within the boundaries of jazz quite firmly is trumpeter Clifford Brown's solo on Sonny Rollins's "Pent-Up House."[11] Heard within the context of mainstream and straight-ahead jazz, it does not push very many boundaries at all, while at the same time it is a brilliant and classic hard-bop solo. It is quite expressive and includes some nice interaction, especially at the climax of the solo when drummer Max Roach responds to Brown's peak. But once the solo and the surrounding context have established a mainstream or straight-ahead style, it stays firmly within those boundaries. Another way to say this is that it is a relatively consistent improvisation, stylistically speaking. Had Brown decided to use more dissonance, or to change his phrasing radically, or to play many rhythms distant from standard swing eighth notes, he would have begun to engage the boundaries of mainstream jazz and the initial context of his solo.

A good example of challenging a boundary is saxophonist and composer John Zorn's solo on his "Latin Quarter."[12] The foundation of this piece is a funky shuffle, but Zorn begins his solo with a radically different idea compared to the surrounding context: he plays one of the most brittle, harsh, and intense screams possible on an alto saxophone. This would be more at home within a free-jazz setting. By including it in the context of "Latin Quarter," Zorn pushes the boundary of what had been established by the performance up to that point. It is part of the meta-freedom of an improviser that he or she not only chooses how to work within the given boundaries, but also whether or how much to push at or stretch or even break those boundaries.

In summary, it is perhaps no coincidence that jazz, as a style of music in which freedom is strongly expressed, was created in the United States, a country founded on the idea of freedom. Wynton Marsalis, speaking about Louis Armstrong, connects the musical freedom in jazz with the ideal of political and social freedom in the United States: "[T]he sound of [Armstrong's] horn was a pure, spiritual essence, the sound of America and the freedom that it is supposed to offer."[13] Diversity, as well, is a value that links freedom in jazz with political and social diversity. Both positive and negative freedom are expressed in jazz, and in particular, positive freedom supports and is connected to some other values in jazz: assertion, initiative, fulfillment, self-expression, the personal, and antiauthoritarianism. Because freedom is such an important part of jazz, it is little wonder that jazz eventually created the substyle of free jazz (isn't the term "free jazz" a redundancy?). Free jazz merely took more seriously the idea that freedom is an essential part of jazz.

NOTES

1. William L. Reese, *Dictionary of Philosophy and Religion: Eastern and Western Thought* (Atlantic Highlands, N.J.: Humanities Press, 1980), s.v. "freedom."

2. Henry Martin and Keith Waters, *Jazz: The First 100 Years*, 2nd ed. (Belmont, Calif.: Thomson Schirmer, 2006), 288.

3. Isaiah Berlin, *Two Concepts of Liberty* (London: Oxford University Press, 1958).

4. Charles T. Brown, *The Art of Rock and Roll*, 3rd ed. (Englewood Cliffs, N.J.: Prentice Hall, 1993), 217, 240–41.

5. Ekkehard Jost, *Free Jazz* (Graz, Austria: Universal Edition, 1974), 8.

6. Frank Tirro, *Jazz: A History*, 2nd ed. (New York: W. W. Norton & Company, 1993), 375.

7. Miles Davis, quoted in Joe Goldberg, *Jazz Masters of the Fifties* (New York: Macmillan, 1965), 231.

8. Ornette Coleman, "Congeniality," *The Shape of Jazz to Come* (Atlantic SD 1317, 1959).

9. Ornette Coleman, "Street Woman," *Science Fiction* (Columbia KC 31061, 1971).

10. Eric Nisenson, *The Making of Kind of Blue: Miles Davis and His Masterpiece* (New York: St. Martin's Press, 2000), 120.

11. Sonny Rollins, "Pent-Up House," *Sonny Rollins Plus 4* (Prestige PRLP 7038, 1956).

12. John Zorn, "Latin Quarter," *Naked City* (Elektra/Nonesuch 9 79238-2, 1989).

13. *Satchmo: Louis Armstrong*, American Masters series DVD (PBS, 1989; New York: Columbia Music Video, 2000).

7

♫

Responsibility

The price of greatness is responsibility.

—Winston Churchill

In chapter 6, we saw how freedom is an important aspect of jazz, but freedom cannot be complete; it is always limited to some extent. In this chapter we will explore one way in which freedom is sometimes limited that is a strong value in jazz in and of itself: responsibility.

Definition of responsibility: Responsibility is the requirement to fulfill the duties and obligations that might be owed to another individual, group, or institution.

For the opposite of responsibility, see chapter 6, Freedom.

CONCEIVING THE MUSIC

Soloists

It is the composer's basic job and responsibility to conceive the music for a composition. However, a jazz soloist is responsible not only for the conception of his or her improvised solo, but its performance as well. The jazz improviser not only accepts the responsibilities of conceiving the music that a composer would otherwise shoulder, but carries even greater responsibilities, those of any performer: interpreting elements of music not normally notated, maintaining technical skills, showing up to the concert on time, maintaining an effective stage presence, and the like. The improviser, therefore, has nearly complete musical responsibility. As Dana Reason says, "It is not possible to claim that the music was not yours to begin with: you are held responsible for a perceived failure or triumph—by you and the audience."[1]

Everyone Else

In a larger sense, every jazz musician, not just the soloist, is similarly responsible for the music that is created because every jazz musician is improvising to a greater or lesser extent. Because every note, typically, is not given or written out for any jazz musician, solo improviser or not, the responsibility for conceiving and executing the music is given to every individual jazz musician, within the limits of style, the particular tune, the norms of the ensemble, and the conditions of the gig. While the musicians in the rhythm section are not soloists, they are improvising their accompaniment, which carries the same responsibilities of the improvising soloist noted above.

Exceptions Are Limited

There are a few cases in which jazz musicians are not responsible for the music they produce. The composer does provide some predetermined material, usually the melody of the piece, as well as its chord progression. This is the foundation from which the jazz musician creates and for which he or she is not responsible. But even in this case, the expectation in jazz is for the musician to take responsibility anyway by embellishing the melody or the chord progression to some extent. The sense of responsibility is so great in jazz that, even in the few musical areas for which jazz musicians are not responsible, they still act as if they are. One way of looking at embellishing a melody or a chord progression is that the musician makes it his or her own. When one makes something one's own in this fashion, one takes responsibility for it.

RESPONSIBILITY TO THE ENSEMBLE

The Jazz Ensemble as a Team

A musical ensemble is a type of musical community, and playing jazz, according to Leroy Williams,

> is like a team effort, the kind you find in basketball or baseball. Everybody has to do their specific job. That's the only way you're going to score. One

guy can't take all the shots in basketball, for instance. He has to lay back at times. You have to give the ball to whichever player has the best shot. It's one big group effort, and when everybody's in harmony, that's when the best things happen. You have to sacrifice your own ideas at times.[2]

Now, any type of musical ensemble can be considered a team. But a jazz combo is much more like a sports team than nonimprovising ensembles because sports are rarely as precisely scripted as ensembles that play compositions without any improvisation. A sports team would have to predetermine literally every single step each member took on every play to match the situation in which an ensemble, playing a composition, has every single note and rhythm predetermined by the composer. A music ensemble playing a composition is heavily scripted. Football is perhaps the team sport that comes closest to being so scripted, but even then, football plays may become improvised. Basketball and hockey are the sports that are most similar to jazz, mostly because play in these sports is continuous and because the very short reaction time required when the athletes improvise is on a general par with the reaction time in jazz.

Personal Behavior: Show Up on Time

Responsibility can mean a commitment to behaving properly. Politeness is the common social value that expresses this aspect of responsibility, but jazz fosters responsible personal behavior in more significant and deeper ways.

If a jazz ensemble (or any musical group) is to be functional, everyone is usually expected to show up for the gig or rehearsal and be prepared and able to fulfill one's musical responsibilities. This responsibility is sometimes expressed as "90 percent of life is just showing up." Another rule of thumb, expressed as a contradiction, is "If you're early, you're on time; if you're on time, you're late." That is, in order to be responsible, one should arrive early in order to have some margin for error, which ensures that the performance will actually begin on time. If, however, one merely plans to be exactly on time but then something unexpected happens (as it sometimes does), then one may be late. This expresses a responsible approach to events like a musical performance in which there is no way to rectify being late. It is not responsible and there is no second chance if a musician is late or does not show up for a performance for which publicity has been distributed, people have paid money to see, and for which they expect something in return at a specified time.

One infamous example of how responsibility functions in jazz, insofar as it affects one's professional life, is that of Charlie Parker. Parker's personal behavior was such that, toward the end of his career and life, even as he was recognized as the world's greatest jazz saxophonist, he had difficulty getting hired for some gigs. Presumably, the rationale for this absurd situation was that another saxophonist who would actually show up for the gig was better than a Charlie Parker who was gaining a reputation for sometimes not showing up at all. While Charlie Parker's irresponsibility is fascinating when considered along with his amazing talent, personal behavior that detracts from the musical product is irresponsible if the music product is prioritized.

RESPONSIBILITY FOR MUSICAL ROLES

A member of a team has a responsibility to the team as a whole to fulfill that member's role or assigned duties. The musical roles and requirements of jazz, as well as any musical style, are similarly a form of responsibility to others in the ensemble as well as to the audience. While there are many things that can happen in jazz that don't need to be coordinated, there are many cases in which the most subtle and intimate coordination is required among the performers, for instance, a saxophone and a trumpet playing a complex melody together. Jazz musicians have a responsibility to carry out their musical duties at a highly skilled and subtle level. In the broadest terms, the various roles in a jazz combo define the basic responsibilities of a jazz musician: drummers keep time, bassists keep time and outline the harmonies, pianists and guitarists define the harmonies, wind instruments play the melodies, and anyone may improvise. The rhythm section in particular fulfills the important if sometimes underappreciated responsibility of just keeping the tune moving along—of providing a stable and reliable foundation for the soloist. For instance, the bassist and the drummer establish the groove, which is the rhythmic foundation for every other rhythmic idea in the jazz ensemble. When locked in with each other, the bassist and drummer are highly responsible to each other, being dependable beat after beat, thousands of times a night.

Show Up on Time Musically

A fundamental responsibility that jazz musicians accept is to play notes and rhythms accurately and in synchronization with the rest of the ensemble. While jazz may be open harmonically (see "Right and Wrong Notes" in chapter 5), it is fairly demanding rhythmically (assuming swing and a steady tempo). To this extent, jazz is about nothing if not about doing the right thing at the right time, and the amount of leeway given a musician to perform, say, a certain note at a certain time, is very small.

Swing, in particular, works to a greater or lesser extent within an extremely small time frame. Consider swing eighth notes at a fast bebop tempo of 300 beats per minute. Such eighth notes follow one another at the rate of ten every second (two every beat, five beats per second). A jazz musician playing at this tempo accepts the responsibility for showing up with the right note with a very short temporal margin of error. This is the responsibility of showing up on time at a very high level.

Wayne Shorter in Weather Report

One remarkable case of responsibility in a jazz ensemble is that of saxophonist Wayne Shorter as a member of the jazz group Weather Report, which was noted for its subtle form of collective improvisation, especially earlier in its history as a group. As coleader Joe Zawinul once remarked, "In this band, either we all solo, or no one solos."[3] Weather Report had equalized and blurred the function and role of each person and instrument in the group such that, sometimes, one couldn't tell if they were all soloing or if no one was soloing.

In this context, Wayne Shorter was in a unique situation. Shorter played the only wind instrument and the only purely melodic instrument; the rest of the group consisted of keyboards, electric bass, drums, and percussion. Shorter's saxophone would easily be heard as a melody, and thereby gain aural prominence, contrary to the goal of equality and collective improvisation. One solution Shorter developed and that can be heard on the collective improvisation sections on the piece "Tears" was to play extremely sparsely so as not to rise above the rest of the ensemble in prominence, thereby maintaining equality among the ensemble.[4] It was a selfless, mature, and highly responsible approach to performance in the context of collective improvisation.

RESPONSIBILITY TO THE CRAFT OF JAZZ

The apparent ease and effortlessness that the best jazz musicians display as they improvise is the result of many, many hours of dedicated discipline and practice. John Dacey and Kathleen Lennon say that "contrary to the stereotype of the unrestrained creative person, most creative people manifest high levels of self-control."[5] This is certainly true in jazz. For many, the discipline and preparation it takes to learn to play jazz is intense and extreme. Jazz musicians often exhibit a high level of dedication and responsibility to practicing their instrument and improvisation in order to perfect their craft. The term "woodshedding" is used by musicians to suggest going to a woodshed to be alone so that one can practice intensely for hours, undisturbed and without disturbing others. Many stories exist about the almost fanatical responsibility jazz musicians exhibit toward practicing jazz, listening to recordings, hearing live concerts, talking about jazz, and thinking about jazz. Paul Berliner says that

> everyone in Max Roach's early circle worked hard; music was a "twenty-four-hour situation for us. We practiced all day, and if we were fortunate enough to be working, we'd gig all night." Afterwards, perhaps at three o-clock in the morning, "we went looking for jam sessions."[6]

An example of underestimating responsibility in jazz occurs with some of the more radical types of free jazz in which a saxophonist, in the typical case, is not playing discrete pitches but instead produces sounds from the saxophone best described as shrieks and screams, imitating an anguished human voice. It is sometimes naïvely believed that the saxophonist does not know how to play the instrument when producing such sounds. But in order to produce these sounds and have them under one's control, one must have significant facility on the instrument and practice such sounds, just like one practices discrete pitches. That saxophone virtuosos such as John Coltrane, Albert Ayler, and Archie Shepp used such sounds in their improvising belies the idea that producing these sounds rests on irresponsibility or incompetence.

RESPONSIBILITY TO THE AUDIENCE

In any musical performance, and certainly in ones that charge admission and for which the musicians are paid, the musician has certain responsibilities to the audience. Some of these concern professional behavior and are the same as the ones that musicians in a jazz ensemble have toward each other: show up on time, be prepared, and the like. More fundamental, however, are responsibilities that concern the nature of the music to be performed. However, for jazz, these responsibilities are vague. There is rarely, if ever, any explicit contract or expectation between the jazz musician and the audience regarding specifics about the music. For instance, at a classical symphony concert one might be able to learn exactly what pieces will be performed before one buys a ticket. While this might happen at a jazz performance ("The Lincoln Center Jazz Orchestra, Featuring the Music of Duke Ellington"), it is certainly not unusual if it does not. All the audience may know before a jazz performance is the name of the headline artist or ensemble, and details such as date and time, location, and admission charge. Any details about the nature of the music to be performed usually are not specified ahead of time. There is no agreement, even an implicit one, that says, "In return for the admission charge, the musicians will perform the following pieces."

Despite the lack of a contract or agreement about the specific nature of the music to be performed at a jazz performance, the audience still has some set of expectations about a jazz performance, and the jazz musician has an implicit responsibility to meet these expectations in some fashion. More as a practical matter and less as an ethical one, the musician must be concerned with meeting audience expectations to some extent if he or she wants to have any sort of career. So, audience expectations can define implicit and practical responsibilities for the jazz musician.

TYPES OF JAZZ PERFORMANCES

There are many different types of jazz performances, each of which carries a different set of audience expectations and the accompanying musician responsibilities. The more common types are listed below, in order of increasing responsibilities for the musician.[7]

Jam session. A jam session is an informal public performance at which anyone may request to perform a few tunes with others who may well be strangers. Usually, a house rhythm section forms the basic band, and they are the only paid performers, if any. The jam session carries the loosest set of audience expectations about the music performed. Because the musicians may have never played together before, and because some musicians may be beginners, an "anything-may-happen" attitude is common. Audience expectations and musician responsibilities are at their lowest, in general.

Casual. Many local, one-time gigs require jazz musicians to play background music, typically for receptions. Audience conversing, socializing, and networking take precedence over the music. The responsibility of the jazz ensemble is to perform unobtrusive music that creates a pleasant backdrop for more important social activities. The usual repertoire is similar to what has been called the "Great American Songbook," pieces by composers such as Cole Porter, George and Ira Gershwin, and Richard Rodgers and Oscar Hammerstein. Even though the music is background music, the musicians still have the responsibility to provide an appropriate background.

Dance. Jazz has a long history as music for dancing. Today, jazz typically provides dance music for weddings, or, with the recent resurgence in popularity of music from the swing era, for swing dances. Dance music perhaps carries the most specific audience expectations and musician responsibilities concerning the nature of the music. Primary of these is tempo. The speed of the beat must not be too fast or too slow for the dancers, and there must be a proper mix of different tempos. The tempo must also be very regular and not waver significantly, although this is a standard competency for jazz musicians. The expected repertoire is similar to the Great American Songbook, especially for weddings, as well as classics from the swing era for swing dances.

Club gig. These occur at smaller venues, usually serving alcohol, at which dancing is not the norm. Different clubs may reveal higher or lower levels of audience conversation during the performance. A club gig is perhaps the purest form of jazz performance; small enough to be intimate and thus encourage focus on the music itself, yet not so formal that the audience cannot converse or interact with the musicians through spontaneous encouragement in response to the music ("Yeah!" or various exclamations). The audience expectations and musicians' responsibilities regarding the music itself are similar to those for a formal concert.

Concert. A (formal) jazz concert takes place in larger venues, and etiquette usually demands little or no talking in the audience. For a concert, as well as club gigs, there is no specific definition of the music as there is for background jazz and dances. Rather, a set of loose expectations may serve to place only broad responsibilities on the musicians. The strongest audience expectation that serves to establish the musicians' responsibilities rests on the musicians' musical personality, defined through reputation and previous work. It is this identity that likely attracts the audience in the first place. A knowledgeable audience understands that, for instance, Diana Krall will likely perform some repertoire out of the Great American Songbook, and that Cecil Taylor probably won't. A jazz musician wanting to be responsible to his or her audience would therefore not disrupt such expectations too much. This is not at all the same as saying that jazz musicians cannot change stylistic directions, and sometimes radically. Rather, it is a question of how abruptly such a change takes place. If, for instance, Diana Krall and Cecil Taylor gave separate performances in which each sounded like the other (!), and the audiences did not expect it, that would be irresponsible to the audience, in terms of the contract implied by charging admission to the concert. Krall or Taylor could adopt the sound of the other without being irresponsible if the audience understood that to be the case beforehand. Perhaps the publicity for such a concert might read, "Diana Krall plays the music of Cecil Taylor." This is a slightly absurd example, but it does define where the practical responsibility to an audience lies.

Studio recording. The notable aspect of performing in a recording studio for our purposes here is that the audience is not present at the performance, and only hears the performance through the subsequent recording. Still, a recording session carries its own unique expectations from and responsibilities to the audience. A recording session carries nearly the same high level of perfection as expected from a composition. In this case, as an exception to the norm, the improviser *can* go back and correct mistakes by recording another take or by editing a take. The audience expectation and widely acknowledged responsibility of the musicians is to create as perfect a recording as possible. The high level of perfection expected of a recording runs counter to a primary value in jazz that accepts imperfection (and which is discussed at length in part III). This is one reason why live performances, as opposed to recordings, are sometimes considered to hold a privileged place in jazz.

Responsibility ultimately comes down to care for others, based on the recognition that our actions matter to others and affect others; so, if we care about others, we will fulfill our responsibilities to them. A jazz improviser has significant musical and social responsibilities to the audience and to fellow bandmates. These responsibilities, especially the musical ones, can be demanding. The tolerances for the timing of musical events can be very small, especially in the case of swing or the groove. But the jazz musician who takes care when establishing a groove with the rest of the ensemble is also taking care when he or she programs the right repertoire for a particular type of performance (formal concert, casual, jam session, or whatever). The primary responsibility, however, for a jazz improviser is the responsibility for creating and conceiving the music itself, a responsibility that is central to jazz as improvised music.

NOTES

1. Dana Reason, "'Navigable Structures and Transforming Mirrors,' " in *The Other Side of Nowhere: Jazz, Improvisation, and Communities in Dialogue* (Middleton, Conn.: Wesleyan University Press, 2004), 77.

2. Leroy Williams, quoted in Paul Berliner, *Thinking in Jazz: The Infinite Art of Improvisation* (Chicago: University of Chicago Press, 1994), 418.

3. Source unknown.

4. Weather Report, "Tears," *Weather Report* (Columbia KC 31352, 1972).

5. John S. Dacey and Kathleen Lennon, *Understanding Creativity: The Interplay of Biological, Psychological, and Social Factors* (San Francisco: Jossey-Bass Publishers, 1998), 116.

6. Berliner, *Thinking in Jazz*, 58.

7. Some of these responsibilities are dependent on the type of venue at which the performance occurs. *The New Grove Dictionary of Jazz*'s summary of the many types of venues (under "Nightclubs and other venues") includes "nightclubs (or clubs), cabarets, casinos and gambling clubs, restaurants, bars, cafes and coffee houses, pubs, taverns, saloons, and speakeasies; ballrooms and dance halls; cinemas, music halls, theaters, concert halls, entertainment centers, and lofts; hotels, inns, roadhouses, and brothels; cruise ships and riverboats; and parks, gardens, and lakesides."

8

♫

Creativity

Creativity represents a miraculous coming together of the uninhibited
energy of the child with its apparent opposite and enemy, the sense of
order imposed on the disciplined adult intelligence.

—Norman Podhoretz

The role of creativity in jazz improvisation is central, as the improviser
supplants the composer as the primary creative agent in jazz. This
chapter will explore creativity as production and as novelty, and will also
explore four arenas for creativity in jazz: improvisation, instrumental
technique, style, and arranging.

Definition of creativity: Creativity requires both production and novelty. To create something is to produce it, which is distinct from novelty,
which requires difference or uniqueness in the characteristics of that
which is produced. One may produce many exact copies of something,
but this does not illustrate creativity because each copy is not different
from the others. Alternately, if person A claims something novel as his or
her own creation but it was actually produced by person B, A has not been
creative, even though the thing may be novel. The word "original" also
carries these two implications. The original is that which comes from the
origin, which is the source of creation or production. Originality also implies the production of something new or unique.

Opposite of creativity: Creativity and tradition are opposites because
creativity is about the new and that which does not yet exist, whereas tradition is about the old and the already existing.

CREATION IN IMPROVISATION

Interpretation

Creation in jazz improvisation is essential and may be contrasted with creation for performers, which is interpretive. Interpretation is the practice by which the performer determines how some elements of music will be performed. A composer, through a traditionally notated Western score, determines certain but not all elements of music. Some aspects of music must be interpreted by the performer because they are not exactly specified in musical notation. Whereas the pitch B♭ exactly defines, for all practical purposes, what the composer intends in terms of pitch, a traditionally notated fermata (indicating a pause), for instance, gives no indication of exactly how long the pause should last. Similarly, a crescendo does not indicate the exact rate at which the music should get louder (quickly or slowly at the beginning, middle, or end?), nor how loud the music should become. Such features are left to the performer to interpret.[1] Some of the elements of music that are interpreted by the performer, in conventional Western notation, are dynamics, timbre, articulation, intonation, rhythmic drive, rubato, and pauses. The composer may specify the placement of some of these elements (for instance, to which notes a crescendo applies), but not some aspects of their realization.

Discrete and Analog Elements of Music

The interpretive elements of music are primarily analog, that is, they are continuously variable. For instance, a fermata can be short or long or any length in between, and tone color can gradually change from bright to dark. Pitches and rhythms, on the other hand, are discrete. While it is possible to vary pitch continuously, jazz makes extensive use of the twelve pitches that make up the chromatic scale as discrete pitches (with the important exception of embellishments like a glissando or a bend). The rhythm of a note is commonly conceived as a discrete point in time, coinciding with its onset.

Informal Editing by the Performer

A performer can take creative liberties with the score by introducing, where none existed before, some of the analog elements of music normally interpreted by a performer, or even by contradicting what the score indicates for these elements. For example, the performer may introduce a crescendo where none is indicated in the score in order to make the music more expressive. This constitutes an informal editing process by the performer. This practice of editing the composer's score is commonplace and constitutes a relatively slight violation of the composer's intent and of the entire system of the composer communicating his or her musical conception, through the score, to the performer for realization.

Pitches and Rhythm

However, there are some elements of music that the performer is not expected to interpret to a substantive extent. A conventional Western musical score specifies pitches and rhythms exactly and conclusively. It is generally understood that the composer intends to leave no room for variation or change with regard to pitches and rhythms (excepting deliberately indeterminate or improvised sections of a composition).[2] So if a performer plays a different pitch or rhythm than the composer had notated, we understand this as a true violation of the composition, or as a mistake. We even understand it to be a violation of the composition in the case of incidents like the one described by Carol S. Gould and Kenneth Keaton:

> Consider, for instance, Lynn Harrell's recent performance of the Haydn cello concerto in D with the Florida Philharmonic. In the second movement he inserted a series of decorative notes. When another cellist asked him after the concert why he had added these notes, Harrell allegedly responded that it sounded better this way (appealing to *causa pulchritudinus*) and that he was tired of playing those same simple notes every time he plays the concerto (appealing to the need for self-expression).[3]

In addition to responsibility for and control over the analog elements of music, the jazz improviser also has responsibility for the creation of the discrete notes and rhythms during a performance. The improviser controls nearly *all* elements of music—analog, as determined by a performer, and discrete, as determined otherwise by the composer—and so has the ultimate role as creator. (The only exception to these responsibilities is that the composer determines the original melody and the underlying chord progression.)

NOVELTY

It is a common expectation in jazz that an improvised solo attempts to produce something novel. A derivative solo, excessively based on what a musician has accomplished previously, is not the highest to which a jazz musician may aspire. Soloists who do not attempt originality or uniqueness are commonly derided. David Hollenberg wrote the following critique of a performance by pianist Ray Bryant:

> How much is improvised? Tonight, Bryant played "After Hours" in a note-for-note copy of the way he played it on the Dizzy, Rollins, and Stitt album on Verve some fifteen years ago. Was it written then? Or worse. Has he transcribed and memorized his own solo, as if it were an archaeological classic? It was fine blues piano indeed, but it is odd to hear it petrified in this way.[4]

The oddness that Hollenberg mentions reflects the expectation of novelty in jazz.

Experimentation

The aesthetics and values of jazz require that the improviser not merely play it safe and perform only those licks or ideas that have been safely performed before, even if they are sure to work. While some tried-and-true ideas are acceptable, and maybe even necessary, the highest level of jazz improvisation involves experimentation, in which the improviser does not know how a creative inspiration will play out, having been just imagined.

Jazz improvisations are experiments and are conducted in real time before an audience, no less. When experimenting, the improviser is in the position of having to manage the experiment as it unfolds. This makes improvisation an audacious and daring maneuver. While the improviser may draw on the value of openness to inspire an improvisation, a particular listener may not embrace a particular musical idea that is the result of an experiment by the improviser (everyone's a critic!). But the values of jazz improvisation say that it is better to have experimented and lost than never to have experimented at all.

The Trickster

Another source of novelty in jazz is tricksterism, which David Feurzeig has identified in pianists James P. Johnson and Thelonious Monk.[5] Trick-sterism sows confusion by stretching expectations so much as to disorient or mislead the listener temporarily. For Monk and Johnson, Feurzeig's best examples show tricksterism with regard to the underlying rhythm, meter, or harmonic progression. Feurzeig analyzes a passage by stride pianist James P. Johnson in which several different rhythmic and metric effects obscure any easy understanding of how the rhythms played are related to the underlying meter. The unusual rhythms threaten to disorient the listener's sense of meter and rhythm completely. Such tricksterism is creative in the sense that it alters the previously established context of time and rhythm, thus showing a novel way of understanding a rhythm in relation to the meter, even if it temporarily disorients the listener.

Free Association

Creativity in jazz improvisation is special because the creative process is laid bare, occurring before one's eyes and ears just as the creative impulse itself happens. The archetypical method by which this happens is free association. While free association is commonly linked with Freudian psychoanalysis, it was first named by Sir Francis Galton in 1879. Galton had the idea to record every single thought that crossed his mind as he walked through Pall Mall in London. Galton concluded that these fleeting, spontaneously occurring ideas come from the unconscious, and that the thoughts that appear are similar to their unconscious sources.[6] It is those same threads of similarity that help the jazz improviser determine what the next note or phrase should be. Free association in jazz improvisation opens up a channel to the unconscious so that it may bring up creative ideas.

In one sense, the essence of all creativity is free association. No creativity happens, at its source, except through free association. Any creative thought, initially, merely presents itself, through free association and as if improvised. Even composers can only get a creative idea initially through free association. At its very beginning, a creative idea always merely appears from the unconscious. One can open a channel to the unconscious, one can call out to it, but it will occur on its own, and the content of it cannot be predetermined; it will be what it is, freely. When jazz musicians say that they stop thinking during an improvisation, they are doing so in order to connect with the unconscious mind so that creative associations may freely occur.

TYPES OF CREATIVITY

Improvisational Creativity

Making an individual, creative, and unique statement in a jazz improvisation is one of the highest musical goals in jazz. Perhaps the only other thing more important in jazz is swing and the groove. However, while swinging and creating a fine groove may be done creatively, it is not necessary that they are. Even if swing and a groove are not creatively interpreted, they may still be satisfactory or even excellent, but to play an improvisation creatively is widely understood to be crucial in jazz. If a jazz musician were to improvise but not play anything creative, that is, merely to improvise patterns or ideas that the musician has performed perhaps many times before, the expected criticism would be that the jazz musician is merely going through the motions.

Instrumental Creativity

Some jazz musicians have approached their instruments and the function of those instruments in a jazz ensemble in innovative ways. This is a significant area of creativity for jazz musicians and can be considered separately from other creative efforts in an improvisation. In some cases, these innovations have been crucial parts of an artist's identity and have helped to define the artist's reputation. A few examples of many: Count Basie was one of the early pianists to move from a stride style to a comping style; Jimmy Blanton is credited with liberating the bass from its timekeeping role, introducing the bass as a solo instrument; John Coltrane extended the range of the saxophone upward, including the use of the higher-pitched soprano saxophone; Rahsaan Roland Kirk played more than one saxophone at a time; Miles Davis was one of the first jazz musicians to use electronic modification (echo, wa-wa, and the like) on the trumpet; Bobby McFerrin greatly expanded the textural, tone-color, and syllabic possibilities of vocal jazz; and Toots Thielemans plays jazz on the harmonica, previously almost unknown in jazz.

Stylistic Creativity

Another method by which jazz musicians express their creativity is through new styles of jazz. What constitutes a new style cannot always be answered clearly, and the boundaries between styles is often blurred, but this should not prevent us from using the concept of style appropriately. Defining a style is a judgment and a matter of context as well as a matter of objective musical criteria. There seems to be some critical mass of societal recognition past which a new style can be recognized and labeled, which then feeds back to musicians who are influenced by this new style, thus creating a positive feedback loop. At some point, when such activity is large or significant enough, and enough people use the term for the new style, a new style can be said to exist.

Jazz has a long history of borrowing from other styles of music for creative inspiration. Even New Orleans jazz, the first style of jazz, had the "Spanish tinge," which was a musical influence from Spanish music that was part of New Orleans's history and cultural heritage. In fact, Latin music is one of the major areas from which jazz has borrowed, ranging from the Spanish tinge, Dizzy Gillespie's fusion of jazz and Afro-Cuban music called *cubop*, and the bossa nova craze of the 1960s, to salsa and other blendings of jazz and Latin music. The single jazz musician who most exemplifies stylistic creativity in jazz is perhaps Miles Davis. While it is rare that one can say that a single person was responsible for any major stylistic innovation in jazz, Miles Davis was a pivotal figure in several innovative styles of jazz: cool, modal, and jazz/rock.

Jazz seems to have an unlimited capacity for blendings and fusion with other musical styles. For nearly any non-jazz musical style one can identify, one can probably find a musician who has attempted to fuse it with jazz. Some of the musical styles that have fused with jazz are Latin, classical, rock, avant-garde, bluegrass, new age, hip-hop, and gospel. This tendency to incorporate nearly any musical style is a major form of openness in jazz, but it expresses creativity as well. By infusing itself with different musical ideas and norms from other styles, jazz continually finds new and creative possibilities.

Arranging Creativity

Another area of creativity in jazz is arranging, which is similar to but narrower than the creation of a new style. Arranging can be viewed as the reinterpretation of previously existing material. It approaches stylistic creativity but is not as extreme, maintaining many or most elements of a style without changing enough so that naming a new style would be more convenient. Reworking even the most traditional material into new contexts is a creative, innovative process that has a strong history in jazz. Some of the specific tasks that comprise arranging are

- assigning melodies, harmonies, and other musical material to specific instruments,
- harmonizing a melody,
- introducing counterpoint (secondary melodies and background figures),
- determining the number of choruses (which may be indeterminate),
- determining who solos when (which also may be indeterminate),
- coordinating larger forms into a coherent whole,
- introducing other formal structures, such as introductions, endings, and interludes, and
- introducing different styles and rhythmic approaches (for instance, playing a Latin jazz tune in swing style).

Arranging is an appropriate topic here, even considering this book's emphasis on improvisation, because arrangements are often improvised as a piece is performed. An arranger may sit at a desk and decide to introduce, say, a Latin rhythmic feel in the trumpet solo for a jazz combo; this arranger is functioning more like a composer, with time to edit and revise. A drummer, however, may spontaneously decide during a performance to play a Latin rhythmic feel at the beginning of the trumpet solo, thus functioning more like an improviser than a composer, even though they are both acting as arrangers, in effect. In this case, the spontaneous nature of the drummer's behavior links it with improvisation.

In summary, then, the jazz improviser adopts the fundamental creative role in music, that of the composer (the person who conceives the music), as well as the fundamental productive role, that of the performer (the person who makes the music manifest). The presence of and emphasis on novelty, experimentation, and free association, even to the point of confounding the listener's expectations (as a trickster) means that the value of creativity in jazz is strong. Its opposite, tradition, also has a role in jazz, and that will be explored in the next chapter.

NOTES

1. There is nothing in principle preventing a composer from using or inventing any notational device to indicate *everything* for the performer in a score, but this is rarely done.

2. The limited exceptions of ornaments, cadenzas, and the like, which do allow the performer to determine pitches and rhythms, do not contradict the primary principle that the performer should not change pitches and rhythms. Not changing a rhythm means, for example, not changing three eighth notes into three quarter notes, and does not mean playing a rhythm a fraction of a section late or early, an analog aspect of music that is a legitimate area of interpretation.

3. Carol S. Gould and Kenneth Keaton, "The Essential Role of Improvisation in Musical Performance," *Journal of Aesthetics and Art Criticism* 58, no. 2 (Spring 2000): 146.

4. David Hollenberg, Review of the Ran Blake/Ray Bryant trio, *Downbeat* 45, no. 10 (May 18, 1978): 42.

5. David Feurzeig, "Making the Right Mistakes: James P. Johnson, Thelonious Monk, and the Trickster Aesthetic" (DMA diss., Cornell University, 1997).

6. Herbert Crovitz, *Galton's Walk: Methods for the Analysis of Thinking, Intelligence, and Creativity* (New York: Harper and Row, 1970).

9

♫

Tradition

Tradition is a guide and not a jailer.

—W. Somerset Maugham

The question of tradition in jazz has received much attention since the neoconservative trend in jazz has flourished. Musicians such as Wynton Marsalis, among others, have embraced tradition, defending it against the idea that tradition reflects a lack of creativity and that tradition and creativity are mutually exclusive. This chapter will explore the role that tradition plays in an art form such as jazz that emphasizes creativity.

Definition of tradition: Tradition has been defined by Edward Shils as "anything which is transmitted or handed down from the past to the present."[1] It is those aspects of a society, culture, art form, or discipline that remain stable or unchanging over time. Tradition is fundamentally conservative; it seeks to define and to preserve.

For the opposite of tradition, see chapter 8, Creativity.

DEFINING JAZZ

The question of tradition in jazz and some recent controversies regarding the neoconservative movement are linked to the definition of jazz. Much ink has been spilled defining jazz, but being clear about what any word means is an inescapable responsibility if we are to communicate effectively, and it is essential to the question of tradition in jazz. Definitions may be vague or problematic, but some sort of starting place is required.

A definition of jazz will help to define its tradition, as tradition in jazz can be seen as the core of its definition.

Definitions Are Limitations

Any word, not just a word that is the name for a musical style, must mean some things and not others in order for communication and understanding to be effective. For instance, the definition of the word "chair" excludes those things on which one cannot sit (for instance, air).[2] This exclusionary function of a definition applies to artistic styles, too. The name of no artistic style, if that name is to mean something, can mean everything or anything. Complete stylistic freedom, openness, and inclusion is impossible, even for a diverse style like jazz that contains so much openness. If jazz were completely open and inclusive, it would be meaningless to speak of the style of jazz because even Beethoven's Fifth Symphony, for instance, note for note, would have to be included within the definition of jazz. That, however, would be absurd, stretching the very idea of a style of music beyond reason. In order to be a style of music, that music must include some sounds and exclude others. The attempt to describe which sounds are included and which are excluded creates a definition. While it may be difficult to separate all sounds into those within the definition of a style and those without, and while such a definition may be imperfect, it is unavoidable if we want to discuss a style properly.

Declining to Define Styles

Although definitions and the limitations they impose on words are unavoidable, one might imagine a way around these limitations: do not use the word at all. If the word "jazz" is problematic, then perhaps we should not use it and only call any music "music." This position claims that if we stop labeling types of music and stop pigeonholing music into styles altogether, then we don't have to include or exclude anything, nor place anything within any boundaries; we may just listen to music and enjoy it, not bothering with definitions.

Identity Remains

However, not only is the style of jazz a well-ingrained and convenient usage, but there is no way around creating identity and boundaries at some point, whether it is a substyle of jazz, the style of jazz, or something at an even broader level. If what might otherwise be called jazz is just, for instance, "good music," one might next question whether the term "music" should retain its identity and definition because it is also creating a boundary like the word "jazz" did. There are plenty of art forms that blend music with theater, the visual arts, and other arts. If one then suggests that we can do away with defining music versus other arts, and just call everything "art," one does not realize that this process never comes to an end, or at least ceases to exploit the usefulness of words and categories. Defining jazz and the jazz tradition cannot be rejected merely because definition depends on boundaries and limitations; this is because boundaries and limitations are impossible to abandon completely. A line must be drawn; the only question is where, and we do our best to decide what is on which side of the line, being grateful for its usefulness and aware of its limitations.

Problematic Examples

Any definition may have difficult cases. For instance, a chair is, broadly, something on which one sits. Now, a chair with its seat tilted slightly upward would still be a chair, but what about a chair with its seat tilted 30 degrees? 45 degrees? 60 degrees? Tilted at 90 degrees (the seat being completely vertical), one could not sit on the seat, one would be leaning against the seat. Because one could not sit on the chair, the chair would lose the very characteristic that made it a chair. One could reasonably argue that the chair was, therefore, no longer a chair. But at what angle is one not able to sit on the seat, and thus at what angle does the chair cease to be a chair? One might also imagine examples of odd types of chairs that might be questioned as fitting the definition of a chair (for instance, a chair missing its seat). Certainly, for a style of music as diverse as jazz, any definition will probably result in many cases for which it might be difficult to clearly determine whether something is jazz, no matter how well the definition is crafted.

Such problems are not enough, however, to prevent our best attempts to craft definitions. The fact that we inevitably find messiness at the boundaries of definitions does not mean that the difficulties outweigh the usefulness of making boundaries and definitions in the first place, especially if one is aware of the limitations. The real problem is ignoring the limitations of definitions and acting as if they should be absolute and perfect. If we can be comfortable with the limitations of definitions and accept that a lesser standard than perfection for definitions is inevitable, then we can accept a definition of jazz.

The Foundations of a Definition

If the style of jazz means anything, it would be impossible for a jazz musician not to base his or her music on tradition to some extent, however small. To understand this, imagine a jazz musician who was so creative and revolutionary that his or her music completely overthrew the jazz tradition. In that case, there would be no reason to call such music jazz. For music to be jazz it must contain some aspect of how we define jazz. Otherwise, we would never think to call it jazz in the first place—we would call it flamenco, or Baroque, or some style of which it was an example. As Wynton Marsalis has said,

> See, if you don't remind somebody of the past, you're not in the idiom you claim that you're in. For somebody to say, "I'm a jazz musician but I don't sound like anything from the past," well, if you don't sound like anything from the past, then you're not a jazz musician.[3]

If there is something in the music that makes us call it jazz, then that aspect of the music is part of the tradition and definition of jazz. Tradition establishes identity, much like definition does. That which identifies is that which is stable and unchanging, just as tradition is. Tradition is logically necessary if we are to talk about something we call "jazz." The question is not whether there is a tradition in jazz, but what that tradition is.

Ultimately, it is more important to enjoy or appreciate music than to worry about how far a definition can be stretched or how much a style must be limited. But the word "jazz" has its usefulness. When we decide to call some music jazz, we do so to refer to some aspects that some pieces of music have in common, as well as to alert our listener or reader that we intend to connect this music with certain other sounds (the rest of the jazz tradition), either implicitly or explicitly. Once we accept defining jazz as a style, in a similar way that we acknowledge that freedom and creativity in jazz cannot be absolute, the groundwork and the necessity are laid for a definition of jazz.

Fuzzy Logic

Most definitions of jazz (as well as other words or ideas) are based on conventional logic and mutual exclusion (something is either A or not-A). But logicians have recently identified "fuzzy logic," which operates on a continuum and not through mutual exclusion. Fuzzy logic establishes partial degrees of truth. Conventional logic assigns complete truth or falsity: either a statement is true or it is not, and there is no in between. But a proposition in fuzzy logic can be somewhat true and not necessarily completely true or completely not true.

> Now if X is a set of propositions then its elements may be assigned their degree of truth, which may be "absolutely true," "absolutely false" or some intermediate truth degree: a proposition may be more true than another propo-

sition. This is obvious in the case of vague (imprecise) propositions like "this person is old" (beautiful, rich, etc.).[4]

Similarly, a definition that defines a class (such as jazz, old people, or beautiful people) may be comprised of a constellation of elements, incomplete combinations of which may be sufficient for an example to meet the requirements of the definition. If more characteristics are applicable to a certain example, then that example may be a better example than another. Fuzzy logic allows for such proportional weighting. Much of the controversy over tradition in jazz, as well as controversies about whether bebop, free jazz, or fusion are truly jazz, is framed in absolute and mutually exclusive terms and not through fuzzy logic.

A Fuzzy Definition of Jazz

Mark Gridley, Robert Maxham, and Robert Hoff have proposed a definition of jazz based on fuzzy logic.[5] They distinguish three different definitions:

Strict definition. Two requirements for jazz, swing and improvisation, are established, and these are necessary and sufficient to categorize an example as jazz.

Family resemblance. Examples of jazz are only required to be related in some fashion to other examples. This produces a wide-ranging, all-inclusive definition of jazz. One can trace a chain of related examples of jazz between very disparate examples (for instance, between Jelly Roll Morton and Cecil Taylor) that allows one to call very different types of music jazz.

Dimension. Various aspects of examples of jazz are evaluated on a continuum, resulting in a relative judgment: one example may be more or less jazzy than another. This is a definition of jazz based on fuzzy logic.

The authors then evaluate these different definitions:

> The overwhelming strength of the strict definition is its simplicity. And this is then the most telling weakness of the dimensional approach because the dimensional approach does not allow you to make an unequivocal statement that a particular performance is jazz. The family resemblances approach and the jazziness approach are more relativistic, and they lead to fewer exclusions, having a flexibility that accommodates jazz as an evolving art form, thereby excluding far fewer performances than the strict definition excludes.[6]

The authors' criticism that the dimensional approach is not unequivocal is actually a strength because it more closely mirrors the empirical situation. With the wide range of subtle influences and many hybrid styles and experiments, it is apparent that there are types of music that are not un-equivocally jazz. Equivocation in the dimensional definition might be a problem if the goal is to craft a definition of jazz that is appropriate for undergraduates (the lead author, Mark Gridley, has written an excellent jazz history textbook). But if the goal is to craft a definition of jazz that fits the empirical situation on the ground and whatever intellectual issues may result, then such equivocation is not a problem, but a strength.

Musical Definition

Scott Deveaux suggests that defining jazz in musical terms is problematic:

> Defining jazz is a notoriously difficult proposition, but the task is easier if one bypasses the usual inventory of musical qualities or techniques, like improvisation or swing (since the more specific or comprehensive such a list attempts to be, the more likely it is that exceptions will overwhelm the rule).[7]

But this is problematic if one imagines only a strict, mutually exclusive, absolute, and perfect definition. This is especially true because Deveaux's alternative to a musical definition is a social one, using African American ethnicity as central to the definition, but this is not without its own fuzziness, such as how white jazz musicians are to be understood, as Deveaux admits. "But on the whole," he says, "ethnicity provides a core, a center of gravity for the narrative of jazz, and is one element that unites the several different kinds of narratives in use today."[8] If African American ethnicity as a core or center of gravity produces a definition that is not absolute or perfect, then there is no reason to reject a musical definition of jazz, because it too can provide a core or center of gravity for a definition. While agreeing that an ethnic definition of jazz can be valid, it is my particular goal here to focus on a musical definition of jazz in order to understand tradition—the musical tradition—in jazz.

A Definition of Jazz and Jazz Tradition

Having argued for a definition of jazz, it is incumbent on me to provide one. The definition I offer here is based on the dimensional definition noted above. It includes a core (which is the tradition), an undisputed area of slightly different substyles, and a disputed area (see fig. 9.1).

The core is the center of the nature and definition of jazz, and defines its tradition. This core is similar to common practice in classical music, which denotes a set of musical practices common to the era of Bach

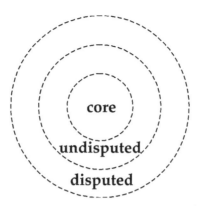

Figure 9.1. A definition of jazz based on dimensional definition, including a core (which is the tradition), an undisputed area of slightly different substyles, and a disputed area.

through Brahms. The tradition of jazz is best seen as just the core of a definition of jazz, and not coequal to all of jazz. I suggest that the following comprise the core of jazz:

- swing/groove
- improvisation
- chorus form
- standard jazz harmony
- the blues
- the combo

The undisputed area is not part of the very core of jazz but is universally or widely considered to be jazz. Some modifications to the core tradition are generally uncontested and not controversial, such as modal and quartal harmonies, Latin jazz, some big-band performances with very little improvisation, and more.

The disputed area contains substyles of jazz that some might not consider jazz (perhaps free jazz, or smooth jazz).

As one moves away from the core into the undisputed and disputed areas, one moves along a continuum of jazziness, and some of the core values disappear. The core does not define a set of required characteristics, merely favored ones, as some may be absent in music that is considered jazz. The question as to when a modification of the core tradition produces music that ceases to be jazz is not be answered easily. Such a question is similar to the question, "When, through all the shades of grey, does black become white?" Some of the discomfort with the difficult examples

Table 9.1.   Selected Jazz Styles and the Core of Jazz

	Swing	Improv	The Core Chorus	Harmony	Blues	Combo
The Tradition						
Big-band era	√	≈	√	√	√	≈
Bebop	√	√	√	√	√	√
Hard bop	√	√	√	√	√	√
Undisputed						
New Orleans	≈	√	√	√	√	√
Modal	√	√	√	≈	≈	√
Latin	X	√	√	√	≈	√
Disputed						
Smooth	X	≈	√	≈	X	√
Free (early)	√	√	≈	X	≈	√

Note: √ is present, X is not present, and ≈ is somewhat present.

at the boundaries of a definition of jazz is the result of not acknowledging that any definition will have problems at the boundaries.

Table 9.1 outlines which elements of the core of jazz are present (√), not present (X), or somewhat present (≈) in various styles of jazz that are categorized as part of the tradition, as undisputed, or as disputed.

My purpose in offering a definition of jazz in table 9.1 is not to establish what is jazz and what is not. One might contest the judgments that make up this definition. For instance, the place that big-band music holds in jazz, as a relatively uncontroversial part of the jazz tradition, might lead one not to include the combo as part of the core of jazz. The larger point is that such a chart depends on fuzzy logic and on a constellation of related musical elements, all of which need not be fully present in any one example in order for that example to qualify as a member of its class. One can speak not only of jazz and non-jazz, but of a core of jazz, undisputed jazz (but not fully within the core), and even disputed jazz. Fuzzy logic is especially necessary for a definition of jazz because creativity is so important in jazz. Creativity can be expressed not only within a traditional improvisation, at the core of jazz, but also at the margins of jazz. A definition of a creative field has to accommodate the margins as well as the core, which fuzzy logic does.

LEARNING JAZZ

The way that most jazz musicians learn to play jazz rests on tradition. The process of learning jazz is one of absorbing the tradition, even to the point of imitating other musicians.[9] (The next step after absorbing tradition and imitating others is learning how to be creative in response to that tradition.) Learning how to play jazz must mean that there is an established tradition which is to be imitated and absorbed.

Types of Competency

What does one learn when one learns how to play jazz? There are three primary areas of competency for jazz musicians:

Instrumental competency. The jazz improviser successfully manages the physical demands of performing on an instrument.

Stylistic competency. The jazz improviser absorbs the stylistic norms of jazz, such as how melodies are constructed, how harmonies are expressed, how rhythms are used in jazz, how swing functions, and the like, and is able to fashion an improvisation that conforms to these norms. This is the area in which the absorption of tradition is most easily seen.

Creative competency. The jazz improviser is able to produce something new and unique, either firmly within the boundaries of the jazz tradition, or creatively stretching and warping those boundaries.

Imitation Was Once Considered Creativity

Imitation is not usually considered a creative activity anymore, but historically, imitation has been connected closely to creativity. Art in the West, as far back as Plato and Aristotle, was seen not as creation, but as imitation. Because the idea of art as imitation was present so early in the history of Western culture, the move to art as creation was a significant one. As Raymond Williams points out, "When imitation, the learning of reality, becomes creation, man making new reality, a critical stage in art and thought [had] been reached."[10] Williams mentions this change in order to overcome the opposition between art as imitation and as creation. If naïve realism is impossible (the green in green grass is not in the grass, but is created from the grass, light, and our nervous system), then reality is interpreted as much as imitated. Interpretation implies a creative act, even if, as in the case of mere perception of green grass, it is one given to all of us by our genetic heredity. To transcend the opposition of imitation and creativity does not mean rejecting either. Williams reveals an important aspect of aesthetics:

> "We mean by art the work of those who are artists, that is specially inspired, and not the work of those who though they write, paint and compose art are not artists, in that they are not inspired." This sounds very silly, spelled out, but we have all learned it, in effect.[11]
>
> In the same light, we imagine that a work of art must do something new and different. But this is not necessary. So far from this being simply

'conventional' art, with the implication that it is less likely to be valuable, it is probable that most great art has been made in these conditions.[12]

In many societies it has been the function of art to embody what we can call the common meanings of the society. The artist is not describing new experiences, but embodying known experiences. There is great danger in the assumption that art serves only on the frontiers of knowledge. It serves on these frontiers, particularly in disturbed and rapidly changing societies. [This was written in 1961, when the even quicker pace of change in Western society in the twenty-first century had not yet occurred.] Yet it serves, also, at the very centre of societies.[13]

This means that artistic expression, even if solidly within a tradition and relying on imitation, is as much art as novel creativity.

Reverence and Imitation of Past Masters

It is often true that young jazz musicians learning jazz fall in love with the sound of established masters and seek to imitate them. The young musician is devoted to studying and learning the music of great musicians, absorbing their improvisatory vocabulary, phrasing, tone, and style in general. In describing their early experiences with jazz, musicians use such powerful words as "mesmerized," "in a cloud," "stunned," and the like.[14] Lester Young was so enamored of "Singin' the Blues," featuring Bix Beiderbecke and Frankie Trumbauer, that he kept a copy of it in his saxophone case for years. It is this type of devotion, much like being in love, that often fuels the great effort it takes to learn jazz. The intense study required in order to imitate another musician successfully usually rests on some type of fanatical or deep devotion. Only that fuel will be enough to power the engine that can produce the vast amount of practice necessary to learn jazz.

This enthusiasm for past masters of jazz helps encourage tradition in jazz. Such idols are already part of the tradition. Their prominence as masters gives them the visibility and status that allow them to be idolized by young jazz musicians. On the other hand, is generally unacceptable in jazz to remain at the level of imitation, no matter how skilled. It is expected that a jazz musician will create a personal style, even if it began in imitation of another's. But because imitation of the tradition is expected to lead to producing one's own creative style does not mean that imitation is without value. It is as much a part of the process as any other part, even if it is the first step.

Personal versus Institutional Connection to Tradition

For most of the twentieth century, musicians learned to play jazz primarily through the jam session and with the guidance of mentors. In the last half of the century, jazz programs in public schools, colleges, and universities provided another way of learning jazz. While jam sessions and mentors still operate, the rise of academic jazz programs has marked a shift in how jazz is learned. This change introduced an institutional approach to learning jazz. In academic jazz programs, values and approaches characteristic of bureaucracy, including the mediated, the indirect, and the impersonal, infiltrate and influence the learning of jazz. In both systems, however, absorbing the tradition of jazz and fealty to it is apparent.

TECHNIQUE FOR ITS OWN SAKE

Musical tradition is usually concerned with technique (in a standard, conventional sense). When Wynton Marsalis talks about "getting to such a place in my art that all will realize that I'm coming from a great tradition,"[15] he is looking at jazz as a craft and hopes to achieve a level of technique such that it will be obvious to anyone how great the music is. How valuable, though, is this part of tradition? Paul Berliner, on one hand, says that "while praising individuals for their technical mastery, musicians rarely appreciate such accomplishment as an end in itself."[16] However, Berliner begins his discussion of instrumental virtuosity with a statement by trumpeter Bobby Rogovin that expresses the opposite idea: "Sometimes, it's exciting just to hear a trumpet played high and fast and clean."[17] It is true that one could appreciate technique merely as a means that accomplishes the true end of, say, emotional expressiveness. But, as is common with opposites, the pendulum can sometimes swing too far in one direction when the opposites are seen only as mutually exclusive. Perhaps technique is sometimes recognized only as a means to another end because technique was the only end conceived at one time, and the pendulum must swing back. I know for myself that, when I was learning my instrument as a child, I was fascinated with the purely mechanical and technical aspect of playing the instrument with facility and did not focus as much on expressiveness. Being able to play my instrument with speed and agility now seems similar to children and puppies running around for the pure physical joy of it, just burning off excess energy, and stands in contrast to a more adult approach that emphasizes emotion and expressiveness.

Is it possible to relegitimize purely technical displays? The best argument for doing so is Art Tatum, perhaps jazz's greatest technical virtuoso, regardless of instrument. Tatum was sometimes criticized for not aiming beyond his technical prowess. Andre Hodeir said that "Tatum does, of course, display great virtuosity and an uncommon flair for harmony. . . . [b]ut his vast imagination strives in vain to enliven themes so intrinsically feeble that only a drastic reappraisal could possibly save them, the very reappraisal which Tatum did not have the courage to undertake."[18] In my opinion, Tatum was much more of a musician than just a technical virtuoso, but his technical displays are still nothing less than brilliant, especially in the sense of the visual metaphor. Babies have all sorts of flashy, brightly colored toys hanging in their cribs, and I imagine that their happy gurgling at the pure redness of a red toy is only the immature version of what it feels like when Art Tatum lets loose one brilliant right-hand run after another at the end of his version of "Tiger Rag."[19] (Perhaps we adults are just playing with bigger toys.)

THE GROOVE HELPS JUSTIFY TRADITION

The groove and swing have not, in the past, been a major focus of study. Two reasons for this are because scholarship and research have tended to focus on the intellectual, not the embodied, and because the field of aesthetics tends to value the novel, not the repetitious. As Susan McClary and Robert Walser have noted, "The body has not been a prestigious topic among scholars of the arts. Aesthetician Roman Ingarden . . . has written: 'We may doubt whether so-called dance music, when employed only as a means of keeping the dancers in step and arousing in them a specific passion for expression through movement, is music in the strict sense of the word.' "[20] Novelty is a prime value for aesthetics, and may be contrasted with repetition. Repetition, as exemplified in the groove, is strongly connected to the body, not only through the many activities of the body that are repetitious (breathing, walking, sex, and more), but also because the response to a great groove is usually expressed through the body: dancing, tapping one's foot, nodding one's head, clapping, and the like.

Recently, however, the groove and swing have found new status as a focus of scholarship and research. Entire books have focused on the groove, and articles about the groove and swing have appeared in scholarly journals.[21] This new focus confirms what listeners and musicians have known for a long time, that the groove and swing are great things. However, the groove and swing need no particular creativity. Swing is certainly a fundamental aspect of jazz, and yet swing requires very little creativity to be successfully accomplished. True, it requires skill and feeling to swing well, and there are different ways to swing: one can fall behind the beat or push ahead of the beat a little bit, and one may do this creatively within an improvisation just like one may spontaneously manipulate any aspect of music in service of improvisational goals. This creativity, though, is not essential to swing. One may swing perfectly well without creatively modifying one's swing, ahead or behind the beat, in any significant way. One can just lock in a groove, swing hard, and stay there all night. Swing and the groove pose no threat to tradition because they require no creativity, and perhaps this is one reason why swing can be cited by jazz traditionalists and neoconservatives as one of the primary elements of jazz.

If the groove and swing, which are so dependent on repetition, can now enjoy respectability in scholarship and research, then tradition should be respected as well. The groove and swing help justify tradition because tradition is no less repetitive than the groove, in its own way. Tradition seeks to repeat, to conserve, and to lock in that which is as firmly established as the beat is when the drummer and the bass player lock in and get together in a groove. The special value of the groove and swing is not their novelty, just as the special value of tradition is not novelty, but exactly the opposite, conserving (repeating) the past.

Creativity does not have to be taken to an extreme in jazz, and one need not make the meta-decision to be creative with some fundamental aspect of jazz to push jazz beyond its tradition. One can play jazz with something less than radical creativity if one emphasizes, for instance, just swinging well and staying within its tradition. One can be faithful to the idea of jazz with a smaller but sufficient amount of creativity and with a healthy dose of swing and the groove, just as one can be faithful to the idea of jazz with a great amount of creativity and with a smaller but sufficient amount of swing.

NOTES

1. Edward Shils, *Tradition* (Chicago: University of Chicago Press, 1981), 12.

2. This assumes literal interpretations of words. Poetry or metaphor might very well imagine a way to sit on air.

3. Scott Walter, "Live with TAE: Wynton Marsalis and Stanley Crouch," *American Enterprise* 8, no. 2 (March–April 1997): 21.

4. *Stanford Encyclopedia of Philosophy*, http://plato.stanford.edu/entries/logic-fuzzy/, s.v. "Fuzzy Logic."

5. Mark Gridley, Robert Maxham, and Robert Hoff, "Three Approaches to Defining Jazz," *Musical Quarterly* 73, no. 4 (1989): 513–31.

6. Gridley et al., "Three Approaches to Defining Jazz," 530.

7. Scott Deveaux, "Constructing the Jazz Tradition: Jazz Historiography," *Black American Literature Forum* 25, no. 3 (Autumn 1991): 528–29.

8. Deveaux, "Constructing the Jazz Tradition," 529.

9. Paul Berliner, *Thinking in Jazz: The Infinite Art of Improvisation* (Chicago: University of Chicago Press, 1994), 95.

10. Raymond Williams, *The Long Revolution* (New York: Columbia University Press, 1961), 8.

11. Williams, *The Long Revolution*, 29.

12. Williams, *The Long Revolution*, 32.

13. Williams, *The Long Revolution*, 30.

14. Berliner, *Thinking in Jazz*, 31.

15. Source unknown.

16. Berliner, *Thinking in Jazz*, 261.

17. Bobby Rogovin, quoted in Berliner, *Thinking in Jazz*, 260.

18. Andre Hodeir, *Toward Jazz* (New York: Grove Press, 1962), 130–31.

19. Art Tatum, *Piano Starts Here* (Columbia PCT-9655E).

20. Susan McClary and Robert Walser, "Theorizing the Body in African- American Music," *Black Music Research Journal* 14, no.1 (Spring 1994): 75.

21. Charles Keil and Steven Feld, *Music Grooves: Essays and Dialogues* (Chicago: University of Chicago Press, 1994); James Lincoln Collier and Geoffrey L. Collier, "Microrhythms in Jazz: A Review of Papers," *Annual Review of Jazz Studies* 8 (1996): 117-39; J. A. Prögler, "Searching for Swing: Participatory Discrepancies in the Jazz Rhythm Section," *Ethnomusicology* 39, no.1 (Winter 1995): 21-54; and an entire journal issue focusing on swing and groove: *Music Perception* 19, no. 3 (Spring 2002).

Part Three

THE OPPOSITES OF JAZZ

10

♫

Individualism
and Interconnectedness

To grow mature is to separate more distinctly, to connect more closely.

—Hugo von Hofmannsthal

In the previous eight chapters I outlined various details of certain values in jazz and how they are expressed. The values can be organized into four groups of opposite pairs:

- individualism and interconnectedness
- assertion and openness
- freedom and responsibility
- creativity and tradition

That jazz should contain such opposition and contradiction is remarkable. But some details of these contradictions can be explored more deeply, and will reveal even further levels of opposition and contradiction. That is the purpose of this chapter and the following three chapters.

INTERACTION

Interaction Expresses Several Values

While most of the following discussion about interaction concerns the opposition between individualism and interconnectedness, interaction expresses those values and nearly all of the other values of jazz discussed in this book. In interaction, musicians have the opportunity to take advantage of the *freedom* that interaction offers and *assert* themselves as *individuals* to produce a new, *creative* musical idea, while remaining *open* to another's idea and responding to it by supporting it in a *responsible* manner, thereby creating a unified group sound and conception that *interconnects* everyone in the group.

Expressing both Individualism and Interconnectedness

Interaction among members of a jazz group holds the individual and the group in opposition not through mutual exclusion. Both values—individualism and interconnectedness—are fully expressed. The individual is given the freedom to improvise any new musical idea, but at the same time, a phrase that is improvised is heard in relation to what others in the ensemble are improvising, and it may contribute to a collective goal (for instance, a dramatic increase in dynamics, density of texture, and the like). The individual remains an individual, but is nonetheless interconnected with the rest of the ensemble. The individual's freedom is not limited just because it is interpreted as part of interaction. An individual may freely improvise anything, as much as any improviser may (even assuming the standard chord progression and chorus form of mainstream jazz), but the context or background in which that improvisation is heard is the collective result of what everyone else is improvising. If improvisation is a single performer acting as a composer during a performance, then interaction is group composition and expands interconnectedness multidimensionally while still fully expressing individualism.

Deciding to Interact or Not

It is common in jazz not to play something exactly as given, but to improvise to a greater degree (as in an improvised solo) or to a lesser degree (by embellishing a composed melody or by the rhythm section accompanying a soloist). If all the notes and rhythms were given to a jazz musician and the musician was expected to play them exactly, the question of the opposition between individualism and interconnectedness in a jazz group would never arise. However, because improvisation is crucial to jazz, it is up to each musician to determine the extent of his or her interconnectedness with the group. The jazz musician must decide, either consciously or unconsciously, how to balance individualism and interconnectedness with the other members of the ensemble. At what point should one introduce an idea into the mix to see if anyone does anything with it? Or should one lay low for a while, playing standard and common ideas, and wait for others to offer an interesting idea? If, for instance, one repeats a rhythm over and over, waiting for others in the group to respond but no one does, how long should one continue to play the rhythm before giving it up? These questions may well be answered intuitively and unconsciously by any particular musician, and asking them here does not require particular answers; they merely illustrate some of the types of decisions about interaction that jazz musicians face.

The Dynamic Tension of Interaction

During interaction, the jazz musician is fully an individual and is fully interconnected with other members of the ensemble. The crucial factor that makes the opposition between individualism and interconnectedness into dynamic tension is the constancy of the question of whether to interact. An improviser has the freedom to interact or not, or to interpret another's musical idea as material for interaction or not. An improviser may make potentially a whole series of ongoing decisions as to whether to engage in interaction. Interaction requires that the musicians walk (even run, for tunes played at fast tempos) along a precipice, or a tightrope, making continuous, split-second decisions. Whether this choice is conscious or not is irrelevant; the improviser cannot help but make, in effect and in practice, a decision to interact or not to play in relation with others. Individualism and interconnectedness are held in dynamic tension because this decision is constantly being made, one way or the other. The two options—to interact or not—are competing, in a sense, all the time.

The Potential of Interaction Not Exploited

There is a range of balance possible between individualism and interconnectedness when viewed as a zero-sum game. Some jazz is not concerned with the opposition between the two, so the musicians merely play individualistically. Each musician articulates his or her particular role (bassists walk a bass line, pianists comp, drummers keep time, soloists improvise). This approach may produce great music without establishing significant interaction among the members of the ensemble.

When the Bill Evans trio raised the level of interaction in a jazz combo to great heights, it underscored that interaction in jazz had occurred to a far lesser degree in the past.[1] When I had developed sufficiently as a jazz musician to understand the potential of interaction in jazz, I was disappointed to hear recordings by some of the great names in jazz history in which they seemed to ignore the potential that the Bill Evans trio had realized. Some musicians seemed to be on autopilot—a swingin', groovin' autopilot, but still without any significant interplay on the level of the Bill

Evans trio. It was as if such groups were interconnected on the microlevel of swing and the groove, and not the larger level of phrases and musical ideas.

Confusing Interaction with Coincidence

Some jazz musicians may sometimes ignore the potential for interconnectedness; some may be aware of the potential for connectedness in jazz but fail to achieve it (someone who, for instance, keeps on suggesting an idea to the rest of the ensemble, which ignores it); and some may take full advantage of the potential for interconnectedness and are always attempting to shape the music in a way that is interconnected with everyone else in the ensemble. However, trying to determine after the fact whether any musical figure is part of interaction can be a difficult thing. Just because two things happen at the same time or one follows the other closely in time does not mean that they should be interpreted to be in relation. One musician may consider a musical idea by another as part of the interconnected web of interaction, but another may not. A jazz musician might improvise something that another musician did not conceive as contributing to interaction but is taken up by others for interaction, or something that that musician did conceive as contributing to interaction but was ignored by others.

Such multiple interpretations create, potentially, a constantly shifting matrix of who interprets what as potential for interaction or not. Interaction is mutually negotiated and interpreted. Trying to analyze whether any musical idea is part of interaction may be more likely in some cases than others because it is an interpretive process, even for the musicians. How are we to determine that an alleged example is actually interaction (that is, intentional interaction), as opposed to a mere coincidence? Because it is a risky proposition to try to get into the heads of jazz musicians after they have performed (or during!) and try to interpret how they conceived the music (unless, perhaps, one is that musician oneself), one can only make informed guesses. Some clear examples of intent may be reasonably inferred, and some examples may be problematic. However, to appreciate the dynamic tension between individualism and interconnectedness in interaction, it is necessary to attempt such interpretation.

Examples of Interaction

Because of the difficulties of inferring interaction, I would like to discuss some examples of interaction that will be less problematic. I will analyze interaction with examples from my own compact disc recording for jazz piano trio, *Active Listening.*[2] Because I composed the songs on the recording, conceived the interactive approach reflected in the title, encouraged the others in the ensemble to take advantage of opportunities for interaction, and played piano on the recording, I am in a unique position to analyze what happened in the music on the recording. I can offer not only an authoritative opinion as to at least one musician's interpretation (mine) of that musician's interaction, but I can also offer my view of the contributions by the other members of the ensemble (whether I thought that any of their contributions were part of interaction, and how). I offer this not to establish whether those contributions by others were objectively part of interaction, but to show how one musician in the ensemble (me) viewed a contribution by another musician, and thereby illuminate the opposition between individualism and interconnectedness in interaction.

It has been suggested by Evan Parker that this type of analysis is unwise. "The mechanism of what is provocation and what is response—the music is based on such fast interplay, such fast reactions that it is arbitrary to say, 'Did you do that because I did that? Or did I do that because you did that?' "[3] While the difficulties should not be underestimated, Parker's example is not intractable, as one cannot respond to something that occurs after the response, and a recording would clearly establish what came first.

The piece I will analyze in this regard is "Groove Tune." While some pieces on this recording used specific approaches to interaction, "Groove Tune" used a very simple and broad one: the goal for the trio was merely to interact in any way imaginable while maintaining a mainstream-style chord progression. The following comments describe the interaction for selected sections of "Groove Tune" from my perspective as the pianist. Sections are identified with timings from the compact disc.[4]

2:55. A standard texture in a harder-driving groove is established collectively and is maintained.

3:14. The single-note piano line breaks the previous, heavier texture of both hands together and raises the possibility of some sort of change and interaction, but no radical change is realized immediately as drums and bass continue as before (although they lighten their texture and dynamics a little).

3:21. The piano ends the single-note line simultaneously with the bass sustaining a long note (with a drop in pitch). My interpretation is that the bassist anticipated the potential resolution of the piano line and interactively followed it (I do not interpret the bass line implying a resolution at that point, so I suspect that the bassist responded to me, and not vice versa).

3:23. It takes the drums a few beats to respond to the piano and bass resolution by stopping the time pattern and playing an accent. Now, without bass, piano, and drums playing standard patterns, new possibilities are opened up because the texture is much thinner (everyone is not playing constantly, as they had been before) and because the absence of the standard texture requires that the trio improvise some texture.

3:24. The piano responds to the lack of a standard texture by playing more softly.

3:25. The bass responds to the piano phrase of 3:24 by imitating the phrase in a call-and-response manner, and the drums also contribute to the lighter feel. This lighter feel has been improvised and collectively established—no plan was predetermined to bring this lighter feel into effect.

3:26. The drums somehow play every note of the bass phrase (except the first note) at exactly the same time as the bass without knowing beforehand that the bass would play that exact rhythm. This is either a coincidence, or bass and drums somehow both independently understood that something prior to this simultaneous phrase implied that very phrase.

3:27. The new, lighter texture is fully established and is maintained.

3:36. The dissonant notes in the piano were an idea that I distinctly recall rejecting as soon as I played it. It was an experiment that was an immediate failure, in my opinion. Even years after making the recording, I have a clear memory of that. Neither bass nor drums were inspired by it (they didn't respond), so I continued onto something else very quickly.

3:43. The piano introduces a new idea: the left hand plays isolated, short, accented notes that accompany the right-hand melody.

3:48. The piano finishes the phrase of short, accented notes with a final short, accented note, and the bass responds in kind.

3:49. The drums play a short, accented note in kind as well. The piano responds to the 3:48 response of the bass by exactly imitating the rhythm of that response. Yet another new idea or texture has been established.

3:58. The bass introduces a resolution of the short, accented notes with a long, sustained, bent note.

4:01. The piano responds to the resolution offered by the bass by sustaining several chords. The group is only two bars away from a major harmonic and formal division in the chord progression, and continues the transition away from the short, accented notes, anticipating the upcoming formal marker.

4:03. The bass anticipates the formal division by walking a bass line a few beats beforehand.

4:05. The formal division is marked by the entire group establishing a new, soft, even texture marked by the bass pedal point, the first few piano chords, and a gentle time feel by the drums.

This illustrates how interaction as group composition can work: the trio spontaneously and interactively suggests, responds to, establishes, and develops unique and specific textures or ideas. Each member is an individual, separately deciding how to interact, but doing so within the context of the others in the ensemble such that an interconnected whole is created.

DIFFERING PERSONALITIES

Jazz embraces the contradiction of a single ensemble containing members who have very different musical approaches. One classic example of this is the great Miles Davis combo from the 1950s with John Coltrane. The opposition between Davis's and Coltrane's improvisatory styles was clear and distinct. Davis was a minimalist and Coltrane a maximalist. It is sometimes said of Davis that the notes he *didn't* play were just as important, if not more so, than the notes he did play. Davis is widely recognized for his masterful use of silence, and for enabling very few notes to speak volumes. Coltrane's prolificacy, on the other hand, is exemplified by his "sheets of sound" technique in which torrent after torrent of notes cascade like sheets of rain, as well as by the following anecdote: "Once in a while, Miles might say, 'Why did you [Coltrane] play so long, man?' and John would say, 'It took that long to get it all in.'"[5]

The great advantage of diversity is revealed through the opposition between diverse elements. Black looks more black when it is right next to white, compared to when black is next to gray. An individual is more strongly affirmed as an individual when he or she is placed in contrast with a partner who is different. In this case, it is through juxtaposition that the personal styles of Coltrane and Davis are opposed. Davis's solo style is juxtaposed with Coltrane's when one's solo follows the other's.

SECTIONS IN A BIG BAND

The modern big band typically has three sections of wind instruments: five saxophones, four or five trumpets, and four or five trombones. Within each section, and excepting improvised solos, the expectation is that each player will blend into his or her section (and each section into the entire ensemble) as much as possible, reducing individuality to a minimum in order to produce a unified and consistent sound. This is accomplished primarily by matching tone color, intonation, dynamics, and articulations. In this case, the value of community—achieving a unified sound—supersedes the value of individualism. Usually only the section leader or the director is allowed to express individuality by deciding exactly which tone colors, dynamics, or articulations should be used at any one point. The rest of the section is expected not to contribute an individual approach, but to imitate the leader exactly. This situation is an exception to the value of individualism in jazz. Here, individualism and interconnection are opposed through mutual exclusion, and collectivism is present.

Perhaps this is one reason why, even though the big band has a long and famous history in jazz, it is the combo that is usually regarded as the primary jazz ensemble. Improvisation tends to be emphasized more in a combo than in a big band. The big band has so many players that a composer is needed to coordinate everybody (with some exceptions). This tends to limit the amount of improvisation compared to a combo. The lack of emphasis on individuality and improvisation in the big band makes it a secondary ensemble in jazz (although still a fascinating one, as issues regarding composition and improvisation are highlighted in some ways).

While not commonly practiced anymore, the big band can function more like a combo and less like a symphony orchestra. An important exception to the usual authority and conformity in the big band is the technique known as a "head arrangement," most notably used by the early Count Basie big band.[6] A head arrangement was not written down like a musical composition, but was developed aurally and collectively by the band, almost equivalent to a jam session that then is frozen into an arrangement. In rehearsal, a trumpet player might improvise a riff that is taught to all the trumpets and then memorized to be used behind, for instance, a saxophone solo. The entire arrangement would be built up more or less collectively this way, emphasizing simple, easily understood elements like many solo improvisations, the blues, riffs, and call and response. This system allowed for negotiation and compromise to a greater extent than allowed by composed and written arrangements.

The presence of individualism in jazz through the ubiquity of the individual solo, a personal sound, diversity, and antiauthoritarianism is opposed to interconnectedness and its related elements of the groove, interaction, community, and democracy. These opposites are expressed through dynamic tension in interaction, through juxtaposition when differing personalities are members of the same ensemble, and through mutual exclusion in the conformity of the big band. Taken together, this results in a significant amount of opposition between individualism and interconnectedness in jazz. However, a similar situation holds for the other three pairs of values that this book explores, and we will now turn to the next pair, assertion and openness.

NOTES

1. Bill Evans, "Autumn Leaves," *Portrait in Jazz* (Fantasy OJCCD 088-2, 1959).

2. Paul Rinzler, *Active Listening* (Sea Breeze Jazz SB-3039, 1999).

3. Evan Parker, quoted in David Borgo, "Negotiating Freedom: Values and Practices in Contemporary Improvisation," *Black Music Research Journal* 22, no. 2 (Fall 2002): 203.

4. An audio excerpt of the music discussed is available at cla.calpoly .edu/~prinzler/Mp3s/GrooveTune.mp3 (the website excerpt starts at the 2:55 timing on the CD).

5. John Coltrane, quoted in Bill Crow, *Jazz Anecdotes* (New York: Oxford University Press, 1990), 325.

6. *The New Grove Dictionary of Jazz*, s.v. "Arrangement."

11

♫

Assertion and Openness

I believe in an open mind, but not so open that your brains fall out.

—Arthur Hays Sulzberger

IN/OUT PROCESSING

Performing any type of music is a process that manages input and output. A musician is receiving input from all the other musicians in the ensemble while at the same time that musician is sending output, in the form of the music he or she performs, to everyone else in the ensemble, as well as the listener. A musician negotiates both channels at the same time, working in two opposite directions at once. Furthermore, managing these inputs and outputs happens continuously. Performing jazz is an ongoing process of attending to the musical environment (the input of what others in the ensemble are playing) while simultaneously helping to determine that environment through the output of what one performs. This is a reflection of the two directions in which openness and assertion are opposed.

Managing this issue is of crucial importance for jazz because both the input and the output have the potential to change the character of the music at any time to the same significant extent that a composer determines the character of a composition. This means that a jazz musician must be highly aware at all times of everything that is happening in a performance in order to appropriately respond in time to sometimes drastic and spontaneous changes in the character of the music, as well as to take advantage of the opportunity to initiate changes. This distinguishes performing jazz from performing composed music. Assuming an ensemble performing a composition has rehearsed, the simultaneous in/out processing is merely a question of monitoring what is expected and has already been determined, and making any necessary adjustments. In jazz, however, spontaneity can change very significant aspects of the music. For instance, the drummer may decide to switch from a swing feel to a Latin feel, or the bassist may play a pedal tone that continues for a long while, or a pianist or guitarist may reharmonize the chord progression. The changes possible are very diverse, and so can change the musical outcome significantly and with minimal warning. This requires the jazz musician to be aware of everything and to be ready for anything, as well as to be a fully functioning, creative, and assertive member of the ensemble.

Dynamic Tension

Dynamic tension is inherent in this in/out processing because the musician must simultaneously and fully process information going in both directions. R. Keith Sawyer interviewed a jazz musician who touched on the dynamic tension of this situation: "It's all a matter of listening to the people you're playing with. . . . This is a real difficulty—you have to be able to divide your senses, but still keep it coherent so you can play, so you still have that one thought running through your head of saying something, playing something, at the same time you've got to be listening to what the drummer is doing."[1]

Conscious and Nonconscious Processes

One argument against viewing this in/out processing as dynamic tension might come from looking at it only as a conscious process. One might suggest that conscious attention to one's inner assertions must alternate with conscious attention to one's outer environment (the rest of the band, the audience, and more). Therefore in/out processing would not truly be simultaneous, and thus not truly illustrate dynamic tension.

There are counterarguments to this position, though. First, even if in/out processing is a quick alternation between receiving and transmitting, and therefore not simultaneous, it would still be a difficult thing to do and might occur quickly enough for the musician to perceive it as simultaneous. More fundamentally, however, Sawyer reminds us that nonconscious processes occur in jazz improvisation, and that "the nonconscious contribution is reported to be salient, continuous, and essential."[2] The musicians that Sawyer interviewed reported both conscious, intellectual thought during improvisation as well as nonconscious processes. They reported that, sometimes, improvisation seemed to come unbidden, from somewhere outside themselves (that is, not present to their consciousness): "But sometimes it just comes out, it falls out of my mouth. . . . When you start a solo, you're still in thinking mode; it takes a while to get yourself out of thinking mode."[3]

The conscious and nonconscious, while opposed, are not mutually exclusive. Sawyer concludes that "in jazz improvisation, it seems that ideation [the stage of creativity at which ideas are generated] and selection [the stage at which ideas are filtered and let through to consciousness] can occur at both conscious and nonconscious levels, and in some cases simultaneously. . . . The conscious levels, which monitor other musicians or attempt to stay aware of the song form, may likewise contribute ideas to the ongoing nonconscious generation."[4]

Viewing the process as a purely conscious one would prevent in/out processing from being constant and therefore from being a true example of dynamic tension. But if the management of in/out processing is a conscious and nonconscious process, it can be constant and therefore truly in dynamic tension. One's conscious attention may be focused on the outer musical environment while one's nonconscious process can help drive one's creative contributions. Alternately, but perhaps less likely, one's consciousness may be attending inwardly to a particularly difficult creative contribution while the outer musical environment is only heard subconsciously.

Sawyer suggests that the dynamic tension of in/out processing is resolved: "There is a constant tension between fully conscious and fully nonconscious performance, and each musician must continuously resolve this tension to achieve a balance appropriate to the moment."[5] Such tension, though, is not really resolved: a resolution that must be continuously re-created is not much of a resolution. Resolution of the tension was perhaps suggested by Sawyer without full appreciation for the possibility of other forms of opposition besides mutual exclusion.

IMPROVISATION AS A WORK IN PROGRESS

There is an opposition between the finality of assertion and viewing jazz improvisation as ongoing and open. There is an element of finality and certainty in assertion because of the immutability of past time. Once an improvisation has been performed, it is over and the improvisation cannot be changed, so we can say that that improvisation was what was asserted at that time by that improviser. But each part of an improvisation can also be viewed as one in a string of responses to similar situations. Part of the openness of improvisation is that it can be seen to continue, into the future, when the next similar situation occurs and the improviser makes another choice, replaying the opportunity he or she had in the past. (Howard Brofsky has analyzed three solos of Miles Davis on "My Funny Valentine" through a similar perspective.[6])

Once one has asserted one's improvisation at a certain place and at a certain time and in certain circumstances, we can say that the improvisation is over, but in another sense it is never really over. The next time the same piece is played, or the next time the same chord progression occurs, or the next time the bassist, for instance, plays a pedal tone instead of walking a bass line, the context in which the improviser makes a choice changes because implicitly included are all the other choices the improviser has made in the past in similar circumstances. This is certainly true to the extent that the improviser wants to maximize creativity so that, when confronted with similar situations, the improviser tries not to choose what has worked or has been tried in the past. The context of all past choices can be crucial for defining what will be creative. As a matter of assertion, an improvisation is over once the last note is played; as a matter of openness, an improvisation continues on to the next similar improvisatory circumstance.

EMBRACING THE UNKNOWN

Even though jazz improvisation can rely on a firm foundation such as the melody, the chord progression, and the chorus form, it is still an encounter with the unknown because the improvisation is not predetermined. The unknown gives jazz improvisation a certain power, and the thing that gives the unknown its power is the danger of what one might eventually find when the unknown becomes known. The unknown would not hold its power over us unless there was some danger possible. On the other hand, we may actively choose, as an example of assertion, the unknown precisely because of the danger implicit in its openness. Something can be exciting, and therefore attractive, exactly because it is dangerous. No one would recognize a roller coaster as such if it went very slowly and peaceably down a track with no sudden corners or no steep hills. The roller coaster is only what it is because it reproduces some aspects of danger within a safe environment. The high speed, the sharp corners, and the steep hills are all dangerous when they occur in real life, but in a roller coaster, they are all safe. Its excitement and allure come from these dangers-without-the-danger. Other chosen activities or recreations may truly be very dangerous, such as advanced mountain climbing, and it is again that danger that helps attract some if not many to these activities.

Certainly, jazz improvisation is not actually dangerous. It's possible that things could go badly for the improviser, but it cannot go too badly because no one is going to fall off a cliff and die. The most that might happen would be an unwanted or unappreciated dissonant note, or no applause at the end of a solo or a gig. Even though an improvisation is not truly dangerous, and even though improvisers may reuse musical material, improvisation is not any less unknown. There are many situations in real life that are unknown at the outset and that are eventually understood to be safe or familiar, but this does not lessen the power of the unknown in those situations. One can walk into a dark, deserted, run-down, multistory house on a dark, stormy night and fear all sorts of dangers and come away without ever meeting ghosts, goblins, or the undead. When the lights are eventually turned on, one will probably see that, for instance, what was feared to be a ghost was merely a white curtain flapping in the breeze that entered through an open window. So the unknown can hold great power over us, through fear, even if those worst fears are realized only a small percentage of the time. Similarly, just because an improviser is never completely creative and often relies on previously performed material in standard ways does not remove the analogous power of the musical unknown, because you never know what can happen, even if the unexpected (either dangerous or musically creative) often does not. But the danger of the unknown in jazz improvisation is a prime reason why improvisation is so exciting. We don't know what's going to happen, and can be as thrilled to find out what happens in a solo nearly as much as we are when a roller coaster turns a corner or speeds downhill.

Jazz improvisation allows us to deal with the unknown, whether as a performer or as a listener. Because jazz improvisation is as unknown as other unknown things, it can allow us to practice and play at confronting the unknown, but in a safe environment. The openness of the unknown, because it is unpredictable, is in dynamic tension with the initiative and assertion it takes to embrace the unknown. One other factor increases this dynamic tension, and that is the fact that jazz improvisation is performed live and often in public. The jazz improviser, performing live and in public, improvises a way through the unknown without anywhere to hide.

NOTES

1. R. Keith Sawyer, "Improvisational Creativity: An Analysis of Jazz Performance," *Creativity Research Journal* 5, no. 3 (1992): 257.

2. Sawyer, "Improvisational Creativity," 257.

3. Sawyer, "Improvisational Creativity," 257.

4. Sawyer, "Improvisational Creativity," 257.

5. Sawyer, "Improvisational Creativity," 257.

6. Howard Brofsky, "Miles Davis and 'My Funny Valentine': The Evolution of a Solo," *Black Music Research Journal* 3 (1983): 23–45.

12

♫

Freedom and Responsibility

I think of a hero as someone who understands the degree of responsibility that comes with his freedom.

—Bob Dylan

PLAYING ANYTHING YOU WANT

There is a maxim about free jazz that says, "You can play anything, but you can't play just anything." This expresses, in the form of a contradiction, the opposition between freedom and responsibility in jazz improvisation. The first part of the saying, "You can play anything," declares the improviser's negative freedom to not have to play what a composer requires. The second part of the saying, "But you can't play just anything," means that it is positive freedom and an affirmative purpose that fully realizes the opportunity for which negative freedom sets the foundation. The saying states, in other words, that one should not do something merely for the sake of doing it, and that there is responsibility associated with one's freedom. An improviser can meet the responsibility to not play anything just to play it if he or she plays what is authentic and honest as determined by the particulars of the musician's individual character and personality. Not playing something just to play it is a higher-level proscription about the purpose of one's freedom, a proscription about the manner in which one is not proscribed, a statement about the responsibility of one's freedom.

116

The improviser can thereby express both freedom and responsibility. As an example, consider the musical technique of banging both hands on the keyboard of a piano. There are times in which such a technique may be responsible, and times in which it may not be appropriate. For instance, Michael Brecker composed a piece called "Nothing Personal" in which one note is notated as an undefined pitch.[1] When I perform this piece, I usually interpret that notation by slapping the piano with both fists, creating an extremely dissonant cluster. My intent in doing so operates within the context of the entire melody, and the cluster has a certain function as part of the melody. If, however, I were merely to bang my hands on the piano without regard to the musical context, just to do it, or perhaps to shock the audience, it could not be called responsible.

One might argue that playing something in an improvisation for no purpose—just to do it—is a purpose itself: a meta-purpose, or a purpose attached to a lack of purpose. This is similar to saying, "Moderation in all things, including moderation." This allows for immoderate things, because if moderation is done in moderation, then occasionally some actions will not be moderate. If one always improvises with a purpose, then, sometimes, one's purpose might be to have no purpose. Sometimes it might be OK to do something just for the heck of it, but we cannot say that doing so was an expression of responsibility, even if it was acceptable in a larger sense. The meta-purpose of having no purpose may be a legitimate part of jazz, but it does not express responsibility.

RESPONSIBILITY FOR CHOICES

There is another way in which responsibility coexists with freedom. A choice is always subject to evaluation, and this means that, except for a perfect improviser (who does not exist), some choices will be evaluated as less worthy than others. Therefore, freedom is not always devoid of costs: stated as a contradiction, freedom is not necessarily free. If one is merely choosing between vanilla and chocolate ice cream, there is no significant cost to that choice, but if we appreciate some improvisations because they are clever, fascinating, humorous, or inspiring, we must also be ready to reject some improvisations because they are plain, uninteresting, or boring. Unless one suggests absolutely no standards, and even if such standards as cleverness, fascination, humor, or inspiration may be intersubjectively determined by the audience and the musicians, failing those standards is part of the landscape. Even before a choice is made, the risk of making a bad choice is implicit. There are musical and aesthetic consequences to choices in jazz improvisation, and when improvisers do not make optimal choices, regardless of who decides what is optimal or how they decide, the improviser takes responsibility for his or her failed choices as much as the credit for successful ones.

The improviser's freedom to make choices and the improviser's responsibility to face the subsequent evaluation of those choices are in dynamic tension. Freedom is fully present because the improviser has the sovereignty to choose to play anything, and responsibility is fully present because, once the choice is made, a negative (or positive) evaluation of the choice is possible. The improviser takes implicit responsibility for a choice at the same time that his or her freedom is being exercised through that choice. The tension in the opposition between freedom and responsibility is most apparent when an improviser takes risks. An improviser might approach the responsibility for bad choices by playing it safe, by not making any risky choices. If an improviser doesn't play it safe, however, and fully exercises his or her freedom, freedom and responsibility are in dynamic tension: a musical choice is more free when it is not limited by a potential negative evaluation of the choice, yet at the same time the musician must accept responsibility for the cost of a potential negative evaluation of that choice. The contradiction between playing freely, as if there are no consequences, when there are consequences and responsibility for playing freely, places freedom and responsibility in dynamic tension. Both are opposed to each other, in contradiction, yet fully expressed. Taking risks in improvisation may or may not be a wise strategy in any particular case, but when such an approach is taken, the improviser negotiates the contradiction between freedom and responsibility.

DISCIPLINE IS THE FOUNDATION OF FREEDOM

There is an opposition between the responsibility of discipline and the freedom that discipline enables. To be able to speak a language, for instance, one must have enough competency to be able to use the language effectively, and this implies standards to which one is responsible. It is through discipline that one achieves such competency and meets those standards, which enable the freedom to say anything in that language. It is genetics that gives us the ability as babies to attempt, through trial and error, to imitate the language of parents and thereby gain competency as a native speaker. For jazz improvisation, it is the self-imposed discipline of practice on an instrument that creates the technical facility and familiarity with the idiom that allows the improviser to use freedom to be creative. Even though creativity and innovation are a part of jazz, jazz is also an idiom with certain competencies. The discipline that is required to become proficient in the language of jazz is the foundation on which creative efforts rest. It is when one is in the process of acquiring competency in jazz as a student that the contradiction between discipline and freedom is most evident. A jazz student who doesn't wonder, "Why are parts of my study of improvisation so unimprovised?" isn't paying attention. Perhaps a closer analogy between language and jazz is poetry. In general, one must be competent with the grammar of English to write English poetry. Even in free poetry, poets generally know the rules of the language in which their free poetry is written. They know when they are breaking the rules of grammar and so understand the effect of what they write.

ART VERSUS COMMERCE

An important question for a jazz musician, as well as other musicians, is, "To what extent should the preferences of an audience be taken into account when determining the nature of the music to be performed?" This question raises the issue of the musician's responsibility to the audience. There are two main schools of thought concerning this question, which I will label "artistic" and "commercial," and four topics—musical content, relation to the audience, rewards, and musical goals—on which each school differs. The following will briefly summarize these schools, and it should be noted that musicians need not follow one school exclusively or consistently.

Artistic

Musical content. Artistic considerations or the demands of personal expression determine the repertoire and how it is played. This stance views jazz improvisation as a highly personal activity in which the spontaneity of improvisation encourages an unfettered imagination and the full expression of an improviser's musical character and personality.

  Relation to audience. In the most extreme forms of this approach, the musician may be hostile to the audience.

  Reward. While perhaps every artist would prefer all rewards at maximum levels, the artistic approach to jazz is driven by musical or artistic rewards. This is summarized by the phrase, "Music for its own sake."

  Values. The artist should follow his or her inner muse. This approach values individualism, freedom, personal expression, and creativity.

Commercial

Musical content. The musician chooses the repertoire with the primary consideration of what the audience will like or prefer. The practicalities of building and maintaining a career for paying audiences create responsibilities to the audience for the jazz musician. Jazz musicians offer their music to an audience in exchange for money, either at concerts or through recordings, so if they expect anyone to pay to listen to their music, they must, like anyone else in business, tailor their product, the music, to their customers, the audience.

Relation to audience. The musician has a responsibility to the audience, and seeks to develop and maintain an audience in order to ensure a successful career. One must be sensitive to the preferences of the audience or there may not be much of an audience at all.

Rewards. The primary reward is money and career security.

Values. Performing music is seen mainly as a form of communication, which requires consideration of and responsibility to the other party, who must be able to understand what the communicator, the musician, seeks to communicate. The musician takes into account how the audience will receive and perceive the music.

Approaches to Managing the Two Schools

When it is not possible to maximize both artistic opportunities and commercial rewards, a musician must balance these two opposite schools. Below I will outline several different approaches to this question that have been used by individual artists or by styles of jazz in general.

Approach #1: Art and Only Art

In this approach, little or no consideration is given to the commercial aspects of jazz and every consideration is given to artistic concerns, or nearly so. This approach is founded on what Robert Francesconi calls the myth of the creative artist:

> There is in jazz the mystique of the suffering artist which depicts the artist struggling to achieve musical excellence against the grasping hands of commercialism. . . . The paragon of the creative individual is the essence of jazz in this mythology. . . . In this value system, success is regarded as an evil to be combated. . . . The audience and its demands are agents of evil, urging the artist to forsake his art and pollute the gift that he possesses. The audience is an encroachment upon the purity of art.[2]

Free jazz and bebop are two styles from jazz history that illustrate this approach to some extent. In every area—repertoire, relation to the audience, rewards, and musical goals—free jazz and bebop musicians tended to place art over the audience. In one of the more extreme examples of this, free jazz has sometimes expressed outright hostility toward its audience.[3] Also, Francesconi considers that the word "squares," which makes a distinction that was important for bebop musicians, contains "a certain measure of contempt for the tastes of the public."[4]

Approach #2: Art First, Then the Audience

This approach values artistic goals but acknowledges the value of commercial goals if they fortuitously happen to coincide. Artistic standards are not compromised, but an audience is still desired. Thelonious Monk expressed this philosophy when he said, "Play what you want and let the public pick up on what you are doing, even if it does take them fifteen or twenty years."[5] Wynton Marsalis has articulated a variation on that approach:

> I'm going to do everything in my power to get the public to understand the real significance and beauty of the music, not by watering it down but by getting to such a place in my art that it will be obvious to all who listen that I'm coming from a great tradition.[6]

Rock musician Frank Zappa has also adopted this model: "If [people in the audience] like [my music], fine. If they don't, they can go out and buy another record."[7] This approach holds that, by being authentic and honest with oneself, the artist has the best chance of creating valuable art that may then be recognized by an audience, or at least recognized by the audience that values sincere and authentic art.

Approach #3: Audience First, Then the Art

Another approach is to establish one's audience and then satisfy artistic goals from a secure commercial foundation. Crucial to establishing an audience is the ability to communicate effectively through the music. The move to jazz/rock by artists such as Chick Corea and Herbie Hancock in the 1970s illustrates this approach. Corea credits a desire to communicate for creating his version of jazz/rock.[8] While this music places the sensitivities of the audience first, the musicians still expect to bring their creativity and personal expression to the task, albeit one bounded by the limits of what the musician estimates that the audience can accept or understand. The emphasis on having the audience understand the music exemplifies the importance of communication in this approach.

Patrice Rushen has developed a variation of this approach that accommodates the audience and the artist, but through time.[9] After initially giving the audience what it wants, the artist then uses the relationship and the trust between the artist and the audience at a later time in the artist's career to help the audience accept music that serves the musician's artistic goals.

Approach #4: Audience and Only Audience

Francesconi quotes guitarist Louis Johnson, who articulates an approach in which the audience is supreme: "You listen to what people like to dance to and change your style with that. . . . The public controls the music."[10] A purer expression of the sovereignty of the audience is rare.

The approaches that do not exclude either art or the audience (#2 and #3 above) express the opposition between artistic freedom and responsibility to the audience. In both cases, the opposition is played out temporally: either the musician who values freedom waits for the audience, in the near or distant future, to appreciate his or her music, or the musician who values the commercial success that comes from meeting the responsibilities to one's audience waits for a strong enough audience base, in the near or distant future, that can accommodate music with greater artistic value. Approaches #1 and #4 above treat art and commerce as mutually exclusive.

The following anecdote illustrates two of the above approaches in a real-life incident. I once played a wedding reception with a very good jazz musician. As is common at weddings, we were playing standards and pieces from the Great American Songbook. I saw teenagers and grandparents dancing and listening, and I saw an audience that was probably not very familiar with jazz, if at all, so I concluded that I should tone down some of the more radical aspects of my improvising in order to make the performance more palatable for a general audience. The main method by which I did this was to embellish the melody of the song as cleverly as I could while still keeping the melody recognizable, rather than improvising a completely new melody for my solos. This, I suspected, would be effective because the audience would have the best chance of being engaged with the music if they could hear a recognizable melody.

In contrast to my approach, this other musician played without much change from his usual style, which was powerful and strong. It was incongruous with the tone of the event, at least as far as I perceived it. In this case, this musician defined a personal style very well and exercised the freedom that improvisation allows, but without any apparent recognition of a responsibility to his audience. It is true that, in order to be responsible, one must know the details of that responsibility. Because no one in the audience stated a preference explicitly, one could argue that the other musician's aggressive style could have met the audience's preferences as much as my embellishments of the melodies. While it may be difficult to estimate precisely an audience's preferences, I think it is reasonable to conclude that my approach was attempting to cater to the audience, whereas my bandmate performed as he did with less regard for the audience.

The responsibility that I expressed in my embellishments of the melody did not preclude creativity nor freedom. I soon found the challenge of being creative only through the means of embellishing a melody to be a fascinating one, and one that I had not fully explored up to that point (but have now established as part of my improvisational technique). The challenge I created for myself was to be clever and interesting within the relatively narrow limits set by embellishing a melody. This challenge was no less a challenge than any other musical one because a musician is more limited by his or her own creativity and imagination than by the musical materials at hand. It is a common exercise to improvise with very limited resources. The purpose of such an exercise is to try to force one's thinking to be more imaginative and creative. So the exercise of freedom need not be limited by acknowledging the responsibility one has to an audience because both freedom and responsibility may be fully realized.

NOTES

1. Michael Brecker, "Nothing Personal," *The New Real Book*, vol. 1, edited by Chuck Sher (Petaluma, Calif.: Sher Music, 1988), 245.

2. Robert Francesconi, "Art vs. the Audience: The Paradox of Modern Jazz," *Journal of American Culture* 4, no. 4 (1981): 75.

3. Edward Harvey, "Social Change and the Jazz Musician," *Social Forces* 46, no. 1 (September 1967): 37.

4. Francesconi, "Art vs. the Audience," 75.

5. Thelonius Monk, quoted in Nat Hentoff, *Jazz Is* (New York: Random House, 1976), 146.

6. Wynton Marsalis, source unknown.

7. Frank Zappa, quoted in Tim Schneckloth, "Frank Zappa: Garni du Jour, Lizard King, Poetry and Slime," *Downbeat* 45, no. 10 (May 18, 1978): 16.

8. Chick Corea, *Piano Improvisations Vol. 1* (ECM 811 979-2, 1971), liner notes.

9. Francesconi, "Art vs. the Audience," 78.

10. Louis Johnson, quoted in Francesconi, "Art vs. the Audience," 76.

13

♫

Creativity and Tradition

Without tradition, art is a flock of sheep without a shepherd. Without innovation, it is a corpse.

—Winston Churchill

The conservative impulse of tradition has long been seen to be in conflict with the liberal impulse of creativity, even in jazz. William Cameron recognized this contradiction back in 1954:

[The jazzman] must subordinate and integrate his musical personality, as expressed through his instrument, into the general group, and he must do this with no score or conductor to guide him. On the other hand, as a soloist, he must produce startlingly distinctive sound patterns which are better, if possible, than those played by any other member of the group. How is this to be done? . . . The soloist must be unique, personal, and "progressive," but in order to meet the other criterion of the esthetic, he must be understood by others who know the idiom. This means, of course, a continual advance into abstraction and esotery, so that contemporary jazz is always musical casuistry, forever seeking new ways to rationalize the impossible.[1]

The jazz esthetic is basically a paradox, tragic in that it is ultimately unrealizable. The comprehensibility of traditionalism and radical originality are irreconcilable.[2]

The paradox is irreconcilable, however, only if one is limited to mutual exclusion as a form of opposition. Understanding Cameron's paradox is possible if one moves beyond mutual exclusion and distinguishes between two types of creativity, one that uses stimulus freedom and another that uses stimulus-bound freedom.

STIMULUS FREEDOM

Stimulus freedom is one way that creativity is expressed.[3] It is, roughly, "thinking outside the box," and can be seen literally in the nine-dot problem (see fig. 13.1). The problem is to connect all nine dots with four straight lines and without the pencil leaving the paper. The solution is to draw the lines outside of the box implied by the nine dots (see fig. 13.2). The type of creativity illustrated by the solution uses stimulus freedom because the solution is free of the stimulus, which is the implied box that lays on top of the outermost dots, that is assumed to be a restriction. This restriction is improperly assumed, however, because drawing lines beyond the box is nowhere forbidden in the statement of the problem.

The nine-dot problem requires stimulus freedom to solve, but all creativity does not necessarily require stimulus freedom. John Dacey and Kathleen Lennon have reviewed some creativity research in which people were asked to make up a story based on an ambiguous drawing (for example, an animal facing a blank rectangle).[4] Most stories that were produced were stimulus-bound, only including the animal and interpreting the blank rectangle in some fashion, perhaps as a window. A few stories were stimulus-free, including things that had nothing to do with an animal and a rectangle. In one example, a chipmunk, a butterfly, starvation, a description of the forest, and monsters were part of the story. Even though one can admire the creativity of the stories that used stimulus freedom, the stories that included only the basics from the drawing, the animal and the rectangle, still required creativity to develop. Stimulus freedom can certainly enhance creativity, and this is seen in the creative stories that included elements not present in the drawing. Stimulus freedom may lead to great creativity, or perhaps creativity of a different type, and sometimes may be required to solve a problem, such as the nine-dot problem, but a lack of stimulus freedom does not equal a complete lack of creativity.

Figure 13.1.   Stimulus freedom, or "thinking outside the box," which can be expressed in a nine-dot problem. The solution is on the following page, in fig. 13.2.

Figure 13.2.   The solution to fig. 13.1.

Tradition Does Not Require Stimulus Freedom

Tradition in jazz requires only stimulus-bound creativity, generally. The whole point of tradition is to define the boundaries within which a jazz musician is creative, and boundaries are what operate in stimulus-bound creativity. This means that there is still, however, some amount of creativity possible within those boundaries. Stimulus-bound jazz musicians are surely creative if only because improvisation is such a strong part of jazz. Jazz that is securely within its tradition is creative, even if this creativity rests on the core of the definition of jazz as well as the necessity for creativity in improvisation. Wynton Marsalis expresses the character of stimulus-bound freedom, what Derek Bailey calls "idiomatic" improvisation,[5] when he says, "Jazz is not just, 'Well, man, this is what I feel like playing.' It's a very structured thing that comes down from a tradition and requires a lot of thought and study."[6]

Some jazz musicians, however, are creative through stimulus freedom, operating beyond the boundaries that the tradition or the core definition of jazz establishes. Creativity may include not only working within the boundaries of a field, but extending the boundaries of the field as well. While the stimulus-bound musician is still creative, stimulus freedom represents a different order of creativity.

Stylistic controversies in jazz about bebop, free jazz, jazz/rock, and other styles can be seen as expressions of the opposition between stimulus-bound and stimulus-free creativity. A new style of jazz is free of the stimulus of the prevailing or previous style. The tension between neoconservatives who seek to maintain tradition and people who bemoan the lack of innovation in jazz, such as Eric Nisenson in *Blue: The Murder of Jazz*,[7] is the result of not understanding that stimulus-free creativity and stimulus-bound creativity are opposed but may coexist. Traditionalists are correct in placing traditional jazz at its core because everything must be defined, but are wrong to reject stimulus-free jazz because stimulus freedom operates as another order of creativity. Similarly, innovators are correct in privileging creativity in jazz because improvisation requires it and all of jazz history demonstrates it, but are wrong to criticize tradition because all creativity must rest on some foundation, and, for stimulus-bound creativity, that foundation is the traditional elements of jazz. Traditionalists who discount new styles of jazz or innovations in jazz are merely complaining that stimulus freedom is not stimulus-bound creativity (that red is not blue), and innovators who discount traditional styles of jazz as old-fashioned or not creative fail to acknowledge stimulus-bound creativity.

The Opposition of Stimulus-Free Creativity and Stimulus-Bound Creativity

The opposition between stimulus-free and non-stimulus-free creativity can be further appreciated after identifying various types of creativity and their implications for jazz, as outlined in table 13.1.

Type 1. The most conservative jazz is jazz that completely conforms to tradition. For some, such conservatism may be as comfortable and satisfying as an old pair of jeans, while to others it may sound boring. In this type of jazz, an improviser would only play ideas that have been tried before and that have withstood the test of time. Playing this type of jazz is one of the first jobs of students of jazz. They learn how to play conservatively and safely within the tradition, and thereby absorb and master that tradition. The opposition between tradition and creativity is resolved in favor of tradition, through mutual exclusion (although creativity must be present to some degree because improvisation is still present).

Type 2. Much mainstream jazz follows the tradition of jazz but still incorporates much creativity. Many people find such jazz interesting but

Table 13.1. Types of Creativity and Their Implications for Jazz

Tradition (Stimulus-Bound)		Creativity (Stimulus-Free)	
Type 1	*Type 2*	*Type 3*	*Type 4*
Completely within the tradition	Within the tradition, but creative	Changing the tradition, but comprehensible	Radically changing the tradition
Standard (tried and true) ideas	New ideas, but similar to standard ones	Some new, nonstandard ideas	Nearly all nonstandard ideas
Comfortable (boring?)	Interesting	Fascinating	Challenging (bewildering?)
Jazz musician students	Young lions	Miles Davis's mid-1960s quintet	Free jazz
Creativity is minimized	Juxtaposition	Dynamic tension	Tradition is minimized

still grounded in the familiar. The improviser is given a significant problem to solve: how to express something new within the boundaries of the tradition. While many jazz musicians operate this way, the "Young Lions" of the 1990s (Wynton Marsalis, Nicholas Payton, Joshua Redman, and others) were well known for their adherence to tradition as well as their fresh look at it. Tradition and creativity are juxtaposed in the sense that they are both present but coexist without any significant conflict.

A good example of this type of jazz would be a creative rearrangement of a jazz standard that only uses elements of music that are within the jazz tradition. An example of this is Tito Puente's version of Dave Brubeck's classic "Take Five."[8] Puente rearranged "Take Five" into the meter of eight, as well as into a Latin rhythmic style. Of course, the whole point of the original "Take Five" is that it is played in the meter of five, so playing it in eight is highly creative. While Puente's arrangement is very clever, the elements of the rearrangement (the meter of eight and the Latin rhythmic feel) are well within the mainstream of jazz.[9] So Puente managed to be very creative completely within the boundaries of the jazz tradition.

Type 3. Tradition can begin to break down when a jazz band changes some of the fundamentals of the tradition. Such music can be fascinating precisely because one can see the tradition changing and mutating, but it is not gone completely. Rather than finding a new solution to an old problem, entirely new questions are asked. A good example of this approach is the music of Miles Davis's quintet of the mid-1960s. This ensemble redefined the rhythm section, blurring the roles of the rhythm section and the horns. The traditional aspects still present (solo improvisations, chorus form, and more) coexisted with some elements radically redefined.

Type 4. When enough of the fundamentals of the tradition are changed to a sufficiently large extent, the result can challenge the entire definition of jazz, and may even confuse listeners. This is jazz at its most revolutionary, and the linkage back to the definition of jazz becomes stretched, or perhaps broken. The first great example from jazz history is the more radical types of free jazz, such as Ornette Coleman's collective improvisation with double quartets on his album *Free Jazz*. Another example is the use of alternate instrumental techniques, like Albert Ayler's shrieks and wailings on his album *Bells—Prophecy*.[10] Enough of the fundamentals of jazz were redefined so that the connection to tradition was stretched to the point of being unapparent to many.

The boundaries between these four types of opposition between tradition and creativity are neither firm nor clear. It would seem to be a matter of judgment in which of the four categories any one particular musical example might be placed. But, as with all categories, they can serve a useful function, highlighting important ideas, even if they cannot easily manage every single example.

When presented as shown in table 13.1, these types of jazz are located along a continuum, which implies the gradation form of opposition (see "Gradation" in chapter 1). But there is a strong element of dynamic tension between stimulus-bound creativity and stimulus-free creativity. When stimulus-free creativity thinks outside the box, the box is being repudiated even as another box, enclosing a larger area, must inevitably be created. While creativity must be bounded by something (a completely creative act is impossible to imagine), it is in the nature of creativity to go wherever the imagination spontaneously leads, regardless of the currently defined boundaries, even if that means rejecting previously held assumptions. The history of jazz illustrates both types of creativity, even if they are in conflict in some ways.

CREATIVITY WITHIN TRADITION

Creativity Rests on the Foundation of Tradition

Any creative improvisation is an improvisation on something.[11] That something must be conceived previously, prior to the improvisation, and therefore places some foundation, some tradition, as part of a jazz performance. A choice is always a choice selected in relation to something. We may focus on the creative aspects of improvisation, but creativity rests on the foundation that tradition provides.

Creativity in jazz generally takes the core tradition and modifies it, drawing on diverse sources. The question is, "How far can one go before the connection between the innovation and its source breaks?" rather than the idea that *any* substantial modification to the tradition is not jazz. If we acknowledge that tradition must be a part of jazz, we must acknowledge that creative modification of that tradition is also part of jazz.

Lee Brown says, "In one sense, the unconventional involves dispensing with structure—or so it might be imagined. In another sense, it involves bending it, using it in unexpected ways, employing it ironically, even flouting it—without trashing it."[12] While I am not willing to reject completely Brown's first sense of the unconventional, his second sense carries the flavor of dynamic tension. The unconventional is thrown into sharp relief and is appreciated much more as unconventional when compared to the conventional. This dynamic tension is also recognized in the following: "A fundamental creative aspiration in jazz is thus very often to find one's own improvisational voice, but to do it in a way that at once both does and does not acknowledge precedent: the aspiration is often to find a style that is both unique and simultaneously deeply historically rooted."[13] When the opposition between creativity and tradition is put in terms of acknowledging or not acknowledging precedent, the contradiction appears as a mutual exclusion and therefore seems impossible to resolve. But when expressed in terms of achieving uniqueness grounded in history, or highlighting the unconventional in terms of the conventional, the contradiction appears as dynamic tension.

The Value of Dynamic Tension between Tradition and Creativity

A tradition or a foundation, as boring or unoriginal as some may view it, is necessary in order to have something to push against when being creative. The resistance that tradition provides to the push of creativity is dynamic tension. This dynamic tension is a positive thing, however, because it heightens our appreciation of both elements in an opposition. Lee Brown offers the following examples:

> True, the elaborate abstraction of the tunes Tatum and Monk played could not be understood except by reference to these works independently of the performer's deconstruction of them. However, far from undermining the inventiveness of jazz improvisers, the use of such materials [standards] underscores it. . . . The wild mockery of George Russell's recorded assault on "You Are My Sunshine" would be meaningless without a grasp of the piece on which it is based.[14]

Russell's version of "You Are My Sunshine" is vivid and distinctive. It creates a mature, nuanced, and haunting arrangement of a plain and simple melody. Not understanding how Russell transforms the original into a subtle and highly effective artistic statement is to miss the full implications of his creativity. Furthermore, the simplicity of the original is also highlighted as we implicitly refer to it when we hear Russell's "wild mockery" of it. Appreciating the original and Russell's creative view of it is heightened through their opposition and the dynamic tension between them.

Miles Davis's Mid-1960s Quintet Relied on Tradition

Eric Nisenson, who has written perhaps the best critique of tradition in jazz, praises the Miles Davis quintet of the mid-1960s as one of the most creative and innovative ensembles in jazz, praise with which I agree. But even this ensemble relied on tradition to some extent. As creative as the constant repetition of the melody by Davis and Wayne Shorter in the ensemble's version of "Nefertiti" is, there are any number of aspects of it that are traditional. The melody is played in unison by a trumpet and a tenor saxophone, a very traditional instrumentation and orchestration in jazz; while the chord progression to "Nefertiti" is unusual, each individual chord is a traditional one in jazz theory. This ensemble's approach did not reject every assumption in the tradition of jazz, so even a group as innovative as this quintet validates and upholds tradition to some extent.

Not Whether but Where to Draw the Line

The debate between creativity and tradition in jazz cannot be *whether* tradition has a role to play in jazz, but *where* the line should be drawn between them; that is, how traditional is too boring and how creative is too different? To some extent, the current controversy about neoconservatism is whether the place in which Wynton Marsalis and other neoconservatives have already drawn the line (swing, blues, and more) is the proper place. Nisenson's *Blue: The Murder of Jazz* is best understood as a critique of where the neoconservatives decided the line should be drawn. It is insupportable to claim that the line should not be drawn at all—it must be.

Absolute Creativity Is Not Possible

By seeing the opposition between tradition and creativity as one of mutual exclusion, Nisenson misses the possibility of dynamic tension: "If the true idea of freedom is at the heart of jazz, then the idea that one must conform to any one sort of sensibility should be repugnant."[15] But complete freedom or nonconformity is impossible. Behavior always exists within a context, and freedom and creativity always rest upon some previously defined foundation. The dynamic tension in freedom and creativity exists because creativity must rest on the tradition from which it pulls away.

Not a Tabula Rasa

Nisenson says, "And like the art of the novel or sculpture or classical composition, jazz is a form of art that is a blank slate the artist fills in out of the grist of his or her own life and experience. These assumptions may seem obvious."[16] Or they may not. The blank slate that Nisenson assumes is similar to the tabula rasa that denies any genetic influence in human development and which has long been discredited. Just as human development does not stem from either nature or nurture solely, but is a subtle and complex blend of genetic and environmental influences, so jazz is a combination of tradition and innovation. Jazz is not a blank slate because its definition limits what it can be. Even the mere act of choosing what piece to play next immediately narrows the universe of possibilities, if only by determining a chord progression and formal outline against which any creativity will be heard. The musicians and the improvisers may certainly warp those givens, sometimes out of recognition, but they are certainly using them as a starting point for their creativity. And most of the time, those starting points are not altered out of recognition, and so remain recognizable as part of tradition.

Beyond providing a foundation for creativity, tradition is also a repository of possibilities with which any single musician might not be familiar. Knowing the recorded history of jazz gives a jazz musician more options. Being familiar with the vast array of creativity that others have demonstrated not only increases the possibilities for further creative variations on those past efforts, but may also spur a musician to imagine very different and creative approaches to jazz. If Tito Puente had never heard Brubeck's "Take Five," he would have never been able to imagine his creative arrangement of the tune.

Using tradition is not only a matter of incorporating what others have done into one's approach. That can be criticized on the grounds that it is not really creative; that is, if one merely copies what another has done (something from the tradition), that is not being creative. But there is another way in which others' creative efforts can be used. Tradition can spur creativity. To take a simple example, the first combos to omit a pianist or guitarist deliberately were creative in regard to instrumentation. One need only generalize from this example to spawn more creative possibilities. One can ask, "What creative possibilities might occur if one did away with some other instrument in the standard jazz combo: bass, for instance?" Not using a bass player may or may not be a fruitful or desirable path. The purpose here is to illustrate how creative possibilities can arise from the past and from tradition.

How Far to Stretch the Givens?

The jazz improviser is in a form of dynamic tension with the given materials—melody, harmony, rhythm, and form—of the piece being performed. At a minimum level, the improviser merely articulates the given harmonies and form, and progresses through them. But at the highest levels of creativity, these givens may be bent, altered, or obscured to a greater or lesser degree. The more they are changed, they greater the tension between the original and the improviser's version of the original. As Paul Berliner says, "Mature artists can obscure the formal elements that guide their inventions in much the same way as the architect, in designing an impressive structure, obscures its underpinnings."[17] The example that Berliner then discusses is obscuring the eight-bar phrase that is so common in jazz. The standard approach would be to begin and end improvised melodies at the boundary between eight-bar phrases, but much more prized is a musical idea that counters this expectation by bridging that boundary. Playing over the boundary of two eight-bar phrases is a common example of creatively playing against the form. Lester Young and Charlie Parker, in particular, were masters of playing over formal boundaries.

The Miles Davis quintet of the mid-1960s explored a form of collective improvisation in which the degree of stretching the form and chord progression could be so great that the connections back to the original piece were all but completely lost. For instance, Wayne Shorter's and Herbie Hancock's solos on the quintet's live version of *Footprints* travel so far away from the original that clear references to the original melody and harmony are few and far between and appear as lifeboats in a sea of uncertainty and creativity.[18] Their creativity distorted the foundation as much as possible without destroying it completely.

Licks and Patterns as a Personal Tradition

On a practical level, no one can be creative all the time. But the improviser must create continually because he or she creates in real time, which flows continuously. So the only hope the improviser has is to be as creative as possible most of the time, and otherwise try to be as tasteful and interesting as possible with tried-and-true, noncreative material. This creates its own tension, according to R. Keith Sawyer: "Jazz musicians frequently discuss an internal tension between their own personally developed patterns—called licks—and the need to continually innovate at a personal level."[19] These licks can be viewed as the individual improviser's own personal tradition, a vocabulary that must be called on in order to keep the improvisation moving forward during those inevitable times in which the improviser is not truly creative. Sawyer also recognizes "the personal tension between technical skill and innovation."[20] The more technically proficient one becomes, the more likely one will fall into a rut that has been constructed out of that technical facility. We tend to do what we do best, and we do best what we have practiced, which is not creative, according to Dieter Glawischnig.

> The basic dilemma concerning all practicing, all studying, all preparing for the real moment of spontaneous playing, for "the act of creation" is, on the one side, you must get your material together by the process of hard work in order to simply play anything. On the other side, creativity could be blocked by repeatedly falling into the trap of reproducing learned habits, something similar to a conditioned reflex. What a nice picture: the musician striving desperately for originality, sitting in a Skinner box, surrounded at best, by one's own phraseology, or all the worse if the repeated repertoire is forced on the youngster by "his master's taste."[21]

To a large extent, the opposition between personal patterns and creativity is a zero-sum game; when one is relying on tried-and-true patterns, one is not being creative. To some extent, such patterns can be seen as what happens when one is waiting for creativity to strike. There is, however, some dynamic tension between the two when one considers that familiar patterns can be seen as the fertile soil in which creativity can bloom. The familiar patterns are the ground, the foundation, from which creativity gets its inspiration. Perhaps creativity will come because the musician got the idea to transpose a familiar lick into a new key, or to vary it in some new way. A starting point gives creativity something on which to work. Furthermore, it is not absolutely necessary that one be creative all the time. As Berliner notes, "mature soloists constantly balance such factors as predictability and surprise, repetition and variation, continuity and change."[22]

Creativity and Tradition Offer Two Separate Pleasures

Nisenson has summarized the theory of a jazz tradition as espoused by Stanley Crouch and Albert Murray: "Playing within this tradition gives a musician a kind of legitimacy, placing him within a community that supports and understands his music, while playing outside this tradition is simply amorphous music-making. Music played outside the tradition was music in a vacuum, unconnected to people's lives."[23] This view of tradition includes the audience as a crucial element. When creativity is maximized, the listener has a greater chance of not connecting with the music because familiarity with a known idiom is a requirement for successful communication. Tradition has the better chance of successfully communicating with a larger audience through a larger common denominator because, by definition, tradition has not just been created, it's been around for a while, so the audience will be more familiar with it. Note that a larger common denominator need not be the *lowest* common denominator: if the music swings well and has creativity within jazz's tradition, which is almost assured if competent improvisation is present, we can still call it excellent jazz.

Another way to see that tradition and creativity are not mutually exclusive is to view them as separate, distinct pleasures. Imagine that you are in a jazz club and the band plays two songs: one is a hard-swinging, soulful tune with a great groove that gets the audience up on its feet, hands clapping; the other conducts an experimental approach to improvisation that few have heard before. One does not need to reject the pleasures of newness and surprise found in the second piece in order to appreciate the pleasures of the groove in the first piece, and jazz is big enough for both if one does not require mutual exclusion as the only means of opposition.

JAZZ EDUCATION

Learning Jazz

It should not be unexpected that students of jazz, once they have progressed sufficiently, begin to question the tradition of jazz by improvising music that runs counter to that tradition and that might therefore risk censure from their teacher. The creativity and personal expression that jazz promises, when carried to its logical conclusion, can lead to a rejection of the boundaries and definition of the tradition of jazz that the student initially must absorb. This situation is similar to that of separation or individuation of adolescents in which they forge their own identity that is separate from that of their parents or family (their tradition). Especially at the initial stages of developing one's own identity as a jazz improviser, one is faced with the question of how to achieve two contradictory goals: faithfulness to the tradition, as might be required by a teacher or mentor, and creatively transforming that tradition into something that expresses the uniqueness of one's own musical personality. The student must learn how to keep tradition and creativity in dynamic tension.

That growth as a jazz musician is not necessarily a straight line from simple to complex illustrates how the opposition between tradition and creativity can be negotiated. Advanced jazz students are sometimes eager to master the most dissonant forms of harmony. Charlie Parker's harmonic style, while controversial during his career in the 1940s and 1950s, is only the starting point for today's jazz students. Some students, in my experience, mistake topics such as advanced harmony, or harmonic styles that occur later in jazz history, as the only ones appropriate for advanced study. An advanced study of jazz, however, might ask the jazz student to imitate the style of Louis Armstrong, which is not as harmonically complex when compared to Charlie Parker or later musicians. To be able to be creative within the more restricted boundaries of Armstrong's traditional harmony requires the student to negotiate the opposition between the closely drawn boundaries and the creativity that is a part of jazz.

Teaching Jazz

There is a dynamic tension between tradition and creativity for jazz educators. Creativity is widely viewed as part of jazz pedagogy, but teachers are also authorities. John Dacey and Kathleen Lennon refer to studies that measure authoritarianism, which includes elements such as dominance, subordination, social hierarchy, and obedience, in American occupations: "State police scored highest . . . followed closely by army officers. . . . Teachers ranked third."[24]

Even jazz teachers are not immune to the authoritarianism that teaching encourages. One example of the authoritarian aspects of jazz education is the prominence of the big band in jazz education, which is out of proportion to its place in jazz history. There are several reasons why the big band is so prominent in jazz education. Not only does the greater size of the big band (sixteen to twenty) increase student enrollments compared to combos and thus help fund jazz programs, but the big band requires more standardization and exercise of authority than jazz combos. It is usual for educational big bands to have a director (the authority) in front of the band, directing rehearsals as well as performances, while it is rare for a teacher to be onstage with a student combo. Most importantly, because the horns in a big band—the trumpets, trombones, and saxophones— are often playing the same rhythms, many details of their performance that might be decided individually and spontaneously in a combo, such as articulation, intonation, rhythm, and swing, are usually predetermined authoritatively by the director.

Some necessities of education—standardization, definitions, and clear rules—are in opposition to the openness and creativity in jazz. These necessities can be risked by teaching creativity as part of jazz. Dacey and Lennon note that "the creative teacher is involved in discovery, risking, pushing the limits, and taking a step into the unknown. This is serious business—dangerous business. When you challenge students to be creative, you lose control."[25] Such loss of control is sometimes not a congenial fit with the demands of the educational bureaucracy. Standardization in education is not, however, in any sort of conflict with tradition in jazz; in fact, the two realms are well suited for each other. They both depend on rules, definitions, and standards.

So the authoritarian aspect of education is itself in dynamic tension when applied to jazz: authoritarianism, on one hand, is well suited to teaching the jazz tradition, but, on the other hand, is ill-suited for encouraging students to be creative, certainly for stimulus freedom (thinking outside the box), and perhaps for stimulus-bound freedom as well. Competent jazz educators will manage this dynamic tension successfully, especially if they are jazz musicians themselves and have some sense of the contradiction.

NOTES

    1. William Bruce Cameron, "Sociological Notes on the Jam Session," *Social Forces* 33 (1954): 179.

    2. Cameron, "Sociological Notes on the Jam Session," 181.

3. John S. Dacey and Kathleen Lennon, *Understanding Creativity: The Interplay of Biological, Psychological, and Social Factors* (San Francisco: Jossey-Bass Publishers, 1998), 99–101.

4. Dacey and Lennon, *Understanding Creativity*, 100.

5. Derek Bailey, *Improvisation: Its Nature and Practice in Music* (New York: Da Capo Press, 1992), xi.

6. Wynton Marsalis, quoted in Paul Berliner, *Thinking in Jazz: The Infinite Art of Improvisation* (Chicago: University of Chicago Press, 1994), 63.

7. Eric Nisenson, *Blue: The Murder of Jazz* (New York: St. Martin's Press, 1997).

8. Tito Puente, "Take Five," *Mambo Diablo* (Concord Picante CJP-283, 1985).

9. The distinction between the meter of eight and the meter of four, in jazz, is largely theoretical. The meter of eight is easily heard as equivalent to the more usual meter of four, with half as many measures.

10. Ornette Coleman, "Free Jazz," *Free Jazz* (Atlantic SD 1364, 1960); Albert Ayler, *Bells—Prophecy* (ESP 1010-2, 1964–1965).

11. The one possible exception might be free jazz; even if one imagines some free jazz based on nothing ("just start playing"), there is still the tradition of playing an instrument, or notes, etc., that is the foundation on which the improvisation would rest.

12. Lee Brown, "Postmodernist Jazz Theory: Afrocentrism, Old and New," *Journal of Aesthetics and Art Criticism* 57, no. 2 (Spring 1999): 239.

13. *Encyclopedia of Aesthetics* (New York: Oxford University Press, 1998), s.v. "Improvisation."

14. Lee Brown, "Feeling My Way: Jazz Improvisation and Its Vicissitudes—A Plea for Imperfection," *Journal of Aesthetics and Art Criticism* 58, no. 2 (Spring 2000): 116.

15. Nisenson, *Blue: The Murder of Jazz*, 74–75.

16. Nisenson, *Blue: The Murder of Jazz*, 47.

17. Berliner, *Thinking in Jazz*, 246.

18. Wayne Shorter, *Footprints*, performed by the Miles Davis Quintet, http://www.dailymotion.com/alternativa/davis/video/745 (accessed July 2, 2006).

19. R. Keith Sawyer, "Improvisation and the Creative Process: Dewey, Collingwood, and the Aesthetics of Spontaneity," *Journal of Aesthetics and Art Criticism* 58, no. 2 (Spring 2000): 157.

20. Keith Sawyer, "Improvisational Creativity: An Analysis of Jazz Performance," *Creativity Research Journal* 5, no. 3 (1992): 260.

21. Dieter Glawischnig, "The Present Boom in Jazz Education—A Trap for Creativity?" *Jazzforschung/Jazz Research* 28 (1996): 80–81.

22. Berliner, *Thinking in Jazz*, 266.

23. Nisenson, *Blue: The Murder of Jazz*, 15.

24. Dacey and Lennon, *Understanding Creativity*, 70.

25. Dacey and Lennon, *Understanding Creativity*, 71.

Part Four

THE MEANING OF JAZZ

14

♬

Is Improvisation Inferior to Composition?

Improvisation is too good to leave to chance.

—Paul Simon

The four pairs of opposite values in jazz improvisation show that jazz improvisation contains a significant amount of opposition and contradiction. But the larger meaning of these contradictions depends on ideas from the philosophies of phenomenology and existentialism. These philosophies stand in contrast to the connections between composition and science. Certain relationships and similarities among composition, product, structural complexity, perfection, and science will be explored. Jazz improvisation, on the other hand, is connected to the experiential, process as well as product, mistakes, phenomenology, and existentialism.

STRUCTURAL COMPLEXITY

Improvised music has been evaluated sometimes as being the aesthetic inferior of composed music. The processes of improvisation and composition differ, and these differences create what have traditionally been considered disadvantages for improvisation. As Bruno Nettl has said, "The improviser makes unpremeditated, spur-of-the-moment decisions, and because they are not thought out, their individual importance, if not their collective significance, is sometimes denied."[1] Ted Gioia has said the same thing in several different ways:

> Yet does not jazz, by its reliance on spur-of-the-moment improvisation, relegate itself to being a second-rate, imperfect art form? [Is not] the best jazz inferior to mediocre composed music? Why, we ask, should the spontaneous prattle of an improvising musician interest us as much as the meticulously crafted masterpieces of the great composers?[2]
>
> Under the pressure of spontaneous creation, the jazz artist had little opportunity to impose on his music the architectonic sense of order and balance that distinguishes the more leisurely constructed arts.[3]
>
> For no matter what a jazz fan may claim, even the best improvised melody suffers by comparison with, for example, a Bach fugue.[4]
>
> One might well conclude then, that regarded as compositions or sounding structures, the musical product of the improviser usually, if not always, falls short of the architectonic (and especially polyphonic) possibilities of conventional Western music.[5]

Lastly, Philip Alperson brings up an important criterion, structural complexity: "Denis Dutton asserted that he did not think it likely that there would ever exist a single jazz improvisation which would compare favorably (or even remotely) with the structural complexity of any of Beethoven's late quartets."[6] Structural complexity is a primary value in Western aesthetics. It is perhaps the single most important aspect of Western composed music on which claims of a composer's genius or a composition's worth are founded, and it is the basis for much musical analysis. Western composers have been very interested in developing complex musical structures.

Formalism

What constitutes structural complexity has been broadly defined by Leonard Meyer as well as by Judith Becker:

> Music must be evaluated syntactically. . . . insofar as the intricate and subtle interconnections between musical events, whether simultaneous or successive, of a complex work involve considerable resistance and uncertainty—and presumably information—value is thereby created.[7]
>
> Western art music is structurally more complex than other music; its architectonic hierarchies, involved tonal relationships, and elaborated harmonic syntax not only defy complete analysis but have no parallel in the world.[8]
>
> Among Western musicologists, our image of musical complexity correlates with levels of hierarchical structures, to the number of musical "lines" occurring simultaneously, to the relationships between similar musical ele-

ments found in different sections of the composition, and in some sense to the length of the composition.[9]

This aesthetic position is sometimes called *formalism*. It places musical value in the relationships among, typically, the pitches and rhythms that make up the composition, as well as larger structures (such as phrases and motifs) that are made from pitches and rhythms. Formalism is sometimes linked with the idea that aesthetic value in music is primarily intellectual, achieved through an understanding of the relations among notes, rhythms, phrases, and motifs, but formalism is also capable of holding that such relations elicit feelings and emotions in the listener, such as the feeling of security or return when a primary theme is brought back after a development section.

Advantages for Composition

At first, it appears unlikely that improvisation can compare favorably with composition in terms of structural complexity, given the different situations in which the improviser and the composer are found. The primary difference is that the composer does not work in real time; that is, the compositional process does not occur when the performance of the composition does. The typical view of this distinction is that, with time available outside and beyond the time it takes to perform a composition, the composer is able to create complex structures that the improviser cannot. Philip Alperson has noted four specific advantages that composition enjoys, discussed immediately below.[10]

Creating an Overall Plan

The fact that the composer has time available for consideration helps the composer to develop an overall plan for a composition, even very complex ones. The entire broad sweep of a composition, as well as its details, can be carefully constructed. Each unit and subunit can be fit into place and coordinated within the entire hierarchy, allowing the composer to create a high degree of structural complexity.

The improviser, on the other hand, is limited by what Ted Gioia calls a *retrospective* method of creating form (as opposed to the *blueprint* method of composition).[11] The ease with which an improviser can look over the entire blueprint of an improvisation is severely limited when compared to how easily a composer can. The improviser can, however, look *backward* at what he or she has just improvised and shape the next phrase based on previous ones to a greater or lesser extent. But this is a severe limitation compared to the advantages a composer enjoys in terms of creating structural complexity.

Revision and Editing

Because composition occurs before a performance, changes in any aspect of the composition may be made prior to its performance. These changes can be of many types: reconsidering major goals or fundamentals of the overall plan; reevaluating several options or trying new ones; correcting mental slips or misjudgments (such as miscalculating the orchestral effect of a certain combination of instruments); or merely correcting notation mistakes. Revision and editing confer a great advantage to composition. According to John Sloboda, "The composer rejects possible solutions until he finds one which seems to be the best for his purposes. The improviser must accept the first solution that comes to hand."[12] The ability to edit a composition is of crucial importance both to the fundamental conditions of composition as well as to the more pragmatic, practical goals of coordinating all the elements of a composition properly, copying parts, and the like.

Notation

Notation has been credited with helping composers achieve structural complexity by Alperson: "It is hardly surprising that, with the development of a sophisticated graphic notation, Western instrumental music has been able to rise to heights of extraordinary complexity."[13] Without a means of notation, composing would be a far different craft. Notation is a powerful tool for conceiving, organizing, and documenting elements of a composition. For an improviser, notation might function as a mnemonic device that refers to some predetermined musical elements, but it does not function as a compositional tool as it does for the composer.

Responsibility of Composition

While the advantages of composition are often noted, it is more rarely recognized that these advantages carry with them a corresponding responsibility. Because the composer has these advantages, he or she can be expected to produce a complete, final, and perfect (within the realm of the humanly possible) product (in principle). With the ability to revise and correct, the composer, unlike the improviser, has no excuse to do otherwise. Complexity and (near-)perfection are reasonable standards because the conditions of composition enable the achievement of those standards.

MISTAKES

Distinct from structural complexity, mistakes are another aspect of jazz improvisation in which it falls short of the standards of composition. If a composer conceives and notates a musical figure or idea that is a mistake—that is, it is not preferred upon later consideration—and then corrects it, the composer's audience never hears or knows of it. (A mistake may occur in the performance of a composition, but that mistake is not the composer's, it is the performer's.) But the improviser does not have the luxury of correcting a mistake. Once a mistake is made, time marches on, the mistake has been made, and the improviser cannot go back and fix things.

Apparent Mistakes

In order to appreciate the significance of mistakes in jazz, we must be confident that some particular case is truly a mistake. Sometimes, what are believed to be mistakes in jazz are actually not mistakes. What might be misunderstood as a mistake can be instead the result of an individualistic and personal aesthetic operating in jazz. A jazz musician is expected to develop an individual and personal approach and sound (see "The Personal" in chapter 2), and this is sometimes mistakenly perceived as deviation from some universal standard that might apply for classical music or some other music but which does not apply in jazz. If one tries to impose such a universal standard, then one might find all sorts of apparent mistakes. Thelonious Monk's dissonant harmony, Miles Davis's range of tone colors, and even the cockeyed angle at which Lester Young held his saxophone are all examples that could be incorrectly judged as mistakes if one ignores the individual and personal aesthetic in jazz. Within this aesthetic, the uniqueness of these examples should be celebrated. As Robert Walser says, "The problem of Miles Davis is that if technical perfection is assumed to be a universal and primary goal, . . . [Davis's] semiotic successes are inaudible."[14] When Davis uses an unfocused tone for dramatic effect, or plays indeterminate notes in a phrase that is, by unenlightened standards, a "mess," it is not a mistake; rather, it is "rhetorically clear."[15] In this example, technique is in service of an individualistic aesthetic sense, and is not a value in and of itself.

Technique in jazz is defined not through a universal standard, but in terms of intent. That is, good technique is that which expresses and makes manifest an improviser's intent, as a matter of positive freedom. The stark dissonances of Thelonious Monk may sound like mistakes to jazz neophytes just like Davis's unfocused tone, but those dissonances are actually the consistent result of clear intent from a great musical mind that saw creative possibilities in harmony and dissonance that no one else in jazz had before. Because some who may not be familiar with the individualistic aesthetic of jazz may make misjudgments about mistakes is not a reason to conclude, however, that mistakes are completely absent from jazz.

True Mistakes

Beyond apparent mistakes that are the result of an individualistic aesthetic remains the possibility of a true mistake in jazz, something that
does not express or manifest the intent of the improviser, or something
that is somehow out of place.[16] There are two types of true mistakes for
jazz improvisers: mistakes of conception, and mistakes of execution.

Mistakes of Conception

The improviser is responsible for conceiving a melody, and this process is
open to mistakes. Alperson quotes Sparshott, who lists several ways in
which an improviser may make bad decisions in this regard, or have a difficult time managing the progression of musical ideas:

> forgetting what he was doing, trying to do two things at once, changing his
> mind about where he is going, starting more hares than he can chase at once,
> picking up where he thought he had left off but resuming what was not quite
> there in the first place, discovering and pursuing tendencies in what he has
> done that would have taken a rather different form if he had thought of them
> at the time, and so on.[17]

Similarly, it is possible to box oneself into a corner in an improvisation, or
to be led by an initial idea to its logical conclusion, which turns out to be
inelegant or ill-advised. The improviser, however, must accept such mistakes in conception because once they are performed, there is no possibility of going back to correct them.

Mistakes in Execution

Even if an improviser's conception is free of blunders, the most mundane
sort of technical difficulty—whether one's fingers, manipulating the musical instrument, accomplish the goal that the improviser's conception
lays out before them—can prevent the successful execution of that conception and result in a mistake. The conception may be inspired, but the
flesh can be weak. An improviser may make technical mistakes such as
any performer of composed music may suffer: irregularities in intonation,
attack, and timbre, playing an unintended note, and so forth.

Mistakes can even find their way onto recordings. One example of a
mistake, in my opinion, occurs in Miles Davis's solo on a recording of the
tune "Four."[18] It occurs at the beginning of his second full improvised
chorus, at approximately one minute and twenty-two seconds into the
recording. Davis plays two phrases, fairly high in the range of the trumpet (especially for Davis at this point in his career, when he was not try-

ing to extend his upper range). The first phrase is approximately three notes, but Davis misses them and bends and slurs them into each other.

Rescuing a Mistake

Davis tries to rescue this mistake by immediately repeating the phrase. This is a standard technique in jazz: if you make a mistake, make it again. That way, it is harder to interpret the first mistake as a mistake. (Who would deliberately repeat a mistake? The informed answer to that question is, "A jazz musician.") While repeating a mistake may rescue it, it is still true that it was a mistake that needed to be rescued, and thus was a true mistake. However, the jazz musician may also use a mistake as inspiration for improvisation, perhaps as a means to try to rescue the mistake. An improviser may find creative possibilities in mistakes because they are outside the normal range of musical ideas for that improviser. This is one way in which the improviser has an advantage over the composer, who cannot deal with a mistake once the performance of the composition has begun.

RESPONDING TO IMPROVISATION'S INFERIORITY

Jazz suffers in comparison to composition through improvisation's disadvantages in creating structural complexity and through the possibility of mistakes. Several writers have responded to these inferiorities of improvisation, but these responses are generally inadequate.

Improvisation as an Expressive and Unique Statement

Ted Gioia, in *The Imperfect Art*, contributes some important concepts for understanding jazz in terms of structural complexity and perfection, but his argument is not developed enough to make it a fully satisfactory answer to the relative lack of structural complexity in jazz. Gioia's alternative to judging jazz in terms of perfection and structural complexity is to ask instead "whether that work is expressive of the artist, whether it reflects his own unique and incommensurable perspective on his art, whether it makes a statement without which the world would be in some small way, a lesser place."[19] Unfortunately, this aesthetic, without further detail, is difficult to accept. It is hard to understand what it means that a work is "expressive of the artist," except as a truism. Anything that anyone produces is expressive of his or her character and personality in some way. This offers no foundation for an aesthetic of jazz.

Furthermore, reflecting a unique perspective and making a statement of some value is not peculiar to jazz, but holds for any art form. Certainly Mozart's compositions and Beethoven's compositions, compared with each other, reflect the composers' unique perspectives. Because this aesthetic is also applicable for compositions, uniqueness adds nothing to crafting an aesthetic specifically for jazz improvisation in terms of its apparent imperfection. Both composition and improvised jazz, as well as any art form that expresses creativity, will reflect an artist's unique perspectives, and yet composition also evaluates its works on standards of perfection and structural complexity, which remain the issues to be addressed for the aesthetics of jazz improvisation. Making a statement, as a criterion for aesthetics, also offers nothing specific for jazz. Any work of art makes some sort of statement. The question that remains is, "Why should we value one statement over another in jazz improvisation?" Gioia's suggestion does not advance the discussion closer to an answer.

Particulars of the Artist

Gioia also believes that "our notions of excellence in jazz thus depend on our understanding of the abilities of individual artists and not on our perception of perfection in the work of art."[20] But how are we able to understand the abilities of individual artists? I don't know what is within the capabilities of specific artists—how much Dizzy Gillespie practiced, or whether Clifford Brown could arpeggiate a dominant thirteenth chord with a sharp eleven in every key with equal facility. In fact, if we only evaluate jazz artists in relation to their own abilities, we are left, again, with only a truism. By logical necessity, an artist will accomplish only what his or her individual abilities will allow. Perhaps Gioia is creating a relative scale for judgment: if improviser X has never done Y, then Y is assigned greater value. But this creates an absurd situation. In general, progress occurs in larger steps the earlier they occur in one's history of learning a discipline, so a teenager who is just learning jazz might make a great leap forward and therefore play an improvisation with more ultimate value, on a relative basis, than a jazz grand master who improvises a complex solo but has been doing so regularly for many years.

By suggesting that jazz must be heard as the creation of a specific person, perhaps Gioia is introducing the idea of the individual in the existential sense, but the lack of further development of this idea by Gioia leaves this possibility at the level of speculation. Without further explanation or discussion, the idea is unsatisfactory. I agree with Gioia and will attempt to provide a fuller explanation of this idea later.

Without an explanation of what we get from hearing improvisation as the work of an individual or from evaluating improvisation only in terms of what the same artist has done or what others have done, Gioia's aesthetic of jazz is not as well formed or detailed as it might be. Gioia begins on the right track by shifting focus over to the artist and not solely on the art itself. The key to an aesthetic of jazz does concern the artist as a person as well as the musical object itself, in a dialectic. However, by not continuing down that track to its logical conclusion, Gioia leaves his aesthetic of jazz ultimately incomplete.

Apologizing for Inferiority

Another response to the disadvantages of improvisation is that it is unfair to expect improvisation to rise to the level of structural complexity in composition. The improviser cannot help but have more difficulties than the composer with regard to creating structural complexity, and so this primary aesthetic standard should be justifiably somewhat lower for the improviser than for the composer. The improviser should not be blamed for a more or less inferior product. Alperson says that "the relevant critical standards for musical improvisations should derive, not from what has been composed or from what has been performed, but rather from what has proven to be possible within the demands and constraints of improvisatory musical activity."[21] While there is a hint of a valuable idea in this view (one that will be expanded later), judging jazz to be inferior and leaving the discussion at that is not a strong platform on which to build an aesthetic of jazz as a valuable and serious art form.

Ignoring Mistakes

One of Sparshott's responses to mistakes in jazz is to tolerate or even ignore the deficiencies of mistakes: "These [deficiencies] are all part of his performance tied together in a single web of intention, a single aesthetic object, though an inconsistent one."[22] This is damning with faint praise. All Sparshott is really saying is that the deficiencies are part of the package, and if that weren't bad enough, for the *coup de grace*, that the package is flawed ("inconsistent") because of the deficiencies. Strictly speaking, Sparshott contradicts himself when he claims that an improviser creates a "single web of intention" because such cannot include, for instance, "what he has done that would have taken a rather different form if he had thought of them at the time."[23] If only the improviser could actually guarantee a consistent, single web of intention, there would be no mistakes of conception, and only mistakes in execution.

Alperson, however, agrees with Sparshott: "In this regard, we attend to a musical improvisation much in the way that we attend to another's talk: we listen past the 'mistakes' and attend to the actual development of a work."[24] While it's true that improvisation is similar in some regard to a casual conversation, there are important differences. Casual conversations are not art, a whole class of professionals don't spend years of their lives practicing how to hold a conversation, audiences don't pay money to hear casual conversations, and casual conversations aren't recorded and sold. This is why listening beyond mistakes is accepted in everyday conversation and why we should view mistakes in jazz differently than mistakes in conversation.

If by "another's talk" is meant a formal speech, then we do listen past mistakes in such cases, but a formal speech is not improvised, and not all such mistakes can be ignored anyway. The significance of mistakes of conception and execution can be distinguished. A mistake of execution can happen to an improviser or a performer, in a composition or an improvisation, and in a piece of music or in speech. More significant than such mistakes, however, are mistakes of conception, for which a composer rightfully suffers criticism. The improviser rightfully does too, because the improviser has taken on the role of the composer in terms of conceiving the music to be performed.

Ignoring the Negatives of Mistakes

Another response to mistakes in jazz has been to ignore their negative consequences or aspects. Reluctance to acknowledge the negative aspects of mistakes prevents a full appreciation of the valuable role that mistakes play in jazz improvisation.

Rhetorical Reluctance

A subtle version of ignoring the negative aspects of mistakes in jazz is included in an article by Robert Walser about a famous performance by Miles Davis of "My Funny Valentine." Davis was infamous for missing notes and for technical flaws, even as he helped create several major styles of jazz. The language that Walser uses to discuss Davis's mistakes is implicit and indirect. Walser comes to the edge of making, but never really makes, a clear statement about the negative aspect of the mistakes of Davis.

Walser only indirectly acknowledges that Davis and jazz musicians in general can make mistakes. He identifies two cracked notes in Davis's solo on "My Funny Valentine," but he indicates that they are mistakes not by directly labeling them as such. He contrasts them with another cracked note that he does explicitly describe as being "done deliberately."[25] Similarly, he softens his indications of mistakes elsewhere by such language as, "Here, he manages to hold onto the note; at other moments in the solo such wagers are not won."[26] Rhetorical reluctance is also seen when Walser mentions Davis's view of his mistakes without offering his own opinion about Davis's mistakes:

> I do not mean to suggest that Davis wanted to make mistakes, or that he was not bothered by them. He had absorbed a dislike of technical failings from many sources. . . . And when Davis had to choose among various takes after a recording session, he is said to have invariably picked the one with the fewest mistakes.[27]

Walser does not actually come out and say how he thinks we should view actual mistakes in jazz. Perhaps his reluctance stems from not clearly distinguishing between apparent mistakes that are fully intended by the artist as part of an individualistic aesthetic and actual mistakes that are unintended. As part of the admirable goal of advocating the view that different tone colors, for instance, are not mistakes but are part of a wider and more individualistic aesthetic, Walser shies away from an honest and complete acknowledgment of true mistakes as actual deficiencies and does not then have an opportunity to include the negative aspects of mistakes within an aesthetic of jazz.

Denying Mistakes

Vijay Iyer suggests that the very idea of a mistake in jazz improvisation is misguided: "It is *never* [emphasis added] clear what is 'supposed' to happen in improvised music, so it makes little sense to talk about mistakes."[28] But "never" is a strong word. Surely an individual improviser can report that a certain note was not intended, even if merely the result of a physical slip. Also, one could make a claim similar to Iyer's for language and it would be readily seen as absurd: if improvisers cannot make mistakes, then a speaker could never say a wrong word. But of course, people sometimes do say the wrong thing. For the same reasons that speakers can misspeak, improvisers can make mistakes.

Mistakes Are Inevitable

Walser makes the point that Davis's mistakes were inevitable because

> Davis constantly and consistently put himself at risk in his trumpet playing by using a loose, flexible embouchure that helped him to produce a great variety of tone colors and articulations, by striving for dramatic gestures rather than consistent demonstration of mastery, and by experimenting with unconventional techniques. . . . [H]e played closer to the edge than anyone else

and simply accepted the inevitable missteps, never retreating to a safer, more consistent performing style.[29]

The impression that Walser leaves is that the inevitability of mistakes in jazz nearly justify their presence; that is, if mistakes are bound to happen, we might as well focus on the positive aspects of Davis's style, such as innovation, that accompany the mistakes. But this, too, does not forthrightly admit the negative aspects of mistakes. It may be true, as Gioia says, that

> improvisation is doomed, it seems, to offer a pale imitation of the perfection attained by composed music. Errors will creep in, not only in form but also in execution; the improviser, if he sincerely attempts to be creative, will push himself into areas of expression which his technique may be unable to handle. Too often the finished product will show moments of rare beauty intermixed with technical mistakes and aimless passages.[30]

To acknowledge this fully and honestly is not admitting defeat for developing an aesthetic of jazz. On the contrary, it is necessary in order to understand some great things that jazz offers. Mistakes, as things unwanted, are another way in which contradiction occurs in jazz. But a full discussion of how that happens is best undertaken after other important ideas are more fully developed.

PROCESS AND PRODUCT, NOT PROCESS WITHOUT PRODUCT

Another way to address the apparent inferiority of jazz is by proposing that jazz concerns process, not product. The move to reject formalism and structural complexity for jazz is partly the result of distinguishing between process and product and linking product, formalism, and structural complexity.

The score of a composition is clearly a product; it is a material thing that is a composer's practical job to produce. The fact that jazz improvisation typically does not use a score leads to the idea that jazz should be looked at as a process, in contrast to the compositional product. If formalism typically analyzes a score to uncover its structural complexity, then might not product and structural complexity be irrelevant for jazz because jazz does not use a score? Also, the process of jazz improvisation is an inherent part of the music of jazz in a way that the process of composing is not. The process of improvisation is necessarily on display during improvisation, whereas, in composition, we only see the result (the product) of the compositional process and not the process itself.

However, some confusion exists concerning the role of process and product in jazz. For instance, David Borgo, among others, links product with formalism and links process with cultural/social studies: "Jazz researchers have often been guilty of emphasizing the analysis of improvised products over a more dynamic and synthetic understanding of the process of improvisation."[31] He also says that "[o]ther more scholarly investigations describe and analyze the music's 'formal' characteristics but ignore the musicians' aesthetic orientation towards in-performance process and real-time interaction and disregard the social, cultural, and historical context for performance."[32]

But there is no inherent mutual exclusion between process and analysis of product. In fact, a better understanding of the process of jazz improvisation is important for fully understanding its product, the music itself. For instance, one could not analyze a soloist's phrase and its imitation and variation by the pianist as a type of motivic development without understanding that in the process of improvisation, a pianist is allowed to imitate, develop, and comment on motifs performed by the soloist and others in the ensemble. Borgo sets up an unnecessary mutual exclusion between product and process. While I will show later that formalism alone may not be able to create an aesthetic of jazz, it is also true that formalism need not be completely rejected. While Charles Keil can be congratulated for focusing on process when he says, "Music is about process, not product,"[33] there can be no plainer statement of opposition as only mutual exclusion, in apparent ignorance of other forms of opposition. In contrast, we will see that there is a dynamic tension between product and process.

It is neither necessary nor advisable in jazz to apologize for lesser structural complexity, to compromise, to ignore mistakes, or to focus on process to the exclusion of product. The way out of such an aesthetic is possible through certain fundamentals of jazz that give it a robust aesthetic on its own terms. This aesthetic is grounded in phenomenology, the experiential, existentialism, and contradiction, as the next chapters will show.

NOTES

1. Bruno Nettl, "Thoughts on Improvisation: A Comparative Approach," *Musical Quarterly* 60, no. 1 (January 1974): 3.

2. Ted Gioia, *The Imperfect Art* (New York: Oxford University Press, 1988), 55–56.

3. Gioia, *The Imperfect Art*, 92.

4. Gioia, *The Imperfect Art*, 105.

5. Gioia, *The Imperfect Art*, 22–23.

6. Philip Alperson, "On Musical Improvisation," *Journal of Aesthetics and Art Criticism* 43, no. 1 (Fall 1984): 22.

7. Leonard Meyer, *Music, the Arts, and Ideas* (Chicago: University of Chicago Press, 1967), 36.

8. Judith Becker, "Is Western Art Music Superior?" *Musical Quarterly* 72, no. 3 (1986): 342.

9. Becker, "Is Western Art Music Superior?" 346.

10. Alperson, "On Musical Improvisation," 22.

11. Gioia, *The Imperfect Art*, 62.

12. John Sloboda, *The Musical Mind* (Oxford: Clarendon Press, 1985), 149.

13. Alperson, "On Musical Improvisation," 22.

14. Robert Walser, "Out of Notes: Signification, Interpretation, and the Problem of Miles Davis," *Musical Quarterly* 77, no. 2 (Summer 1993): 359–60.

15. Walser, "Out of Notes," 357.

16. Who determines intent and purpose in mistakes may be problematic. Cases could be made for the informed listeners, musicians in general, or the musician who makes a mistake as the entity who may determine intent and purpose. Of course, there may very well be disagreement among informed listeners or musicians as to whether a particular musical figure is a mistake. But such disagreements on some examples should not cause us to reject the very idea of a mistake in jazz when, probably, informed listeners and musicians would agree about many other examples.

17. Sparshott, quoted in Alperson, "On Musical Improvisation," 23–24.

18. Miles Davis, "Four," *Workin' with the Miles Davis Quintet* (Prestige P-7166, 1956).

19. Gioia, *The Imperfect Art*, 68.

20. Gioia, *The Imperfect Art*, 69.

21. Alperson, "On Musical Improvisation," 27.

22. Sparshott, quoted in Alperson, "On Musical Improvisation," 24.

23. Sparshott, quoted in Alperson, "On Musical Improvisation," 24.

24. Alperson, "On Musical Improvisation," 24.

25. Walser, "Out of Notes," 355.

26. Walser, "Out of Notes," 353.

27. Walser, "Out of Notes," 356.

28. Vijay Iyer, "Embodied Mind, Situated Cognition, and Expressive Microtiming in Afro-American Music," *Music Perception* 19, no. 3 (Spring 2002): 408.

29. Walser, "Out of Notes," 356.

30. Gioia, *The Imperfect Art*, 68.

31. David Borgo, "Reverence for Uncertainty: Chaos, Order, and the Dynamics of Musical Free Improvisation" (Ph.D. diss., University of California, Los Angeles, 1999), 17.

32. Borgo, "Reverence for Uncertainty," 14.

33. Charles Keil, "The Theory of Participatory Discrepancies: A Progress Report," *Ethnomusicology* 39, no. 1 (Winter 1995): 1.

15

♫

Phenomenology and Experience

Few people even scratch the surface, much less exhaust the contemplation of their own experience.

—Randolph Bourne

Phenomenology is a philosophy that emphasizes how the world is perceived by an individual; a person's experience is the paramount consideration. It emphasizes subjectivity and particularity to a great extent. Ivan Soll and C. S. Wyatt offer two views of phenomenology:

> [The German philosopher Edmund] Husserl conceived the task of Phenomenology, hence the task of philosophy, as describing phenomena—the objects of experience—accurately and independently of all assumptions derived from science. He thought that this activity would provide philosophic knowledge of reality.[1]
> [P]henomenology is less a rejection of science . . . than it is an embracing of the human emotional experience of life. Phenomenologists suggest what we experience matters more to our decisions than how the experience can be scientifically analyzed.[2]

It is this focus on experience that is crucial to understanding the meaning of jazz improvisation.[3]

SCIENCE IS INCOMPLETE

Phenomenology maintains that science is not a complete description of reality and cannot address crucial aspects of human existence. A brief outline of this stance is provided by David Stewart and Algis Mickunas:

> Phenomenology is thus concerned with conscious experience beyond its scientific treatment through empirical means. For instance, empiricism limits knowledge to that gained through sense perception. However, phenomenology would include as phenomena for study anything in one's experience or of which one may be conscious, such as moods, feelings, values, desires, or even mathematical entities. Phenomenology claims that objective, materialistic investigations are only part of the entire story, and thus also rejects the claim sometimes made for science that science can discover everything, a view phenomenologists call "scientism."[4]

TRANSCENDING CARTESIAN DUALISM

Descartes distinguished between mind and body and subject and object in his dictum *Cogito ergo sum* (I think, therefore I am). Stewart and Mickunas point out that this dualism first led to science ignoring consciousness as an area for investigation, and then led to science treating consciousness as another empirical phenomenon for study. However, Stewart and Mickunas continue, phenomenology holds that science cannot validly treat consciousness in this way because consciousness is a different kind of object than all the other objects in nature that science studies, and because the techniques of quantification and experimentation cannot deal with some aspects of consciousness.

Phenomenology attempts to transcend the Cartesian duality of subject and object that provides the foundation for science by considering that consciousness is "intentional," that is, consciousness always has an object (in Cartesian terms) or content toward which consciousness is directed (or "intended"). Because of this essential link, phenomenology holds that the subject and object cannot be separated in the manner of Cartesian dualism. Reality is viewed as a dialectic relationship between an intentional consciousness and the necessary content of that intention, or between what would be called the subject and the object in Cartesian terms.

> Another implication of the intentionality of consciousness is that it shifts the emphasis from the question of the reality of the world to the meaning of that which appears to consciousness. All questions about the reality of the world are suspended, put out of the question for the moment. Once consciousness is extricated from naturalistic psychological [and scientific] biases, the prob-

lem of getting out into the "real" world is eliminated. The intimate connection between consciousness and the content of consciousness is then fully manifested, for consciousness is never empty and abstract but concrete and tied to the world of experience.[5]

SCIENCE AND COMPOSITION

Christopher Small has also critiqued science in a way consistent with the critique of science by phenomenology and in a way reminiscent of existentialism, although Small cites neither phenomenology nor existentialism in his writing. Small links science to composition, in contrast to aligning improvisation with experience and phenomenology.[6]

Dualism

Small characterizes science as founded on the split between subject and object. That is, science is abstract knowledge divorced as completely as possible from experience, a body of facts and concepts existing outside and independent of the knower.[7] Small also contrasts the scientific with the experiential in terms similar to those of phenomenology: "Science . . . [transforms] everything upon which it is brought to bear into an object, as something to be observed, not experienced."[8] Science is also cumulative, thus ensuring that knowledge is not dependent on any one individual's experience. "Scientific knowledge was—and is—viewed as an abstract body of knowledge and theory existing outside, and independently of, the person knowing, such knowledge increasing quantitatively over time, so that each generation knows more than the preceding."[9]

Small also points out the difference between objective scientific observation and experience. While a scientist who reads a dial to take a measurement is nominally undergoing an experience, the experiential and phenomenological aspects of this situation are not important to the scientific endeavor. Experience, in the phenomenological sense, implies what the scientist, as an individual, went through while taking such a reading. Of course, these concerns are irrelevant to science. The scientist's experience is irrelevant to the nature of the data the scientist collects. However, the point here is not what is relevant to science, but the difference between an experience and a scientific observation. An observation is only concerned with objective, public facts, while an experience must include internal, subjective factors as well. Small recognizes phenomenology's linking of subject and object in contrast to the objective knowledge of science: "Knowledge [is not] an abstract and absolute thing, but [is] a relationship between the knower and the known, as a function as much of the knower as it is of the known."[10]

Composition, Knowledge, and Experience

Small holds that art and science are fundamentally opposed because art is linked with experience and science is opposed to experience through the subject/object duality. Small states that "art is knowledge as experience."[11] Furthermore, he says that Western common practice music is art tainted by science. He notes that the rise of this music began at the same time as scientific rationalism.[12] The abstractness and logic inherent in composing music of great structural complexity is paralleled by science:

> We have seen how the splitting off of man from nature, of observer from observed, was necessary before science could begin its work of discovery and conquest. Similarly, the abstract and logical nature of classical music . . . would not have been possible without the ability of the composer to separate himself, to distance himself, from his composition. Indeed, when Paul Henry Lang says "The essence of all these types of music is causal relationship achieved by the grouping of many small units into larger ones and finally into a great system of architecture," he might equally have been a nineteenth-century physicist expounding his essentially mechanistic view of the cosmos. . . . It may seem strange to speak of classical music, whose essence seems to be the expression of personal emotion, as abstract and logical, but this, as we have already seen, is the case. The logical transparency of this music parallels the vision of nature held by . . . [science.][13]

Henri Pousseur has said, "Tonal harmony is in fact the type of musical language in which the most transparent logic reigns, in which logic is truly made flesh."[14] All the implications or characteristics of abstractness, logic, distancing, science, composition, and classical music are not necessarily related, but they are linked through a constellation of mutually supportive values.

Expanding Small's link between science and Western compositions, we can see that the concepts of repetition and product also link composition with science.

Repetition

Scientific experiments are designed so that they may be repeated by others in order that results may be verified. It is a fundamental aspect of a composition that it is also designed to be repeated by others, essentially unchanged, through different performances. Although some variation in interpretive aspects, such as dynamics and phrasings, will occur in different performances of a composition, the composition need not be defined by these interpretive differences. If some number of different notes were played in a certain repetition of a composition, the resulting performance would not be the same composition. If a mistake in performance occurred, it would be acknowledged as a performer's error, not an error of the composition itself. Like a theory or a hypothesis that an experiment seeks to prove, a composition can be considered a separate thing from any specific, single performance (experiment) of it.

Product

The point and goal of science lies in its product. The process of science is only important insofar as it achieves progress toward improving its product, which is knowledge. The focus for science is the knowledge that results from investigation, not the investigation in and of itself.[15] As Small says, "[t]he experiences that Galileo underwent in order to obtain that knowledge are irrelevant to the nature of the knowledge itself; we are concerned, not even with the mental processes which went into it, but only with the final product of the thinking."[16] Similarly, in composition, we are not given access to the composer's experience or process, but only to the final product. Even if we could see a more or less complete history of the drafts used in composing a piece, that would be only a documentation of the process of composing. The focus in composition is on the final product because only the final product is revealed to the audience.

IMPROVISATION LINKED TO EXPERIENCE

In contrast to science and composition, the nature of improvisation has much in common with the nature of experience, which connects improvisation to phenomenology. Certain aspects of experience are exactly the same as certain aspects of improvisation and are not shared with composition. Improvisation is connected to the experiential by placing the improviser in a situation that shares important characteristics with any experience in life.

Time

Improvisation and experience are connected because the process of improvisation takes place in real time, as do experiences. The improviser must accept what has been improvised and cannot halt the process once begun or go back and change things, just as the ability to move freely in time is not a characteristic of experience in the real world. In contrast, a composer is able to transcend the time of a composition and compose at any point in the time of the composition. The improviser is a real-time composer, and the nature and constraints of real time align improvisation with experience because experience is also a real-time process.

Not Repeatable

Every experience is unique, and an experience cannot be repeated. Even if one attempted to repeat an experience, the second experience could not take place at the same time as the first, and so would be different at least in that regard. Other differences would also be likely, such as knowledge or remembrance of the first experience, as well as the effect of intervening experiences between the original experience and its repetition.

Improvisations are not repeatable either. It is only a hypothetical possibility that an improviser could literally repeat an improvisation note-for-note by spontaneously generating the same improvisation twice. Also, if the improviser played an improvisation from memory, it would not be an improvisation, it would be merely a memorized performance. Even considering successive improvisations on the same tune as improving a single improvisation (see "Continuation" in chapter 5) does not make the later versions repetitions of the previous ones. Congruency of notes and rhythms at least would be necessary in order to call a later improvisation a repetition of a prior one. The uniqueness of an experience and the uniqueness of an improvisation are the result of the fact that both occur in real time.

The composer Cornelius Cardew assigns improvisation a great beauty based on its inability to be repeated, and believes that this aspect of improvisation reflects the essence of all music: "From a certain point of view improvisation is the highest mode of musical activity, for it is based on the acceptance of music's fatal weakness and essential and most beautiful characteristic—its transience."[17] We shall see later that other weaknesses and contradictions are crucial for an aesthetic of jazz.

Immutable

Once an experience happens, it cannot be changed because one cannot go back in time. An improvisation, once performed, cannot be changed either. In contrast, it is one of the basic conditions of composition that the composer can change any part of a composition at any time during the compositional process. Improvisations are, therefore, like experiences in this regard, and compositions are not.

Nonmediated

An experience cannot be mediated; that is, it is impossible for one to experience something for another. Similarly, there is no mediation in improvisation: the performer and the composer are the same person—the improviser. In composition, however, the score mediates between the composer and the performer, and the performer mediates between the composer and the audience.

Uniting the Mind and Body

Another important idea that links improvisation to phenomenology and to experience is the unity of the mind and body, in contrast to the Cartesian duality of mind and body. The mediation between composer and performer in composition reinforces this Cartesian duality. Composition separates the mental conception of the music from the physical execution of it, making composition primarily a mental activity and leaving its physical realization to the performer. Improvisation, in contrast, unifies the conceiver of the music and its executor in the body of the same person, the improviser, whose body and mind must be present and coactive during the process of an improvisation.

Daniel Belgrad offers a paradigm for spontaneity that applies to jazz and is based on the unity of the mind and body as well as intersubjectivity. In contrast with objectivity, which distinguishes subject from object and establishes a split between mind and body, intersubjectivity "emerge(s) through a conversational dynamic . . . determined by the interaction of body, emotions, and intellect."[18] David Borgo also unites the mind and the body by claiming that "action and experience are not subordinate to their representation or conceptualization."[19] He means that the body's actions and experiences are not necessarily preceded by the mind's conscious conception of an action or an experience.

An improviser does not necessarily function like he or she has a body that is separate from a mind and which works in coordination with the mind, but, more characteristically, functions like he or she has a body/mind. This unity is evident in the reliance in improvisation on rote kinetic and physical learning of musical patterns and other material, in addition to the commonly recognized mental and compositional aspects of improvisation. Improvisers train their bodies as much as their minds. In spontaneous improvisation the mental conception of musical material and its physical execution may be simultaneous and not separated, and thus the mind/body dichotomy is overcome. Improvised music at its purest is not music that is mentally conceived and then executed very quickly after its conception, but is music that is mentally/bodily conceived and thus executed.

Consider how one speaks in everyday conversation. The process is transparent and immediate (at least as perceived by the speaker). One does not characteristically work out in advance a paragraph, sentence, phrase, or word in conversation. One merely exercises one's will to speak and, presto, one speaks. It is done with no apparent separation between conception and execution. One can, for convenience, separate the two factors in this dichotomy and speak of mental conception and physical execution, but in the actual process of everyday conversation as well as improvisation, they are unified, at least from a phenomenological perspective. Learned improvisation patterns are physically as well as mentally and aurally ingrained, and improvisation is a function of the body as well as the mind.

A great statement of intersubjectivity and the unity of the body and the mind was Charlie Parker's advice to Sonny Criss: "Don't think. Quit thinking."[20] Parker's advice is best read not as a rejection of the mind or intellect, but merely a rejection of its separation from the body and emotion. When mind, body, and emotion are unified, we do not describe it as "thinking," which refers only to the mental and not the physical or emotional. Parker's advice rejects thinking as a way to emphasize this point rhetorically.

Embodied

Recently, cognitive scientists have reconceived cognition as something embodied, in contrast to viewing it as data processing or information management. The perception of the outside world by the mind through the body (that is, through the senses) overcomes the mind/body split. Vijay Iyer says, "In the embodied viewpoint, the mind is no longer seen as passively reflective of the outside world, but rather as an active constructor of its own reality."[21] Similarly, with jazz improvisation, the musician is no longer seen as passively reflective of the composer's intentions, but rather as an active constructor of his or her own music.

"Thrown"

The concept of "thrownness" in phenomenology creates an important link between phenomenology, experience, and improvisation. Thrownness refers to the fact that people, in experiences and in life, are always thrown into situations. That is, it is a characteristic of existence that one's situation or experience is always presented to oneself immediately and automatically. One is always in some sort of situation, one cannot help it, and one is always responding to a situation (even doing nothing is one type of response to a situation). One can only continue through a situation or experience to the next.

The improviser is also found in a similar position. The improviser is thrown into improvising. Once the time has come to improvise, the improviser can only go forward as best he or she can. Not playing is even as much a part of the improvisation, as doing nothing is a response to a situation or experience. (Miles Davis made doing nothing into a full-fledged aesthetic through the notes he didn't play gaining more importance than the notes he did play.) The composer, on the other hand, is not thrown into composing because the composer can transcend the time of the composition. The composer can leave the process of composing at any time and that will have no essential effect on the composition.

Overlap

Much if not all music can exist in real time as a performance, and so shares that characteristic with the experiential. It should be made clear that linking improvisation with experience does not have anything to do with the listener's experience of hearing a composition or an improvisation. In both cases, of course, listeners undergo the experience of hearing music. To the extent that any performance of music occurs in time, all music is also aligned with the experiential to some degree.

Recording an Improvisation Is Irrelevant

The fact that a recording may be made of an improvisation does not remove the qualities of embodiment, nonmediation, and nonrepeatability from the improvisation, even though the improviser need not be physically present when a recording of an improvisation is played and even though one can play a recording of an improvisation many times. A recording is a documentation of an act, be it an improvisation or a composition; it is not the act itself. From the standpoint of the improviser or composer, a recording of an improvisation is not a repetition of the improvisation, just as playing a video recording of someone eating a meal does not mean that that person has eaten another meal and actually received more calories and sustenance. We commonly ignore this distinction when we enjoy recordings of improvisations, and we do so with no great harm, but recordings still do not make improvisations any less embodied, nonmediated, or unrepeatable.

The Experiential Is the Realm of Art

While Small never mentions the field of phenomenology, he considers it the goal of music (and art in general) to explore the realm of experience, which aligns it with phenomenology. "The reality of experience, a reality in fact of greater significance in our lives than the structure of atoms or of galaxies, is inaccessible to scientific method, and it is this reality that art proclaims and explores."[22] For Small, like Cornelius Cardew, improvisation holds a special, if not primary, place in the pantheon of the arts. By sharing fundamental aspects of experience, improvisation is especially suited to explore the world of experience, which Small holds to be the primary duty of art.

Raymond Williams also believes that the primary role of art is to communicate experience: "To succeed in art is to convey an experience to others in such a form that the experience is actively re-created—not 'contemplated,' not 'examined,' not passively received, but by response to the means, actually lived through, by those to whom it is offered."[23] The best example of this, for Williams, is a musical one: "Rhythm is a way of transmitting a description of experience, in such a way that the experience is re-created in the person receiving it, not merely as an 'abstraction' or an 'emotion' but as a physical effect on the organism—on the blood, on the breathing, on the physical patterns of the brain."[24]

Improvisation Is Humanistic

One of improvisation's fundamental values is thus humanistic. Improvisation provides an analogue for what it is like to be an experiencing, living human being. One may view the improviser as a person experiencing some situation in real life. The improviser demonstrates how to get through an experience because the method and process of improvising has so much in common with experience. In improvisation and in life, we experience things in real time, we must be embodied, we cannot repeat things, we cannot go back and change things, no one else can live life for us, we are thrown into experience, and we are bodies and minds. Carroll Pratt once famously said that "music sounds the way emotions feel."[25] The analogous formulation for improvisation is "improvisation sounds the way experiences happen."

SHIFTING AWAY FROM PRODUCT

The move away from a single-minded emphasis on musical product is important for jazz improvisation. Understanding the process of jazz improvisation—the conditions under which jazz is improvised and how jazz improvisation unfolds—cannot only change how we understand an objective musical structure, such as a pianist imitating a soloist's musical figure, but can also change the meaning and significance that we impart to the objective musical structure. We can ask, "What is the context of the music, under what conditions (process) is it created, and what different meaning might we find in a musical object when we acknowledge or appreciate such a context?" While I will show that product is not irrelevant, it is certainly not the entire story, either, because we cannot fail to impart a context or meaning. Even asserting that there is no imposed context and that our only focus is on the objective notes and rhythms themselves is a context, in the same way that no decision is a decision itself when viewed from a broader standpoint. Both process and product have a role to play and can coexist as opposites.

In strictly formalist terms, it is true that, in general, the conditions of jazz improvisation do not favor structurally complex music as much as composition does. But to evaluate jazz solely on this basis ignores crucial aspects of jazz, even as structural complexity can remain a part of the jazz aesthetic. Jazz also brings an existential, humanistic element to the creation of music because of the nature of its process and the conditions of its creation. If we want to listen to jazz improvisation with full regard for its special qualities, then we must listen with regard to the situation of the improviser, which mirrors that of ourselves. That jazz mirrors the experiential leads us to assign different meanings to jazz improvisation than to composition.

There are several areas in which the context of jazz improvisation is crucial for a complete appreciation of it. These areas are witnessing the creative process, the jazz improviser as explorer, and the direct connection to the unconscious source of creativity.

Witnessing the Creative Process

It is sometimes remarked that one value of improvisation is that it displays, for all to see, the creative act. "One great attraction of improvised performances is precisely the opportunity to witness, as it were, the shaping activity of the improviser who creates an artistic utterance unmediated by another human being. It is as though we are able to gain access to the artist's mind at the moment of artistic creation."[26] But why is this valuable? Seeing the creative process may be interesting, much like one might spend a pleasant afternoon in the studio of a painter, for instance, observing the techniques that the painter uses and following the development of a work in progress. But the fact that the creative process is coincident with the creative product in jazz improvisation gives improvisation a unique and crucial aspect that depends on the experiential.

Lee Brown offers one example of appreciating this crucial element: "I am interested in [the improviser's] on-the-spot gambits and responses. If things are going well, I wonder if he can sustain the level. If he takes risks that get him into trouble, I worry about how he will deal with it. If he pulls the fat out of the fire, I applaud."[27] The true value to pulling the fat out of the fire, and the reason why we might applaud, depend on the fact that we view the creative process in improvisation as it unfolds. If a composer were to compose the same musical structure as the improviser who has just made a risky move succeed—an exactly equal musical product in objective, formalist terms—we might very well have heard a musical structure of great value, but it means something completely different coming from a jazz improviser. An improvisation affords us an opportunity that is completely absent in composition because when the fat is needing to be pulled from the fire in improvisation, the outcome is not certain. No one knows exactly what will happen next, including, quite possibly, the improviser, and everyone knows that as well.[28] But in a composition, everyone knows that the outcome has already been fixed, even if we don't know what it is yet. We know that the end of the story has already been written.[29]

To go on a ride with an improviser is a completely different thing than going on a ride with a composer in a composition. Going on a ride with an improviser is like the experience itself, with the same type of uncertainty that accompanies any experience in real life because no one knows what will happen next. Going on a trip like a composition is one thing because you know that the driver knows the ultimate destination even if you do not, but improvisation is a completely different thing because you not only do not know the destination, you know that the driver does not know it, either. Frank Oteri brings up a similar point about the experience of sports: "For example, many times over the years when making plans to go out to dinner with my sports friends, they insisted there be a television nearby so they could watch a game. 'Why don't you just tape it on your VCR and watch it later?' I'd query them with my music-archivist sensibility. They thought I was nuts. . . . 'What's the point of watching the game if you know how it's going to turn out?' "[30] The improviser may be the navigator, pilot, and engine all at the same time, but the listener is sitting right next to the improviser in the passenger seat, wondering where on earth everyone is going to wind up. In composition, there is no doubt that the course of the trip has already been laid out and will play itself out accordingly.

THE JAZZ IMPROVISER AS EXPLORER

The title of Ted Gioia's *The Imperfect Art* implies a criticism of jazz improvisation: it fails to live up to the standards for complexity and structure compared to composition. But holding jazz up to the highest formalist criteria, being disappointed when it fails to achieve those criteria, and making excuses for jazz nonetheless (the process is the important thing, somehow) is a little bit like criticizing Lewis and Clark for not taking the shortest and easiest route to the Pacific Ocean, as well as apologizing for how difficult their journey was. It is illogical as well as a category mistake to expect Lewis and Clark to have taken a beeline (or even the shortest realistic route) to the Pacific, as if they already had the route laid out for them, when the whole point of their journey was to discover *any* route, even as they obviously desired the perfect one and strove to find it. Lewis and Clark's route to the Pacific, structurally, may not have been the perfect route, but the fact that they were trailblazing, not knowing how to get to where they wanted to go, makes their lesser structure, the more indirect route, all the more amazing. They did not fail in a quantitative sense (that is, traveling some number of miles when they could have traveled fewer miles); rather, their task was qualitatively different. They were explorers, not tour guides consulting maps to find the best route. There is no apology necessary for not meeting the standard of the absolutely shortest route; Lewis and Clark were operating in a completely different realm and context, and yet, they strove to find the shortest or easiest route.

The jazz improviser is also such an explorer. The musical problems inherent in any work of music may or may not be solved in the best manner by the improviser, but they are discovered as they occur. In contrast, travelers on an already defined route, including performers of composed music, know where things are going to wind up. Paul Berliner says that "when evaluating a performance, the improviser typically favors inconsistency in the service of spontaneous, creative exploration over consistency in less extemporaneous invention."[31]

Direct Connection to an Unconscious Source of Creativity

Another example of how important process can be for jazz improvisation concerns different types of creativity. Because jazz improvisation is unmediated, its creativity can be of a different type than that typically available to a composer. Improvisation encourages a direct connection to the unconscious sources of creativity because it must be ongoing and because it unites the mind and body as well as conception and execution.

We can distinguish between two types of creativity. Both may occur with composers as well as improvisers, but the conditions of composition and improvisation link one type more closely with composition and the other with improvisation. Given that the composer has as much time as he or she wants to ponder solutions to compositional problems, one can imagine the composer in a "Eureka!" moment when creativity and inspiration hit and the composer finds the correct and perfect solution to a compositional or aesthetic problem, perhaps one that has been simmering in the back of the composer's mind for some time. Such moments for the improviser are limited in comparison because the improviser does not have the luxury of extended contemplation, waiting for the "Eureka!" to hit. The composer can wait for a "Eureka!" moment to strike, but if the improviser waits, the moment will have passed. While the improviser is not completely excluded from such moments, what the improviser does more characteristically is to open up a direct, ongoing channel to the unconscious sources of creativity and then let things flow continuously, as a real-time process, through the mind/body.

I can recall a specific instance in one of my performances in which this opening of a channel to the source of creativity happened quite distinctly, and it stands in contrast to the "Eureka!" moment that is more characteristic of composition. I was performing with a jazz combo, and the soloist before me took an imaginative, creative, and highly expressive solo. It was wonderful. Strategically and consciously, as that solo was ending, I thought to myself, "How can I possibly follow that?" I decided to adopt what is probably a common strategy used by others. I decided to try to do something completely different than the soloist before me had, in order not to compete with his solo. There was no sense in trying to beat that soloist at his own game, because he had done such a marvelous job.

Although I deliberately set out to deploy a certain strategy, that strategy relied on me being nonconscious. Just before my solo started, I emptied my mind, blanked my thoughts, and merely waited for some musical idea to appear. My perception of this process was that it was accompanied by a calm and open feeling, without struggle for a creative idea or a particular desire for it. Then, I played something. It was one of the most creative ideas I've ever had, very different from the previous musician's solo, and quite successful (at least in my opinion). Tellingly, it did not appear as a "Eureka!" idea that I then decided to execute. Rather, it was only after I had started to execute it that I was consciously aware of what the idea was. It was a clear example of how improvisation transcends the mind/body dualism. Such a dualism is present in a "Eureka!" moment: after the composer is struck with the creative insight, it is a separate act to implement or execute the idea, the implementation of which typically involves conscious and considered decisions. In my case, however, the conception and execution of the idea were coincident (at least as far as I could tell). By calming and blanking my conscious mind, I made a connection with the unconscious source of creativity as well as my body and then allowed that creativity to conceive an idea and execute it through my body simultaneously.

Phenomenology links jazz improvisation with the experiential, and this stands in contrast to the link between composition and science. Phenomenology also contributes to a fuller understanding of jazz improvisation through its influence on another kind of philosophy, existentialism, which is the topic of the next chapter.

NOTES

1. Ivan Soll, "Existentialism," *World Book Online Reference Center*, www.world-bookonline.com/wb/Article?id=ar188480 (accessed August 8, 2004).

2. C. S. Wyatt, "Existentialism: Definitions," *The Existential Primer*, www.tameri.com/csw/exist/ex_lexicon.html#lexicon (accessed December 13, 2005).

3. By "experience," I mean the experiential—what it is like to have the experience of being alive, of being conscious of the passage of time, etc.—and not "being experienced," that is, having lived through many events in the past that give one an advantage for negotiating similar events in the future.

4. David Stewart and Algis Mickunas, *Exploring Phenomenology*, 2nd ed. (Athens: Ohio University Press, 1990), 4.

5. Stewart and Mickunas, *Exploring Phenomenology*, 9.

6. Christopher Small, *Music, Society, Education* (London: John Calder, 1980).

7. Small, *Music, Society, Education*, 4–5.

8. Small, *Music, Society, Education*, 61.

9. Small, *Music, Society, Education*, 64.

10. Small, *Music, Society, Education*, 90. One ill-founded response to this situation is extreme relativism: that, because the investigator influences what is being investigated, any conclusion drawn from an investigation is based on one's own approach and biases. Of course, this conclusion does not follow because it ignores the second half of the equation: knowledge is based on the known as well as the knower. While the knower may have great influence, he or she does not have complete discretion to define what is known because there is an outside world with which the knower is interacting. Both the knower and the known limit what is known.

11. Small, *Music, Society, Education*, 4.

12. Small, *Music, Society, Education*, 81.

13. Small, *Music, Society, Education*, 82–83.

14. Henri Pousseur, quoted in Small, *Music, Society, Education*, 13.

15. The process in question here is not the process of some natural occurrence, say, the formation of a coral reef. That process is an appropriate topic for scientific investigation. Rather, the process in question is the process of how science discovers knowledge about that coral reef, or any other natural phenomenon. This process of discovery is largely irrelevant for scientific knowledge. If some other process of investigation proves to be superior to another, then the one that produces better results, that produces a better "knowledge product," will always be favored. The only criterion for process in science is how that process contributes to the final product.

16. Small, *Music, Society, Education*, 64.

17. Cornelius Cardew, "Towards an Ethic of Improvisation," in *Treatise Handbook* (London: Edition Peters, 1971), quoted in David Borgo, "Reverence for Uncertainty: Chaos, Order, and the Dynamics of Musical Free Improvisation" (Ph.D. diss., University of California, Los Angeles, 1999), 55.

18. David Belgrad, *The Culture of Spontaneity: Improvisation and the Arts in Postwar America* (Chicago: University of Chicago Press, 1998), 5–6.

19. Borgo, "Reverence for Uncertainty," 24.

20. Charlie Parker, quoted in Ira Gitler, *Swing to Bop* (New York: Oxford University Press, 1985), 71.

21. Vijay Iyer, "Embodied Mind, Situated Cognition, and Expressive Microtiming in Afro-American Music," *Music Perception* 19, no. 3 (Spring 2002): 389.

22. Small, *Music, Society, Education*, 97.

23. Raymond Williams, *The Long Revolution* (New York: Columbia University Press, 1961), 34.

24. Williams, *The Long Revolution*, 24.

25. Carroll Pratt, "Music as the Language of Emotions," in *Lectures on the History and Art of Music* (New York: Da Capo Press, 1968), 64.

26. *Encyclopedia of Aesthetics*, s.v. "Improvisation."

27. Lee Brown, " 'Feeling My Way': Jazz Improvisation and Its Vicissitudes—A Plea for Imperfection," *Journal of Aesthetics and Art Criticism* 58, no. 2 (2000): 121.

28. An exception to this would be aleatoric composition, in which the composer deliberately leaves significant aspects of the work to be determined by the performer (much like an improviser). This type of composition omits one of the hallmarks of composition, the ability to determine in final form significant aspects of the work.

29. Hearing a piece of music, whether improvised or composed, on repeated listenings does not deny this perspective. Even though we may know exactly where the music is going on a second hearing, we are also able to either (1) suspend our memory in order to more closely re-create the authentic uncertainty of first hearing the work, or (2) reacknowledge that the improviser did not know where the improvisation will lead, so that we are merely gaining the advantage of the memory of the original ride that was uncertain when the improviser led us there. This is one reason why live jazz retains an authenticity that recorded jazz does not. Without a recording, one can only go on the ride for the first time, just as in an experience.

30. Frank Oteri, "Harnessing the Random Element," *NewMusicBox* http://www.newmusicbox.org/page.nmbx?id=23ls00 (accessed December 13, 2005).

31. Paul Berliner, *Thinking in Jazz: The Infinite Art of Improvisation* (Chicago: University of Chicago Press, 1994), 273.

16

♫

Existentialism

Man is free at the moment he wishes to be.

—Voltaire

Phenomenology strongly influenced existentialism, and some important ideas in phenomenology also appear in existentialism. Existentialism holds that individuals must make their own decisions and must
accept the consequences of those decisions (even not deciding is making
a [meta-]decision not to decide). Existentialism further says that there are
no objective, absolute standards to guide one's decisions and behaviors.
The only possibility, therefore, is that individuals must find their own
way as best as they can, making their own decisions and taking responsibility for doing so. Jean-Paul Sartre said, "Man is nothing else but what he
makes of himself. Such is the first principle of existentialism."[1] Ralph
Harper explains this more fully: "Man can not rest on his human nature;
it is not enough just to be. One must be someone; one must make oneself
continually in order to be real. One must make one's self felt, throw one's
weight around."[2] Existentialism insists that individuals freely choose,
rather than rely on received wisdom. Steven Crowell holds that "my
moral act is *inauthentic* if, in keeping my promise for the sake of duty, I do
so because that is what 'one' does (what 'moral people' do). But I can do
the same thing *authentically* if, in keeping my promise for the sake of duty,
acting this way is something I choose *as my own*, something to which,
apart from its social sanction, I commit myself."[3]

THE VALUES OF JAZZ AND EXISTENTIALISM

Individualism, assertion, freedom, and responsibility are the four values of jazz discussed in this book that are most strongly reflected in existentialism. This can be seen in the following summary of existentialism by Ivan Soll:

> The existentialists conclude that human choice is subjective, because individuals finally must make their own choices without help from such external standards as laws, ethical rules, or traditions. Because individuals make their own choices, they are free; but because they freely choose, they are completely responsible for their choices. The existentialists emphasize that freedom is necessarily accompanied by responsibility. Furthermore, since individuals are forced to choose for themselves, they have their freedom—and therefore their responsibility—thrust upon them. They are "condemned to be free."[4]

Jazz improvisers, as individuals, similarly make their own choices, are thrown into an improvisation, and are responsible for their choices. There is no one on the bandstand to blame except the improviser when an improvisation does not work out very well. Also, when an improvisation does go very well, there is no doubt as to whom credit is owed: it must be the improviser.

Choice in existentialism is continuous, just like improvisation, according to Crowell: "We are 'condemned to be free,' which means that we can never simply *be* who we are but are separated from ourselves by the nothingness of having perpetually to re-choose, or re-commit, ourselves to what we do."[5] Jazz musicians commit themselves to their task with every beat and with every note.

The ideas of the philosopher Friedrich Nietzsche were important precursors to existentialism. Steven Crowell compares the aesthetics of art to what might be called Nietzsche's existential aesthetics of life:

> To say that a work of art has style is to invoke a standard for judging it, but one that can not be specified in the form of a general law of which the work would be a mere instance. Rather, in a curious way, the norm is internal to the work. For Nietzsche, existence falls under such an imperative of style: to create meaning and value in a world from which all transcendent supports have fallen away is to give unique shape to one's immediate inclinations, drives, and passions; to interpret, prune, and enhance according to a unifying sensibility, a ruling instinct, that brings everything into a whole that satisfies the non-conceptual, aesthetic norm of what fits, what belongs, what is appropriate.[6]

To apply this to art and jazz, we can view jazz improvisation as being similar to Nietzsche's existential view of life. The improviser must "create meaning and value" through a style of music in which "all transcendent supports [namely, the composer] have fallen away." The improviser "give[s] unique shape to [the improviser's] immediate inclinations, drives, and passions" through the spontaneous process of improvisation. The improviser, however, rather than mindlessly wandering through an improvisation, will "interpret, prune, and enhance according to a unifying sensibility."

EXISTENTIALISM AND THE BLUES

Another way in which existentialism and jazz are linked can be seen in the blues. The blues are fundamentally connected with existentialism. The connection between existentialism and the blues also connects jazz with existentialism, since the blues are a major part of jazz: nearly every substyle of jazz throughout all of jazz history has incorporated the blues, and many if not most jazz musicians play the blues as a fundamental part of jazz.

Shelby Steele has located existentialism in the blues through Ralph Ellison's *The Invisible Man*:

> Throughout most of the novel the invisible man merely exists in the sense that he allows others to define and direct the course of his life. He looks to the world outside himself for meaning and direction. Only when the hostile forces of that world force him underground does he confront himself, assume responsibility for his own life, and begin to build what he calls a "plan of living." . . . [The] invisible man [affirms] the presence of an inner "margin of freedom," an inner space that is free from the pressures and constraints of the outside world, a space in which he is free to redefine himself.[7]

Defining oneself is a core aspect of existentialism. Steele then shows how the blues are connected to the novel and to existentialism, quoting Ellison:

> The blues is . . . an assertion of the irrepressibly human over all circumstance whether created by others or by one's own human failings. . . . [T]he blues posit the sufferer's right (freedom) to redefine his pain and thereby transcend it. This act of redefinition is existential . . . ; it moves the individual sufferer . . . from helpless suffering to self-control, and from victimization to self-determination. It assumes that the individual, no matter what his circumstances, has the freedom, within limits, to assign his own meaning to the world. The blues act on the world in an existential manner by positing the inner freedom necessary for remolding and reshaping meaning.[8]

This is also what jazz does. Jazz allows the improviser to assign the improviser's own perspective and meaning to the piece on which he or she improvises. Jazz requires that the improviser use the freedom inherent in jazz improvisation to remold and reshape the piece on which the improviser improvises, and thereby remold and reshape the meaning of the improvisation. Steele also acknowledges contradiction in the blues and existentialism:

> The blues work by juxtaposing possibility against circumstance and the human sadness the blues decry. In the fact of defeat they pose the possibility of victory, sadness is opposed with the possibility of happiness and loneliness is confronted with the possibility of fellowship. For many this juxtaposition may seem absurd. For example, it seems hopeless for an old man trapped in an endless cycle of poverty in an inner city to relieve his lonely despair by believing in the possibility of a life without such despair. As outsiders we can see that it is very unlikely that his material circumstances will improve. But the blues say there is an inner freedom, based on an internal sense of possibility, that provides this man with enough space in which to existentially redefine himself and thereby gain some control over his despair.[9]

The contradiction between an objective assessment of the old man's possibilities and what the old man might will for himself through the blues is just what existentialism says exists for everyone.

SELF-DEFINITION

Jazz musicians make themselves in a direct musical way and in the same way that existentialists say applies to the entire human condition. The jazz improviser stands onstage naked in a way unlike any other musician who does not improvise. No one can bail out the improviser if the next note is not forthcoming, or if a mistake is made. If existentialists say "it is not enough just to be," jazz says "it is not enough just to play notes that are given by a composer." Rather, the improviser is responsible for both the conception and the execution of the music. Furthermore, the improviser is in an existential situation made more exposed and vital because the decision-making process is in full view of the audience, and is done in real time.

AUTHENTICITY

Authenticity in existentialism carries a special meaning, one that implies awareness of strengths and limitations as well as having to assert one's strengths in light of those limitations. This type of authenticity savors the dynamic tension between one's strengths and limitations. The following explanation of authenticity by Salvatore R. Maddi highlights this dynamic tension: "[S]earch your memory for the times you understood and accepted yourself the most, when you were aware of your vanities, sentimentalities, follies, and weakness, yet could somehow assert the importance of your life. You could anticipate with vigor your future experiences even though you could not entirely predict or control them, and this frightened you."[10] William Day finds a similar contradiction in what he calls "moral perfectionism," whose distinctive features are "a commitment to speaking and acting true to oneself, combined with a thoroughgoing dissatisfaction with oneself as one now stands."[11]

Being authentic means that one is in full awareness of the limitations of one's abilities and the possible uncertainties resulting from action based on one's limited abilities. Even though one may feel frightened or anxious because the future is uncertain and because one has limitations and foibles, one is able to move ahead anyway. Being authentic means consciously and fully facing the actual situation as it is presented, with eyes wide open. It implies that, even though the situation is not perfect, one has made a conscious choice to proceed anyway. (This approach may be contrasted with other behaviors that people exhibit when confronted with an imperfect situation; for example, people sometimes ignore their reality through denial, blame it on someone else, or become angry.)

The jazz improviser is in an authentic position. The conditions of improvising allow the improviser to be authentic, in the face of limitations or imperfections, because the improviser does not have any choice. The music must continue, and the improviser is forced to move on and figure out what the next notes will be, and not doing anything is just as much a decision as anything else. It is just the improviser and the next note staring at each other. Crowell acknowledges as much when he writes, "Authenticity defines a condition on self-making: do I succeed in making *myself*, or will who I am merely be a function of the roles I find myself in?"[12] This holds true very directly for the jazz musician. Jazz musicians have certain roles, such as improviser, rhythm section member, accompanist, or timekeeper. Only a perfunctory, nominal jazz musician would perform only these roles and do nothing else, without bringing himself or herself, as personally defined, fully to the task at hand. One might play like a perfect metronome in order to fulfill a role in a jazz ensemble, but if one didn't feel the groove, enjoy it, and imbue the performance with that feeling and joy, one would not be an authentic jazz musician, in the existential sense.

A dramatic description of an authentic jazz improvisation was written by saxophonist Art Pepper. He ended his autobiography, *Straight Life*, by recounting a performance with saxophonist Sonny Stitt, who laid down an implicit but significant challenge for Pepper to try to match or beat the great solo Stitt just played, a seemingly impossible task:

> [He] looked at me. Gave me one of those looks, "All right, suckah, your turn." And it's *my* job; it's *my* gig. I was strung out. I was hooked. I was drunk. I was having a hassle with my wife, Diane, who'd threatened to kill herself in our hotel room next door. I had marks on my arm. I thought there were narcs in the club, and all of a sudden realized that it was *me*. He'd [Stitt] done all those things, and now I had to put up or shut up or get off or forget it or quit or kill myself or do *something*.
>
> I forgot everything, and everything came out. I played way over my head. I played completely different than he did. I searched and found my own way, and what I said reached the people. I played myself, and I knew I was right, and the people loved it, and they felt it. I blew and I blew, and when I finally finished I was shaking all over; my heart was pounding; I was soaked in sweat, and the people were screaming; the people were clapping, and I looked at Sonny, but I just kind of nodded, and he went, "All *right*." And that was it. That's what it's all about.[13]

Pepper's solo was existentially authentic. He had his limitations—being drunk, strung out, having marital problems, afraid of narcotics officers—but realized that he could not escape the responsibility of responding to Stitt, and he found a way to assert himself with amazing results.

Existentialism is a very honest philosophy. It encourages facing the world straight on, as it is given to us, unblinkingly. Similarly, and with much of the flavor of existentialism, improvisation in its highest form can bring out a truer, more honest reflection of the deepest parts of an improviser's musical personality. One reason for this is because improvisation is spontaneous. Something spontaneous and unmediated can be a truer reflection of the self than something considered and reworked. Consider spontaneous words that one might blurt out. Such words can reveal what one is truly thinking or feeling. In contrast, if one has time to consider or deliberate how those words might be changed for some purpose, one can twist or spin the original impulse and edit, much like a composer, those words that might otherwise reveal a truth that we may not want revealed. When being spontaneous, however, we can expose our inner selves without any of the conscious filters we might otherwise assume. This is honesty as existentialism requires. Psychoanalysis uses this honesty through the technique of free association, in which a client spontaneously responds to prompts from the analyst. Free association is based on the principle that the spontaneous utterance can reveal the true self. David Lichtenstein says, "Nevertheless the appreciation of this form of discourse [free association], the idea that truth must reside there, is fundamental to psychoanalysis, truth defined as new utterances that attain authority."[14]

THE UNACCOMPANIED SOLO

Perhaps the existential nature of jazz is nowhere more obvious than in an unaccompanied solo. Without the usual foundation of a rhythm section, we can more easily imagine the soloist (a saxophonist, perhaps) as existentially pitted against the limitations of his or her technical abilities, the instrument itself, and the materials of music (the notes, scales, and rhythms from which the improviser will create a melody), as well as the limits of the musician's imagination and creativity. We watch the saxophonist in this challenge and can, perhaps, imagine what that must be like because we know that we ourselves, in our lives, are also pitted against the limitations of our physical bodies, the social relationships from which we build our lives, and the limits of our imagination and creativity in living our lives. So when the saxophonist executes a brilliant maneuver, we might applaud because we know what it's like to do something similar in our lives (hopefully), and when the saxophonist stumbles and misses an opportunity, we know what that's like as well because we've done something similar in our lives (probably). When we imagine ourselves strongly asserting something all by ourselves, we can hear the solo saxophonist in a different light. We can understand better what it means to be an individual, existentially alone in the world in the manner in which we enter the world and in the manner in which we leave it.

RISK

Risk is a fundamental part of existentialism. Because existentialism holds that one is responsible for one's decisions and there are no absolute, objective standards to help one make a decision, there is always the risk that one will make a poor decision (even in the absence of an objective standard). Similarly, when a jazz musician improvises, the element of risk is always present. Not only is the possibility of mistakes always present, but the improviser may be having an off night: even the greatest do. Eric Nisenson recounts the time that Sonny Rollins gave a lackluster performance that barely deserved the label.[15] Inspiration comes and goes, and no one is inspired 100 percent of the time. Pianist Keith Jarrett has put the idea of risk in terms that any existentialist would immediately understand: "Jazz is about risking everything to your personal muse and accepting the consequences."[16]

The jazz improviser is out on a risky tightrope, executing no previously defined plan in front of a demanding, sometimes fickle lot of strangers and perhaps a few friends that is called an audience. The improviser is on this tightrope in a way that a composer is not. It is the difference between performing the same backflip, for instance, on a tightrope with a safety net and without a safety net. The objective structure of the act itself is the same, but the different context changes everything about our appreciation of the objective event. A composer need not risk a compositional disaster like the improviser risks. There is no reason, in principle, why a composer should not have solved all the problems posed in a composition. But for the improviser, anything is possible, both brilliance and disaster, and anything *should* be possible if the improviser is challenging himself or herself at the highest levels. A mistake or a bad decision risks disaster, so we are thrilled at the performer's courage and daring at attempting risky moves in those circumstances, and our opinion of the improviser would decline if the improviser did not take any risks and played it safe.

JAZZ AND LIFE

Some writers have made a comparison between improvisation and speaking.[17] People improvise conversations every day, and the parallels between conversation and jazz improvisation are fruitful and well considered, if limited at some point. But this analogy—between something from everyday life and jazz improvisation—can be carried much further. Jazz improvisation can be compared to life itself, existentially. We are all thrown into life, just like the improviser is thrown into an improvisation. In both cases, we cannot help but go on, we try the best we can, and even doing nothing is doing something. Sometimes our decisions are amazing ones, sometimes they are bad ones, and sometimes we just get plain lucky.

Don't we improvise our entire lives, in the broadest sense? There is certainly no plan—a composition?—that tells us exactly what our next step in life should be: what job should we take, where should we live, who should we marry, or what should we say in every situation. Halpern, Close, and Johnson say that "anyone can improvise. We all do it every day—none of us goes through our day-to-day life with a script to tell us what to do."[18] If only we had a score to show us the way! Instead, we are forced to improvise our way through life, without the ability to go back and reconsider things, fix mistakes, or make different decisions—without all those things a composer can do.

When we come upon a problem in life for the first time—whenever we have any experience in life for the first time—no amount of previous wisdom, transmitted through the ages, or advice from elders or friends, can substitute for the experience of going through that situation and learning for ourselves how it feels and how our personal abilities, limitations, and inclinations will lead us through to the other side, smoothly or not. It's only after we have gone through an experience that we truly understand it. That means that we have to improvise our way through an experience, at least initially. Living life is the most elemental form of improvisation. Even in succeeding situations that are similar to earlier ones, we still improvise our way through them, although now we have some experience on which to draw, just like a jazz improviser who is improvising on a chord progression that he or she has played before. Every new experience or tune is probably similar in some way to a previous experience or tune, and we draw on that past experience to help us through it.

Ralph Waldo Emerson, in his seminal essay "Self-Reliance," expressed an outlook on life that would immediately resonate with a jazz improviser:

> If our young men miscarry in their first enterprises, they lose all heart. If the young merchant fails, men say he is ruined. If the finest genius studies at one of our colleges, and is not installed in an office within one year afterwards in the cities or suburbs of Boston or New York, it seems to his friends and to himself that he is right in being disheartened, and in complaining the rest of his life. A sturdy lad from New Hampshire or Vermont, who in turn tries all the professions, who teams it, farms it, peddles, keeps a school, preaches, edits a newspaper, goes to Congress, buys a township, and so forth, in successive years, and always, like a cat, falls on his feet, is worth a hundred of these city dolls. He walks abreast with his days, and feels no shame in not "studying a profession," for he does not postpone his life, but lives already. He has not one chance, but a hundred chances.[19]

Similarly, the jazz improviser always has another chance when the next tune comes around. Therefore, the improviser can improvise without being restricted by feeling as if this one chance is life or death.

It is because the process of improvisation is exactly that of experience and life that they are linked so strongly. Ted Gioia's retrospective method, in which each improvised figure can only be related to what has already been played and not to what will be played, has its parallel in life in the philosophy of the existentialist Søren Kierkegaard, who said, "Life is understood backwards but lived forwards."[20] So is improvisation.

Improvisation lacks a predetermined blueprint that guarantees it the same high degree of structural complexity that we expect in a composition, but this ultimately means little because the lack of such a plan and structure only mirrors what it means to be alive. If improvisation was able to function somehow with a predetermined plan that ensured compositional complexity, it would lose its ability to mirror what our lives must be. Improvisation, even with all its messiness, is an analogue for life and experience, despite its limitations, because life is inescapably messy.

George Lewis has commented on a famous saying by Charlie Parker, who "once said that 'music [jazz] is your own experience, your thoughts, your wisdom. If you don't live it, it won't come out of your horn. . . .' The clear implication is that what you do live does come out of your horn."[21] What we live is rarely perfect. So, while we can enjoy compositions in part because we are able to get a glimpse of perfection that we might have in our lives, we can also appreciate improvisations because they show us what our lives are actually like: sometimes messy, sometimes brilliant, sometimes mundane, and, hopefully, reaching for brilliance and perfection as much as possible. How perfection is part of the imperfect process of jazz improvisation is the subject of the final chapter.

NOTES

1. Jean-Paul Sartre, quoted in Ralph Harper, *Existentialism: A Theory of Man* (Cambridge: Harvard University Press, 1965), 100.

2. Harper, *Existentialism*, 100.

3. Steven Crowell, "Existentialism," *Stanford Encyclopedia of Philosophy*, http://plato.stanford.edu/entries/existentialism/ (accessed December 7, 2004).

4. Ivan Soll, "Existentialism," *World Book Online Reference Center*, www.worldbookonline.com/wb/Article?id=ar188480 (accessed August 8, 2004).

5. Crowell, "Existentialism."

6. Crowell, "Existentialism."

7. Shelby Steele, "Ralph Ellison's Blues," *Journal of Black Studies* 7, no. 2 (1976): 151–68.

8. Ralph Ellison, quoted in Steele, "Ralph Ellison's Blues," 162.

9. Steele, "Ralph Ellison's Blues," 162–63.

10. Salvatore R. Maddi, *Personality Theories: A Comparative Analysis* (Pacific Grove, Calif.: Brooks/Cole Publishing Company, 1996), 155.

11. William Day, "Knowing as Instancing: Jazz Improvisation and Moral Perfectionism," *Journal of Aesthetics and Art Criticism* 58, no. 2 (Spring 2000): 99.

12. Crowell, "Existentialism."

13. Art Pepper and Laurie Pepper, *Straight Life: The Story of Art Pepper* (New York: Schirmer Books, 1979), 476.

14. David Lichtenstein, "The Rhetoric of Improvisation," *American Imago* 50, no. 2 (Summer 1993): 233.

15. Eric Nisenson, *Blue: The Murder of Jazz* (New York: St. Martin's Press, 1997), 167.

16 Keith Jarrett, "The Virtual Jazz Age," *Musician* (March 1968): 36.

17. Alan M. Perlman and Daniel Greenblatt, "Miles Davis Meets Noam Chomsky: Some Observations on Jazz Improvisation and Language Structure," in *The Sign in Music and Literature*, edited by Wendy Steiner (Austin: University of Texas, 1981), 169–83; Charles Suhor, "Jazz Improvisation and Language Performance," *Et cetera* 43, no. 2 (Summer 1986): 133–40; Luke O. Gillespie, "Literacy, Orality, and the Parry-Lord 'Formula': Improvisation and the Afro-American Jazz Tradition," *International Review of the Aesthetics and Sociology of Music* 22, no. 2 (December 1991): 147–64.

18. Charna Halpern, Del Close, and Kim Johnson, *Truth in Comedy: The Manual of Improvisation* (Colorado Springs, Colo.: Meriwether Publishing, 1994), 9.

19. Ralph Waldo Emerson, "Self-Reliance," in *The Complete Essays and Other Writings of Ralph Waldo Emerson*, edited by Brooks Atkinson (New York: Random House, 1940), 162.

20. Quoted in Phil Oliver, "On William James' 'Springs of Delight': The Return to Life," *Stream of William James* 2, no. 3 (Fall 2000): 15.

21. George Lewis, "Improvised Music after 1950," *Black Music Research Journal* 16, no. 1 (1996): 119.

17

♫

The Contradiction of
Perfection in Jazz

When you come to a fork in the road, take it.

—Yogi Berra

The connection between existentialism and jazz is based on the conditions and process of jazz improvisation. As important as this is for our appreciation of jazz, it does not mean that formalism and product need be completely rejected. Rather, process and product can coexist as opposites, and viewing them in this manner will lead to a humanistic and existential approach to formalism and structural complexity in jazz.

MATERIAL AND PERFORMANCE PRODUCTS

First, we may distinguish two different types of product: material and non-material. The product created when a composer composes is a composition, which is embodied materially as a musical score. But a broader conception of product is possible. A performer's product, so to speak, is music, performed and audible. A product need not necessarily be a physical thing, like a score or a recording, but is, most broadly, merely the result of some action or behavior. The improviser is a performer, so the improviser produces an audible musical product. But the improviser is also acting as a composer, too, determining not only notes and rhythms, but nearly all other aspects of music as well. We may correctly reject the material product of the composer's score as irrelevant for the jazz improviser because scores are not characteristically used in jazz as a compositional tool, and this rejection can then lead to a valuable focus on process, as we have seen. But this should not lead to a complete rejection of product in the broader sense because the improviser, as a performer, is creating a non-material product, the music of a performance. Regardless of how it is created, the product of a jazz ensemble is the music it creates, whether that music is notated, recorded, made tangible in any form, or not.

THE TOPIC OF THE STUDY OF MUSIC IS MUSIC

Formalism focuses on the musical product, conventionally conceived as the score. Formalist scholars have analyzed jazz by transcribing improvisations and analyzing the resulting score, as if a composer had composed it. This tradition of jazz analysis has come under attack by critical theory scholars of jazz. One encyclopedia summarizes several "putative errors of the [formalist] tradition, by the lights of the new theory. . . . The essentialist is also typically an internalist [formalist], that is, a theorist who mistakenly fixates on formal features of the music at the expense of externals. By contrast, the critical theory of jazz holds that we can only get at the heart of jazz by placing the music within its cultural context."[1] Lee Brown calls the critical theory position "externalist," in contrast with an internalist or formalist approach. He has characterized critical theory that does not incorporate formalism as "close to incoherent":

> Consider the explanation of Howard McGhee, the trumpet player, that when his generation of African-American players came out of the army after World War II, feeling that their music had been stolen by the white music system, they cultivated music that sounded "wrong," thereby frustrating white players who tried to join in and play. With such remarks, we might initiate an externalist account of the beginnings of modernist bebop jazz.
>
> However, if the account remained merely externalist, it would not tell us anything about the music itself. After all, what is of interest to the ear is that the music sounded hostile, by comparison with classic swing's generally friendly demeanor. A purely externalist account would not hook up with the music's mechanics, and would therefore give us no idea why music of that sort has that message in it.[2]

One can argue that the cultural context of jazz should be studied, but it is logically demonstrable that, no matter how illuminating its cultural context, the study of music must ultimately, at some point, return to the music itself. Stated as a tautology, the topic of the study of music is music. Even if the cultural context illuminated the music so well that our ideas about the music were revolutionized, note that what is getting illuminated is the music itself.

While any jazz scholar may legitimately restrict research to a more or less narrow or limited topic, jazz scholarship as a whole must return ultimately to the musical object, whether in the material form of a score or a recording, or in the immaterial form of a live performance, unless we propose never to hear music; but that would make jazz scholarship an absurd enterprise. As Henry Martin says, "[W]e should never neglect what brought us to jazz itself: the music, and our emotional and aesthetic response to it."[3] If the focus of thinking about music is music, then we must ultimately return to the music, even if we are enlightened for having temporarily abandoned treating the music as an isolated object. If music is audible, there must be a musical product, and the product in all music is, well, *the music*. So as long as we listen to actual music, we will be concerned with product, whether it is the material product of a composer's score or the immaterial product of the music of a performance.

John Brownell has argued that product and the musical object is not an appropriate focus for the study of jazz improvisation, especially when analyzed through the written, material object of the score: "Improvisation is essentially a performance practice, and it is inappropriate to apply to it analytical models developed in the context of the written record."[4] "The object in the analysis of improvisation is itself a phantom, and rather than analyzing music, what ends up being analyzed is the frozen record of a process."[5] Brownell views Thomas Owens's study of Charlie Parker's improvisations as one example of a processural analytic model that "reveals fundamental departures from previous analytic (product-oriented) approaches. Rather than subject a small number of improvisations to detailed analysis in an effort to identify evidence of development and variation, Owens examines a large number of Parker's solos with a view to identifying statistical similarities. He compiles a catalog of sixty-four melodic devices and ranks them according to frequency."[6]

But Owens's study is no less focused on the musical product than the analytic models that Brownell surveyed. Owens analyzed transcriptions of Parker's improvisations, using, no less, that hallmark of product in the study of music, music notation. Brownell's view of Owens's study as an example of a processural analytic model is further flawed when Brownell contrasts it with the "notism" of Gunther Schuller's study of Sonny Rollins:

> [F]or Schuller, Rollins' "thematic" approach is aesthetically superior. Its superiority, to Schuller, lies in its use of devices that are normally considered to be indicators of quality in composed music. Development of themes, coherence, deliberation, and consideration of material employed (as opposed to whatever the player "happens to hit upon") are the hallmarks of well-crafted compositions. I propose the term "notism" for this critical attitude. Notism

springs from a fixation on the object of analysis rather than on the process from which it springs.[7]

But analyzing the product of improvisation, even the notes and rhythms of an improvisation, need not necessarily imply the standards of compositional excellence. Brownell confuses an analytic approach with critical standards. The standards that Brownell says Schuller and others bring from composition into improvisation, such as development of themes or coherence, is not the necessary result of looking at improvisation as product. One could just as well analyze the processural aspects of improvisation by using what is really just a convenient tool, the score (a transcription of the improvisation), just as Owens has done. The tool of notation is a shorthand for the "real" (audible) thing, but one can effectively use the tool if its nature— its usefullnesss and its limitations—is kept in mind. The standards and the tools of analysis can be separated from a focus on product or process.

Brownell says that, "Like Schuller with Sonny Rollins, Stewart finds evidence in Clifford Brown's improvisations of structural development and variation, the hallmarks of compositional quality."[8] Assuming that this is a criticism, what are we then to do with development and variation, two of the standard if not omnipresent techniques of jazz improvisation (as well as composition)? Development and variation is essential to all but the most static forms of music. They may be hallmarks of composition, but composition certainly does not have exclusive rights to them. Every jazz improviser develops and varies musical material to some extent.[9]

The two processural models that Brownell outlines—formulaic improvisation, similar to that used in epic poetry, and linguistic models—are fruitful analytic approaches. Whereas Brownell views the opposition between processural models and analytic/product models as one of mutual exclusion, they may be merely juxtaposed, each contributing a valid perspective.

It is indicative of the confusion surrounding process and product that nowhere in Brownell's review of processural models for improvisation are there any critical standards, and Brownell confuses the standards with the approach when he identifies the critical standards of notism but also defines notism as being fixated on the object. He confuses the standards with the analytic approaches that don't necessarily require those standards, and when he offers an alternative, the processural models, no mention of critical standards is made.

CONTEXT AND PRODUCT CAN COEXIST

The larger context in which we view jazz, beyond formalism, contains not only the social and cultural aspects of jazz on which critical theory focuses, but the conditions and processes of improvisation as well. As we have seen, consideration of this larger context can lead to some very important ideas about jazz, such as the humanistic implications of jazz, or the significance of an improviser pulling the fat out of the fire compared to a composer doing so. This larger context does not change our understanding of the musical object as an isolated thing. It is not so much that our understanding or analysis of an isolated musical object changes, but that the meaning and significance that we impart to the musical object changes.

But doing so does not mean that focus on product should disappear completely. To understand this, let's start with the following: "Improvisation, on the other hand, may . . . inspire novel approaches to music analysis that focus more attention on the human and cultural aspects of music making than on the formal structure of the musical work."[10] David Borgo accurately identifies a topic for research that is distinct from formalistic analysis. This topic is the social, cultural, historical, and human context of jazz performance. But consider whether social, cultural, and historical contexts are used to further the understanding of the product, the music itself, or not. If not, we have two very different research topics—a formalist approach to jazz that focuses on the musical object, and social/cultural studies of jazz that do not refer back to the musical object. There is no substantive connection between the two other than they are both studying jazz. They are doing so in two separate arenas, and therefore there is no reason to suspect that they both are not valid, interesting, and useful in their own right. It is an example of either/or thinking, of only being able to see one type of opposition—mutual exclusion—to deny one research agenda because another is valuable. Critical theory's valuable emphasis on culture does not deny the value of formalism, and vice versa. In the other case, insofar as social, cultural, and historical contexts are used to understand the musical product of improvisation, their utility is then in service of a more enlightened understanding of the music itself. These two cases mean that, however, one is left with either (1) a return to a focus on the music itself, albeit from a position enlightened by social and cultural studies, or (2) two distinct research agendas that can not deny one another. Either way, jazz scholarship is allowed a focus on product and the music itself, despite recent efforts to shift focus away from product.

Much of the recent acknowledgment of the importance of process in jazz improvisation, as well as critical theory's critique of formalism and product, is the result of assuming mutual exclusion between product and process, rather than conceiving their opposition in other terms. Process as well as social and cultural factors can change the context in which we view the musical product, and therefore the meaning and significance we give it, which are also important concerns in the study of music. Yet, we may also understand music by understanding the music itself. These two goals are not so much pointed directly at each other in mutual exclusion as they are pointed in opposite directions.

Critical theory might have a valid complaint against formalism if formalism explicitly denied social or cultural concerns. This complaint, however, should be balanced by its less frequently heard but no less valid counterpart, stated by Ted Gioia:

> Many [free jazz musicians] saw their music as inherently political. They saw that they could, indeed must, choose between participating in the existing structures—in society, in the entertainment industry, in the jazz world—or rebelling against them. . . . This overt linking of free jazz and sociopolitical criticism went so far that Ekkehard Jost, a historian of the movement, lamented that the "autonomous musical aspects of the evolution of free jazz—i.e., those aspects which escape a purely sociological analysis—often were ignored." The music risked being relegated to a secondary, utilitarian role, valued for what it symbolized rather than for what it was.[11]

These opposites can coexist, too. Music can be what it symbolizes as well as what it is.

PERFECTION AND STRUCTURAL COMPLEXITY

If formalism and product can be a part of how we understand jazz improvisation, then perfection and structural complexity might be, too. But we have already seen how the conditions of jazz are not advantageous in this regard. This contradiction will be illuminated by considering the performer's interpretive role versus improvisation.

The role of a performer as an interpreter also supports product and formalism as a part of jazz. Carol Gould and Kenneth Keaton have discussed the many ways in which performers interpret a composition. They challenge the view that the improviser is in a fundamentally different situation than the performer because both determine many aspects of a composition. They "submit that jazz and classical performances differ more in degree than in kind."[12] However, there is an important difference in kind that reveals a legitimate role for product and formalism in jazz. Understanding this difference depends on recognizing the function of the elements of music that a performer may interpret.

Pitch and Rhythm Creates Structure

We have seen how composers and performers are responsible for determining different elements of music (see "Creation in Improvisation" in chapter

8). Traditionally, it is the discrete musical elements of pitch and rhythm that are those elements of music under the strictest control by the composer, are assumed to not be changed by the performer, and create the relationships and structures that are the focus of formalism.[13] Recognition of musical relationships and structures has an intellectual component to it, and this relies on the discrete character of pitch and rhythm. Perceiving and appreciating relationships and structures requires some intellectual recognition of same (although it does not rule out an emotional response as well). Part of the reason for this is because two elements in a relationship must be discrete elements in order for that relationship to be formed, and some intellectual function is required to make a connection between the separate elements. One must realize intellectually that two or more musical events are related in order for a relationship to be established and perceived. For instance, when the composed melody (the "head") returns in jazz after the improvisations, a relationship and structure is established between the initial head and the one after the solos, as a result of their identity. This structure is a common one in jazz, and may well be accompanied by an emotional response of security, of having returned home after a journey.

Interpreted Elements Are Immediately Appreciable

Alternately, it is the analog elements of music, such as dynamics or tone color, that the composer traditionally does not determine completely, and that the performer interprets, that strike us more immediately and viscerally, with no necessary relationship to another musical event, and which tend to induce an emotional response (but do not prohibit an intellectual response). For instance, the brittle tone color of Miles Davis's Harmon mute or the thunder of McCoy Tyner's loud left-hand octaves are appreciable immediately and viscerally. Appreciating them is not dependent on recognizing a connection between them and some other event or structure in the music. They hit us immediately. (An immediately appreciable musical event that takes some amount of time to unfold is different from forming a relationship between two musical events separated in time.) While it is possible that we may connect an analog event with some other musical event or structure, we need not do so. One of the distinctive things about the analog elements of music is that they can be appreciated immediately, without reference to any other musical structure.

Structure Is Not Privileged Over the Visceral

Our understanding of jazz may gain from the distinction between the composer's responsibility for pitches, rhythms, and the resulting relationships and structures, and the performer's interpretation of dynamics, articulations, and the resulting visceral effects, while not privileging one over the other. The visceral in jazz and music is highly attractive to many, including myself. Rather than the relationship between the visceral and structure in jazz being mutual exclusion, they are juxtaposed. Because the jazz musician is a performer as well as a composer, the performer's analog realm of dynamics, articulations, and tone color assume a great importance in jazz. Can one say unequivocally that Miles Davis's tone color is more or less important than his structural use of silence? That this is an impossible question to answer indicates that the two realms are fused into an organic whole in jazz.

The Improviser Creates Structure

The improviser does have a crucial difference of kind with the performer. By taking over the composer's task of determining pitches and rhythms, the improviser has the responsibility of creating musical relationships and structure, a responsibility that the performer does not have to any great degree. This is significant: creating relationships is a distinct means of creating musical value compared to using visceral effects. (Some might argue that creating relationships is the primary means, although mistakenly, I think.) Entering into this significant aesthetic realm makes the difference between improvisers and performers a difference of kind as well as one of degree. It also provides one reason why complex musical structure can be a goal in jazz. The improviser must create those discrete elements of music, pitch, and rhythm, that are traditionally used to create relationships and structure because the composer is not creating them. The hallmark of jazz is improvisation, and a fundamental duty of the improviser is taking responsibility for creating pitches and rhythms, which are the primary means of creating musical relationships and structures.

Furthermore, given the responsibility for determining those elements of music that traditionally create relationships and structure, there is no reason to exclude structural complexity from the aesthetics of jazz improvisation. We can not deny jazz the highest goal in areas—notes, rhythms, and the resulting relationships and structures—for which the improviser takes responsibility. To do so would be to reject an opportunity that is inherent in the conditions of jazz.

Dynamic Tension and Complex Structure

It is another measure of the dynamic tension in jazz that the conditions of jazz encourage structural complexity, because the improviser is responsible for pitches and rhythms, which composers use to create complex structure, and yet also discourage structural complexity, because the improviser does not have the advantages that the composer does. Jazz improvisation can include the challenge of producing a perfect musical product even though the conditions of improvisation make it more difficult, just as Lewis and Clark wanted the shortest and easiest route to the Pacific but understood that their circumstances would probably make their route longer and more difficult. An explorer as well as an improviser accepts the dynamic tension of wanting to find the most perfect solution and understanding that such may be less likely, just as, existentially, we want to make the best decisions in our lives but understand that much of life is a crapshoot anyway and leading a perfect life is highly unlikely. The improviser has the following as potential goals: the creation of a perfect, complex musical structure and the creation of an improvisation that is also highly expressive emotionally and grooves well, too. The improviser, however, understands that succeeding at all these goals might not happen for every single performance because of inherent limitations. This is a different aesthetic than that of composition, the conditions of which encourage the idea that perfection and complexity are attainable. This condemns neither improvisation nor composition. Even in the worst case, if we assume that perfection is not possible even for composition, it is nonetheless valuable even as a wonderful fantasy, that we flawed humans may get a glimpse of perfection that inspires us to be less flawed.

JAZZ RESOURCES

Even though jazz has some disadvantages compared to composition in creating structural complexity, it can still do fairly well in this regard, perhaps more so than might first be imagined. Even if jazz is held to formalist standards, some level of deficiency in creating complex structure does not necessarily mean insufficiency. The jazz improviser has several techniques that allow him or her to improve the chances that structural complexity can be produced, even in an improvisation.

Improvisers Improve

The sure way to get better at something is to practice. As an improviser practices the craft of improvisation, both on stage and off, the ability to produce complex musical structures can increase. This was made vivid to me when I heard alto saxophonist Phil Woods live, when he was middle-aged. My reaction to his playing was that it was like fine wine. Everything he did was so smooth and secure, in addition to being quite complex. Most likely, he achieved this high level of performance as a result of the many years of practice and thousands of hours of professional experience that honed his craft.

Performing a Piece Many Times

One way to look at jazz improvisation is to view each time a musician improvises on the same piece as one in a single series of improvisations that gradually develops a superior approach to that piece. Throughout a career, an improviser might play common pieces hundreds of times. During each one, the musician must solve a similar musical problem. By attempting to work out a solution to such a problem hundreds of times, the improviser may gradually improve his or her approach. The danger, of course, is that the improviser will find what may seem to be an optimal solution and then just keep performing it without trying to find new and creative ways to solve the same problem.

Chorus Form Limits

One advantage the improviser has is the chorus form. The great majority of mainstream jazz pieces have a chorus form, which is a chord progression, often thirty-two measures in length, that is repeated throughout the entire performance and which forms the basis for the improvisation. This foundation means that the improviser does not have to create all the music from scratch. In fitting an improvisation to the given chord progression and chorus form, the improviser is given a head start.

Motivic Development

Another area in which the conditions and process of jazz improvisation help create structural complexity is motivic development. Jazz improvisers typically rely on previously worked out patterns, motifs, and their variation and development. This allows the improviser to create a complex series of relationships among a motif and subsequent variations. While a motif may not be repeated and varied many times in a row, it often returns under similar circumstances, and a return occurrence of it will create a relationship, sometimes a quite complex one, between it and the original occurrence of that motif.

Overall Shape

Just as classical music and other forms of music rely on a finite number of standard forms (sonata, theme and variations, and more) that do not inhibit structural complexity, jazz relies on some standard methods of creating a broad, overall structure for an improvisation. The most obvious and common one is that of a gradual increase in intensity, with a climax near the end, followed by a brief dénouement. While other shapes for the overall intensity curve of an improvisation are possible, having this standard one helps the improviser achieve one element of structural complexity—a broad, overall shape—underneath which are the complex details of how that shape is produced.

One Element Not Possible

The one area in which the jazz improviser is not likely to create a complex structure is long-range harmony. The chorus structure defines the basic harmonies for an entire improvisation, removing this area from significant development by the jazz improviser. The improviser may introduce substitute chords, and often does, but usually these are only local harmonic embellishments. While harmony is a very significant area in which jazz improvisers create complexity, the chorus form prevents much creativity in this area on a long-range basis.

MISTAKES

If product is an appropriate focus in jazz improvisation, and if perfection is an acceptable challenge, then how do we view mistakes in jazz?

The Positives of Mistakes

Mistakes can have a positive function in jazz. R. Keith Sawyer says that "mistakes perform the valued function of interrupting the prearranged ideas and forcing an innovative alternative."[14] A mistake can alert the improviser to opportunities and possibilities not normally considered. A mistake is unexpected, and so can shake the improviser out of the normal ways of thinking and improvising and offer new ways of viewing the problem at hand.

Aren't Mistakes Bad?

While a mistake may function positively, this does not necessarily remove the negative aspect of a mistake. Both the positive and negative aspects of a mistake can coexist. However, in his article on the mistakes of Miles Davis, Robert Walser does not acknowledge the obvious: mistakes are bad. That is, no one wants mistakes (certainly not Davis, as Walser indicates), they are to be avoided, and they detract from the success an improvisation would otherwise enjoy.

We are quickly led to absurdities if we don't acknowledge the negativity of mistakes. For instance, if we ignore the negativity of mistakes because they are inevitable, and conclude that we must accept them, we might then ask, "How many mistakes can we tolerate?" Clearly, there must be a limit on the number of mistakes that are acceptable. If any number of mistakes were acceptable, then you could have an improvised solo full of nothing but mistakes, which not even Walser, and very few listeners, musicians, or scholars, I suspect, would find acceptable. Not even free jazz is all mistakes (although some might think it sounds that way). If there were not a limit on mistakes, then we would be just as happy listening to incompetent musicians, or anyone at all, marveling at how their failed attempts are an analogue for the mistakes that we make in our lives (although perhaps few would want to be reminded of or live through such mistakes via such music). Critical standards—any standards—would disappear.

But this means that some mistakes—certainly those beyond some limit—must be viewed as negatives and cannot simply be glossed over or ignored. Moreover, if those mistakes past that limit can be interpreted as negatives, then we might as well acknowledge *any* mistake as a negative, just as common sense demands, even if jazz improvisation is fated to include mistakes. Ultimately, a clear, unafraid estimation of mistakes as *bad*, at least partially and in some cases, is necessary, nearly by definition. The necessity of mistakes has been admitted by no less than Ornette Coleman: "From realizing that I can make mistakes, I have come to realize that there is an order to what I do."[15] In dialectic fashion, order and disorder (mistakes) coexist, just as the positive and negatives aspects of mistakes coexist, too.

Existentially Required

Mistakes need not doom jazz, yet still function as a negative, because jazz is an analog for the experiential and for life, in which mistakes figure prominently. And yet this does not mean that one is free to play any mistake as if mistakes somehow don't count. It is exactly because mistakes still do count as negatives that, contradictorily, they contribute positively to understanding jazz as a humanistic, existential practice.

One challenge for the jazz improviser is to create complex, perfect structures under the conditions of imperfection. If a jazz musician improvised a brilliant, complex maneuver, carrying the audience along for a thrilling ride, and then, at the moment of truth, at the highest climax of the solo, took a misstep, or made a crucial mistake, we might respond on a naïve level with disappointment and a lesser regard for the musician, especially as a technician; but on a more enlightened level, understanding the risk taken and the conditions under which the improviser works, we might respond with admiration and an honest respect for someone who has attempted something great and far above what might be expected normally, as if the improviser had the luxuries afforded the composer, even as we understand that the improviser ultimately fell short. Mistakes in jazz can be a noble failure, and not just a careless or unprepared failure or a measure of inferiority

compared to composition. The nobility of failure is a lesson for ourselves
and our lives, and that is the larger lesson we hear in jazz improvisation.
Stated as a contradiction a long time ago by Saint Augustine, "This is the
very perfection of a man, to find out his own imperfections."[16] This still
does not permit mistakes in jazz at will. All it does is encourage jazz musicians to take risks in the service of creating brilliant, complex structures.

Limits vs. Optimism

To admit the limitations of mistakes, imperfection, and the disadvantages
for creating structural complexity in jazz goes against deep and powerful
traditions of perfection and boundless optimism that have long been part
of the national culture in the United States, the birthplace of jazz. Donald
McCullough, in a book dedicated to embracing the negatives inherent in
limitations, summarizes this:

> [We are] a determinedly optimistic culture that runs on a can-do confidence
> in every individual's ability—given a positive attitude and hard work—to
> overcome all obstacles on the way to success [perfection]. This spirit has
> flourished, in part, because of geography: the seemingly boundless expanse
> of our continent promised new opportunities, and this promise energized
> and focused our expectations. In the words of Parker Palmer, "We resist the
> very ideas of limits, regarding limits of all sorts as temporary and regrettable
> impositions on our lives. Our national myth is about the endless defiance of
> limits: opening the western frontier, breaking the speed of sound, dropping
> people on the moon, discovering 'cyberspace' at the very moment when we
> have filled old-fashioned space with so much junk that we can barely move.
> We refuse to take no for an answer."[17]

To add one more example: football's Super Bowl, part of the American
myth if anything is, rarely if ever acknowledges anything less than perfection; that is, the Super Bowl is winner-take-all. Only the team that wins
the Super Bowl is truly acknowledged. Only lip service is given to the accomplishments and success of the loser of the Super Bowl, which team is
actually the second greatest of all teams, has accomplished great things,
and should be envied by all the other teams who didn't make it to the Super Bowl. But their accomplishments are largely overlooked in our focus
on the best, the number-one team.

CONTRADICTIONS IN JAZZ AND LIFE

Obviously, perfection has its advantages. It is an example of either/or thinking, however, to deny any useful function for imperfection. Rather, perfec-

tion and imperfection can be held in dynamic tension. Perfection is a laudable goal, and the improviser can achieve it more often than might be imagined, but the conditions of improvisation encourage imperfection, which then give the improviser the opportunity to mirror the experiential and, ultimately, the conditions of our lives through improvisation; and, lastly, the improviser can do both at the same time. By striving for perfection, perhaps achieving it sometimes, and perhaps failing in some (hopefully) small way, the improviser demonstrates both contradictory aspects of improvisation.

Contradiction in jazz resides in the fact that great structural complexity is a legitimate goal in jazz improvisation despite improvisers facing inherent limitations in creating structural complexity, even as the same conditions that create those limitations also create existential and humanistic values in jazz beyond structural complexity. Even though mistakes and lesser complexity are nearly inevitable in jazz improvisation at some point, they are no reasons for improvisers to reject the goal of perfection and complexity. Lee Brown says, "We find ourselves slipping back and forth between our hopes for the ultimate quality of the music and our fascination with the activity by which it is generated—even when those actions appear to threaten the quality of the resulting music. The strain [dynamic tension] contributes to the music's fascination rather than detracting from it."[18] While we can not blame Lewis and Clark for their errors or wanderings in reaching the Pacific, they still strove to take the easiest, shortest route, and highly valued such a path. Jazz musicians can rightly strive to create structural complexity and to minimize mistakes at the same time that its existential context and analogy with experience give jazz other meaning as well.

We may improve how we work through a situation or experience in life. Sometimes we do so skillfully, although gradually, with the help of past experiences; sometimes we do so with the help of others who have gone before, although such advice or wisdom can only go so far; and sometimes (most of the time?) we do so by just muddling our way through each new challenge as it is presented to us, sometimes brilliantly and sometimes, not despite of, but because of all the contradictions inherent in our situations and our lives—just like jazz improvisers.

NOTES

1. *Encyclopedia of Aesthetics*, s.v. "Jazz."

2. Lee Brown, "Postmodernist Jazz Theory: Afrocentrism, Old and New," *Journal of Aesthetics and Art Criticism* 57, no. 2 (Spring 1999): 239.

3 Henry Martin, "Jazz Theory—An Overview," *Annual Review of Jazz Studies* 8 (1996): 4.

4. John Brownell, "Analytical Modes of Jazz Improvisation," *JazzForschung/ Jazz Research* 26 (1994): 19.

5. Brownell, "Analytical Modes of Jazz Improvisation," 15.

6. Brownell, "Analytical Modes of Jazz Improvisation," 18.

7. Brownell, "Analytical Modes of Jazz Improvisation," 15.

8. Brownell, "Analytical Modes of Jazz Improvisation," 16.

9. It is difficult if not impossible to imagine any music that does not develop or vary musical material (except perhaps a single note sustained without variation, but even then one could argue that the mere passage of time makes that same note at, say, 5 minutes of duration different in some way than that note after, say, 5 seconds of duration.

10. David Borgo, "Reverence for Uncertainty: Chaos, Order, and the Dynamics of Musical Free Improvisation" (Ph. D. diss., University of California, Los Angeles, 1999), 58.

11. Ted Gioia, *The History of Jazz* (New York: Oxford University Press, 1997), 338–39.

12. Carol S. Gould and Kenneth Keaton, "The Essential Role of Improvisation in Musical Performance," *Journal of Aesthetics and Art Criticism* 58, no. 2 (Spring 2000): 146.

13. It is not impossible, however, to create relationships and structures with analog elements.

14. R. Keith Sawyer, *Group Creativity: Music, Theater, Collaboration* (Mahwah, N.J.: Lawrence Erlbaum Associates, 2003), 60.

15. Ornette Coleman, *The Shape of Jazz to Come* (Atlantic SD 1317, 1959), liner notes.

16. Attributed to Saint Augustine, *Augustine of Hippo Quotes*, http://www .quotesplace.com/i/b/Augustine_of_Hippo (accessed December 13, 2005).

17. Donald McCullough, *The Consolations of Imperfection: Learning to Appreciate Life's Limitations* (Grand Rapids, Mich.: Brazos Press, 2004), 13–14.

18. Lee Brown, "'Feeling My Way': Jazz Improvisation and Its Vicissitudes—A Plea for Imperfection," *Journal of Aesthetics and Art Criticism* 58, no. 2 (Spring 2000): 121–22.

Bibliography

PRINTED MATERIALS

Alperson, Philip. "On Musical Improvisation." *Journal of Aesthetics and Art Criticism* 43, no. 1 (Fall 1984): 17–29.

Augustine. *Augustine of Hippo Quotes*. http://www.quotespalace.com/Augustine-of-Hippo/index.html (accessed December 13, 2005).

Bailey, Derek. *Improvisation: Its Nature and Practice in Music*. New York: Da Capo Press, 1992.

Balliett, Whitney. *Improvising: Sixteen Jazz Musicians and Their Art*. New York: Oxford University Press, 1977.

Becker, Howard. *Outsiders: Studies in the Sociology of Deviance*. New York: Free Press, 1963.

Becker, Judith. "Is Western Art Music Superior?" *Musical Quarterly* 72, no. 3 (1986): 341–59.

Belgrad, Daniel. *The Culture of Spontaneity: Improvisation and the Arts in Postwar America*. Chicago: University of Chicago Press, 1998.

Berendt, Joachim E. *The Jazz Book: From Ragtime to Fusion and Beyond*. Revised by Günther Huesmann, translated by H. and B. Bredigkeit with Dan Morgenstern and Tim Nevill. New York: Lawrence Hill Books, 1992.

Berlin, Isaiah. *Two Concepts of Liberty*. London: Oxford University Press, 1958.

Berliner, Paul. *Thinking in Jazz: The Infinite Art of Improvisation*. Chicago: University of Chicago Press, 1994.

Borgo, David. "Negotiating Freedom: Values and Practices in Contemporary Improvised Music." *Black Music Research Journal* 22, no. 2 (Fall 2002): 165–88.

———. "Reverence for Uncertainty: Chaos, Order, and the Dynamics of Musical Free Improvisation." Ph.D. diss., University of California, Los Angeles, 1999.

Brecker, Michael. "Nothing Personal." In *The New Real Book*. Vol. 1, edited by Chuck Sher. Petaluma, Calif.: Sher Music, 1988.

Brofsky, Howard. "Miles Davis and 'My Funny Valentine': The Evolution of a Solo." *Black Music Research Journal* 3 (1983): 23–45.

Brown, Charles T. *The Art of Rock and Roll*. 3rd ed. Englewood Cliffs, N.J.: Prentice Hall, 1993.

Brown, Lee. "Postmodernist Jazz Theory: Afrocentrism, Old and New." *Journal of Aesthetics and Art Criticism* 57, no. 2 (Spring 1999): 235–46.

———. "Feeling My Way: Jazz Improvisation and Its Vicissitudes—A Plea for Imperfection." *Journal of Aesthetics and Art Criticism* 58, no. 2 (Spring 2000): 113–23.

Brownell, John. "Analytical Modes of Jazz Improvisation." *Jazzforschung/Jazz Research* 26 (1994): 9–29.

Cameron, William Bruce. "Sociological Notes on the Jam Session." *Social Forces* 33 (1954): 177–82.

Cardew, Cornelius. "Towards an Ethic of Improvisation." In *Treatise Handbook*. London: Edition Peters, 1971.

Cobb, William. "The Empty Board #13: The Dialectic of Go." *American Go Journal* 33, no. 1 (Winter 1999): 8.

Collier, James Lincoln, and Geoffrey L. Collier. "Microrhythms in Jazz: A Review of Papers." *Annual Review of Jazz Studies* 8 (1996): 117–39.

Conflict Resolution Program of Santa Cruz County. *Conflict Management Tools & Skills: A One-Day Workshop*. Santa Cruz, Calif.: Conflict Resolution Program of Santa Cruz County, 1995.

Corbett, John. "Jazz Experiments: Cutting Edge Research." *Downbeat* 61, no. 7 (July 1994): 50.

———. "Writing around Free Improvisation." In *Jazz among the Discourses*, edited by Krin Gabbard. Durham, N.C.: Duke University Press, 1995.

Crovitz, Herbert. *Galton's Walk: Methods for the Analysis of Thinking, Intelligence, and Creativity*. New York: Harper and Row, 1970.

Crow, Bill. *Jazz Anecdotes*. New York: Oxford University Press, 1990.

Crowell, Steven. "Existentialism." *Stanford Encyclopedia of Philosophy*. http://plato.stanford.edu/entries/existentialism/ (accessed December 7, 2004).

Dacey, John S., and Kathleen Lennon. *Understanding Creativity: The Interplay of Biological, Psychological, and Social Factors*. San Francisco: Jossey-Bass Publishers, 1998.

Day, William. "Knowing as Instancing: Jazz Improvisation and Moral Perfectionism." *Journal of Aesthetics and Art Criticism* 58, no. 2 (Spring 2000): 99–111.

Deveaux, Scott. "Constructing the Jazz Tradition: Jazz Historiography." *Black American Literature Forum* 25, no. 3 (Autumn 1991): 525–60.

Doerschuk, Bob. "McCoy Tyner." *Keyboard* 7, no. 8 (August 1981): 28–38.

Emerson, Ralph Waldo. "Self-Reliance." In *The Complete Essays and Other Writings of Ralph Waldo Emerson*, edited by Brooks Atkinson. New York: Random House, 1940.

Encyclopedia of Aesthetics. New York: Oxford University Press, 1998.

Feurzeig, David. "Making the Right Mistakes: James P. Johnson, Thelonious Monk, and the Trickster Aesthetic." DMA diss., Cornell University, 1997.

Fischlin, Daniel, and Ajay Heble. "The Other Side of Nowhere." In *The Other Side of Nowhere: Jazz, Improvisation, and Communities in Dialogue*, edited by Daniel Fischlin and Ajay Heble. Middleton, Conn.: Wesleyan University Press, 2004.

Francesconi, Robert. "Art vs. the Audience: The Paradox of Modern Jazz." *Journal of American Culture* 4, no. 4 (1981): 70–80.

Gillespie, Luke O. "Literacy, Orality, and the Parry-Lord 'Formula': Improvisation and the Afro-American Jazz Tradition." *International Review of the Aesthetics and Sociology of Music* 22, no. 2 (December 1991): 147–64.

Gioia, Ted. *The Imperfect Art*. New York: Oxford University Press, 1988.

———. *The History of Jazz*. New York: Oxford University Press, 1997.

Gitler, Ira. *Swing to Bop*. New York: Oxford University Press, 1985.

Glawischnig, Dieter. "The Present Boom in Jazz Education—A Trap for Creativity?" *Jazzforschung/Jazz Research* 28 (1996): 77–81.

Goldberg, Joe. *Jazz Masters of the Fifties*. New York: Macmillan, 1965.

Gould, Carol S., and Kenneth Keaton. "The Essential Role of Improvisation in Musical Performance." *Journal of Aesthetics and Art Criticism* 58, no. 2 (Spring 2000): 143–48.

Gridley, Mark, Robert Maxham, and Robert Hoff. "Three Approaches to Defining Jazz." *Musical Quarterly* 73, no. 4 (1989): 513–31.

Halpern, Charna, Del Close, and Kim Johnson. *Truth in Comedy: The Manual of Improvisation*. Colorado Springs, Colo.: Meriwether Publishing, 1994.

Hamilton, Andy. "The Aesthetics of Imperfection." *Philosophy* 65, no. 253 (July 1990): 323–40.

———. "The Art of Improvisation and the Aesthetics of Imperfection." *British Journal of Aesthetics* 40, no. 1 (2000): 168–85.

Harper, Ralph. *Existentialism: A Theory of Man*. Cambridge: Harvard University Press, 1965.

Harvey, Edward. "Social Change and the Jazz Musician." *Social Forces* 46, no. 1 (September 1967): 34–42.

Hentoff, Nat. *Jazz Is*. New York: Random House, 1976.

Hodeir, Andre. *Toward Jazz*. New York: Grove Press, 1962.

Hollenberg, David. Review of the Ran Blake/Ray Bryant trio. *Downbeat* 45, no. 10 (May 18, 1978): 40–42.

Iyer, Vijay. "Embodied Mind, Situated Cognition, and Expressive Microtiming in Afro-American Music." *Music Perception* 19, no. 3 (Spring 2002): 387–414.

Jarrett, Keith. "The Virtual Jazz Age." *Musician* (March 1968): 34–36.

Jost, Ekkehard. *Free Jazz*. Graz, Austria: Universal Edition, 1974.

Joyce, James. *Ulysses*. New York: Vintage Books, 1961.

Keil, Charles. "The Theory of Participatory Discrepancies: A Progress Report." *Ethnomusicology* 39, no. 1 (Winter 1995): 1–19.

Keil, Charles, and Steven Feld. *Music Grooves: Essays and Dialogues*. Chicago: University of Chicago Press, 1994.

Leonard, Neil. *Jazz: Myth and Religion*. New York: Oxford University Press, 1987.

Lewis, George. "Improvised Music after 1950." *Black Music Research Journal* 16, no. 1 (1996): 91–122.

Lichtenstein, David. "The Rhetoric of Improvisation." *American Imago* 50, no. 2 (Summer 1993): 227–52.

Lindemann, Erika, and Daniel Anderson. *A Rhetoric for Writing Teachers*. 4th ed. New York: Oxford University Press, 2001.

Litweiler, John. *The Freedom Principle: Jazz after 1958*. New York: William Morrow, 1984.

Maddi, Salvatore R. *Personality Theories: A Comparative Analysis*. Pacific Grove, Calif.: Brooks/Cole Publishing Company, 1996.

Martin, Henry. "Jazz Theory—An Overview." *Annual Review of Jazz Studies* 8 (1996): 1–17.

Martin, Henry, and Keith Waters. *Jazz: The First 100 Years*. 2nd ed. Belmont, Calif.: Thomson Schirmer, 2006.

McClary, Susan, and Robert Walser. "Theorizing the Body in African-American Music." *Black Music Research Journal* 14, no.1 (Spring 1994): 75–84.

McCullough, Donald. *The Consolations of Imperfection: Learning to Appreciate Life's Limitations*. Grand Rapids, Mich.: Brazos Press, 2004.

Meyer, Leonard. *Music, the Arts, and Ideas*. Chicago: University of Chicago Press, 1967.

Monterose, J. R. *Straight Ahead*. Xanadu, 1975.

Nettl, Bruno. "Thoughts on Improvisation: A Comparative Approach." *Musical Quarterly* 60, no. 1 (January 1974): 1–19.

Nisenson, Eric. *Blue: The Murder of Jazz*. New York: St. Martin's Press, 1997.

———. *The Making of Kind of Blue: Miles Davis and His Masterpiece*. New York: St. Martin's Press, 2000.

Oliver, Phil. "On William James' 'Springs of Delight': The Return to Life." *Stream of William James* 2, no. 3 (Fall 2000): 14–15.

Oteri, Frank. "Harnessing the Random Element." *NewMusicBox*. http://www.newmusicbox.org/page.nmbx?id=23ls00 (accessed December 13, 2005).

Oyserman, Daphna, Heather M. Cooñ, and Markus Kemmelmeier. "Rethinking Individualism and Collectivism: Evaluation of Theoretical Assumptions and Meta-Analyses." *Psychological Bulletin* 128, no. 1 (2002): 3–72.

Pepper, Art, and Laurie Pepper. *Straight Life: The Story of Art Pepper*. New York: Schirmer Books, 1979.

Perlman, Alan M., and Daniel Greenblatt. "Miles Davis Meets Noam Chomsky: Some Observations on Jazz Improvisation and Language Structure." In *The Sign in Music and Literature*, edited by Wendy Steiner, 169–83. Austin: University of Texas, 1981.

Pratt, Carroll. "Music as the Language of Emotions." In *Lectures on the History and Art of Music*. New York: Da Capo Press, 1968.

Prögler, J. A. "Searching for Swing: Participatory Discrepancies in the Jazz Rhythm Section." *Ethnomusicology* 39, no.1 (Winter 1995): 21–54.

Reason, Dana. " 'Navigable Structures and Transforming Mirrors': Improvisation and Interactivity." In *The Other Side of Nowhere: Jazz, Improvisation, and Communities in Dialogue*, edited by Daniel Fischlin and Ajay Heble. Middleton, Conn.: Wesleyan University Press, 2004.

Recording Industry Association of America. "2003 Consumer Profile." www.riaa.com/news/marketingdata/pdf/2003ConsumerProfile.pdf.

Reese, William L. *Dictionary of Philosophy and Religion: Eastern and Western Thought*. Atlantic Highlands, N.J.: Humanities Press, 1980, s.v. "freedom."

Roberts, Hugh. "Improvisation, Individuation, Immanence: Thelonious Monk." *Black Sacred Music* 3, no. 2 (Fall 1989): 50–56.

Rothman, Tony, and George Sudarshan. *Doubt and Certainty*. Reading, Mass.: Helix Books, 1989.

Rychlak, Joseph. *The Psychology of Rigorous Humanism*. New York: John Wiley and Sons, 1977.

Sawyer, R. Keith. "Improvisational Creativity: An Analysis of Jazz Performance." *Creativity Research Journal* 5, no. 3 (1992): 253–63.

———. "Improvisation and the Creative Process: Dewey, Collingwood, and the Aesthetics of Spontaneity." *Journal of Aesthetics and Art Criticism* 58, no. 2 (Spring 2000): 149–61.

———. *Group Creativity: Music, Theater, Collaboration*. Mahwah, N.J.: Lawrence Erlbaum Associates, 2003.

Schmitt, Richard. *Beyond Separateness: The Social Nature of Human Beings—Their Autonomy, Knowledge, and Power*. Boulder, Colo.: Westview Press, 1995.

Schneckloth, Tim. "Frank Zappa: Garni du Jour, Lizard King, Poetry and Slime." *Downbeat* 45, no. 10 (May 18, 1978): 16.

Shils, Edward. *Tradition*. Chicago: University of Chicago Press, 1981.

Sloboda, John. *The Musical Mind*. Oxford: Clarendon Press, 1985.

Small, Christopher. *Music, Society, Education*. London: John Calder, 1980.

Soll, Ivan. "Existentialism." *World Book Online Reference Center*. www.worldbookonline.com/wb/Article?id=ar188480 (accessed August 8, 2004).

Stanford Encyclopedia of Philosophy. http://plato.stanford.edu/entries/logic-fuzzy/, s.v. "Fuzzy Logic."

Steele, Shelby. "Ralph Ellison's Blues." *Journal of Black Studies* 7, no. 2 (1976): 151–68.

Stewart, David, and Algis Mickunas. *Exploring Phenomenology*. 2nd ed. Athens: Ohio University Press, 1990.

Suhor, Charles. "Jazz Improvisation and Language Performance." *Et cetera* 43, no. 2 (Summer 1986): 133–40.

Talbott, William. "PHIL 102A, Test of Transparencies for Week #1 (Sept. 30–Oct. 4)." http://faculty.washington.edu/wtalbott/phil102/trweek1.htm (accessed September 3, 2005).

Tirro, Frank. *Jazz: A History*. 2nd ed. New York: W. W. Norton & Company, 1993.

Triandis, Harry. *Individualism and Collectivism*. Boulder, Colo.: Westview Press, 1995.

Walser, Robert. "Out of Notes": Signification, Interpretation, and the Problem of Miles Davis." *Musical Quarterly* 77, no. 2 (Summer 1993): 343–65.

Walter, Scott. "Live with TAE: Wynton Marsalis and Stanley Crouch." *American Enterprise* 8, no. 2 (March–April 1997): 20–23.

Weber, Max. *Economy and Society*. Vol. 1. New York: Bedminster Press, 1968.

Williams, Raymond. *The Long Revolution*. New York: Columbia University Press, 1961.

Williams, Martin. *The Jazz Tradition*. Oxford: Oxford University Press, 1983.

Wilmer, Valerie, ed. *As Serious As Your Life: The Story of the New Jazz*. Westport, Conn.: Lawrence Hill & Company, 1980.

Wyatt, C. S. "Existentialism: Definitions." *The Existential Primer*. www.tameri.com/csw/exist/ex_lexicon.html#lexicon (accessed December 13, 2005).

RECORDINGS

Ayler, Albert. *Bells—Prophecy*. ESP 1010-2, 1964–1965.
Coleman, Ornette. "Congeniality." *The Shape of Jazz to Come*. Atlantic SD 1317, 1959.
——. "Free Jazz." *Free Jazz*. Atlantic SD 1364, 1960.
——. "Street Woman." *Science Fiction*. Columbia KC 31061, 1971.
Corea, Chick. *Piano Improvisations Vol. 1*. ECM 811 979-2, 1971.
Davis, Miles. "Four." *Workin' with the Miles Davis Quintet*. Prestige P-7166, 1956.
Evans, Bill. "Autumn Leaves." *Portrait in Jazz*. Fantasy OJCCD 088-2, 1959.
The Firesign Theater, *How Can You Be in Two Places at Once When You're Not Anywhere at All*. Mobile Fidelity Sound Lab MFCD 834, 1969.
Puente, Tito. "Take Five." *Mambo Diablo*. Concord Picante CJP-283, 1985.
Rinzler, Paul. *Active Listening*. Sea Breeze Jazz SB-3039, 1999.
Rivers, Sam. *Dimensions and Extensions*. Blue Note BST 84261, 1986.
Rollins, Sonny. "Pent-Up House." *Sonny Rollins Plus 4*. Prestige PRLP 7038, 1956.
Tatum, Art. *Piano Starts Here*. Columbia PCT-9655E.
Weather Report. "Tears." *Weather Report*. Columbia KC 31352, 1972.
Zorn, John. "Latin Quarter." *Naked City*. Elektra/Nonesuch 9 79238-2, 1989.

VIDEOS

Miles Davis Quintet. *Footprints*. http://www.dailymotion.com/alternativa/davis/video/745 (accessed July 2, 2006).
Satchmo: Louis Armstrong. American Masters series. DVD. Columbia Music Video, 2000.

Index

About the Author

Paul Rinzler received his doctorate in theory/composition with a secondary emphasis in jazz pedagogy from the University of Northern Colorado. He joined the faculty at Cal Poly State University in San Luis Obispo, California, in 1997 as director of jazz studies after having taught jazz classes at the University of California, Santa Cruz, for twelve years. He recorded a jazz piano trio CD, *Active Listening* (Sea Breeze Jazz 3039), on which *Cadence* magazine noted "impressive trio interplay" and "rich dialogues." He appears as a special guest artist on the recent collective improvisation CD *Short to the House* (GeoJazz Records MD 2020).

Rinzler has been awarded several National Endowment for the Arts grants, including a Jazz Performance Grant. His compositions have been performed in New England, California, and the Midwest. Scarecrow Press re-released Rinzler's *Jazz Arranging and Performance Practice* in paperback, and his *Quartal Jazz Piano Voicings* has recently been published. His articles on jazz have appeared in journals such as the *Annual Review of Jazz Studies* and *Jazz Research*, as well as the *New Grove Dictionary of Jazz*. In addition, his listening guide software that accompanies the jazz history text *Essential Jazz: The First 100 Years* has recently been published.

DATE DUE	RETURNED